Praise for Sea Fare

When she isn't catching fish on hidder
fascinating cultures, like Papua New Guinea, or nanging out wim
characters, she is serving up the most amazing meals ... and sharing her
recipes and secrets. Victoria Allman is as good a writer as she is a cook. I
loved reading the book. I wish I could have eaten it.

—Rita Golden Gelman, author of
Tales of a Female Nomad, Living at Large in the World

Chef Victoria Allman became hooked on travel following a trip to the
Bahamas more than 10 years ago. Since that time she's caught, sautéed,
simmered and served her way through the Caribbean, Mediterranean,
North America, Europe, Africa, and the South Pacific from Australia to
Tahiti. *Sea Fare – a Chef's Journey Across the Ocean* is her travel memoir of
food, lust, finding true love and high seas adventure.

—MiamiARTzine

Allman's recipe is equal parts foodie-centric, glamour and adventure,
making for a delightful literary repast.

—Seabourn Club Herald

Part memoir, part romance, part travelogue and part cookbook.
Anyone who enjoys travel writing and exotic cuisine will love *Sea Fare*.

—The Key West Citizen

Sea Fare serves up a plate full of enthralling stories and delectable
recipes giving readers a taste of what it's like to stand in the flip-flops of
a megayacht chef, in all of its exotic and harrowing glory.

—The Crew Report

Her story is personally infused with her very human doubts, triumphs
and joys. Clearly written, *Sea Fare* includes 30 simple, fresh recipes and
while reading it, I felt like I'd taken a trip myself.

—The Urban Coaster

Happy Birthday, Yusuf!

Enjoy your journey :)!

From Nelly
xxx
02.12.2014

Sea Fare

A Chef's Journey Across the Ocean

A Culinary Odyssey

Victoria Allman

Author of: *SEAsoned*
A Chef's Journey with Her Captain

Printed in the United States of America
ISBN: 978-1-935254-83-6

Book Design by Nadene Carter

First printing, 2009
Second Edition, 2011

Permissions:
Cover photos courtesy of Emile Bootsma
Author photo courtesy of Suki Finnerty, Broad Reach Productions
Norman's Cracked Conch Chowder reprinted by permission of Norman Van Aken River Café
Spring Asparagus and Brown Beech Mushroom Soup reprinted by permission of River Café

Contents

Acting on wanderlust breeds fantastic discoveries. Making it a lifestyle transforms dreams into reality. In Sea Fare, Victoria presents a global collage of unscripted culinary experience.

—Chef David Shalleck,
author of *Mediterranean Summer*

Author's Note

The places, events, and adventures that I write about here are all real. However, I've taken liberty within each story with the timeline of events, condensing many trips or days into one for narrative purposes. The chapters appear geographically and somewhat chronologically. Because of the numerous trips during the eight years I've been yachting, they jump all over the globe, back and forth from one continent to another. Just like my life.

Dolphins Off the Bow

"**D**olphins off the bow!" Patrick shouted over the roar of the engine. "Two on your right, and four more coming from behind." He glanced over his shoulder to make sure I was still holding on and nudged the boat throttle a little more to gain speed.

I was fifteen feet behind him, being pulled through the crystal-clear Tahitian water by a rope, and could see the school of dolphins ahead. They surfed at the bow of the boat. Then leaping, they broke the surface, momentarily in flight before gracefully splashing back in—our own private Sea World show. Taking a deep breath, I ducked beneath the surface in time to see one bottle-nose dolphin break away from his traveling partners. He dove beneath the boat no more than ten feet away from me, and there, suspended in teal like a Wyland painting, radiating serenity, he watched me watch him. He held eye contact for what seemed like an eternity, bubbles streaming out his blowhole like a leash to the surface. His body contracted in a slow underwater ballet. Propelled by his spring-loaded tail, he glided past, alternating from a sleek torpedo to a curve like the hook of an umbrella handle, gaining power before descending into the depths and out of sight. I heard the chattering clicks and chirps of his friends and saw their shadowed movements as they vanished as well. I was alone again.

I surfaced, took a deep breath, and shouted a triumphant, "Yeah!"

This is what living on the water is all about, experiencing life with no filter to limit the sensations. Like those dolphins, I, too, swim in Tahitian waters, diving down deep to truly touch the world around me, feeling at home wherever I am, and thankful for the wanderlust that guides me.

* * * *

My mother swears she knew I was going to be a chef when, at the age of eight, I packed my doll carriage and announced I was running away from home. Having seen this independent streak before, my mother said, "Okay, you can go but tonight we're having your favorite for dinner: turnips." Naturally, I ran away, but only for the afternoon. I was home for dinner, possibly being the only child in history to be bribed with turnips.

And become a chef I did—chef on a yacht. I seem to possess that peculiar craziness and offbeat eccentricity needed to survive in this profession. I've traveled to more than forty-five countries, discovering that perfectly ripe mango that would drizzle juice down my chin when I bit into it, learning to make intricate dim sum bundles from a master chef in Hong Kong, and eating warthog, grilled over a wood fire while on safari in South Africa. It may seem like a crazy life, but sometimes crazy is just downright normal.

The Yachting World

I was a long way from home. For the first time, I stood on the beach, my toes digging in the sand, while the Atlantic Ocean swirled around my ankles. Sunlight baked my arms and warmed my body. A sea breeze blew strands of hair off my face.

I smiled: Back home, the first snowflakes were falling in the mountains.

During the seven-day journey, I'd driven my car past prairie wheat fields, around the Great Lakes, and down the Appalachians to Florida, a state so vastly different from home that I had to stand in the ocean, gathering strength before heading to my job interview. As I walked across the street to the marina parking lot, I got my first look at a yacht. In front of me, twelve large snow-white boats gleamed in the sun. They looked like floating palaces.

At the end of the row, I saw a sleek, blue-hulled boat with a low, sexy profile. It stood out from the rest. This boat had more of a classic boat look than the others with their multi-leveled decks, helicopter pads, and pristine whiteness. This boat had character. I walked toward it, admiring the varnished wooden cap rails and bleached blond teak decks. With only one level above the main deck, it had clean lines, and to me it looked more like a boat than the cumbersome, over-stuffed pillows I had just passed. I was relieved to see the name *Pari* in bold font on the back of the boat (the stern, I would soon learn).

"What does a chef from the mountains in Canada know about the ocean?" was Captain Mike's first question when we met on the dock.

The answer: "Not much." I'd arrived in Lauderdale from Calgary in one piece but had yet to comprehend what I was getting myself into. The crew placement agent had set up this interview. I innocently believed I just had to convince the captain that I knew what he was talking about when he spoke of port and starboard, aft-bridges, fly bridges, bulkheads and spring lines.

Mike was nothing like the Captain Ahab I had envisioned. He wasn't a salty, nor did he have long grey hair and a beard. He didn't even wear a sailor's cap or have a pipe hanging from his mouth. Instead, he was a young, blond surfer who'd spent his youth in the Navy. The first thing he did was give me a tour around the boat. We started in the engine room, where he pointed out the two diesel engines and two generators.

He spoke like a kindergarten teacher, explaining they made their own energy to run the boat. "We make all our own water as well by converting seawater to fresh with the water-maker but it's in limited supply, so no long hot showers for you. A quick in and out to conserve the water for guests is okay. I'll know if you're wasting water." He spoke with such authority, I felt I was being reprimanded, already. And this was just the interview.

The owner's salon continued the classic look, with warm, honey-colored wood walls and royal blue couches. Windows wrapped around the entire room. My bare feet sank into a beige carpet as soft as an alpaca. A dining table in the center sat six.

"Most of the meals you serve will be outside on the aft deck table. This," Mike motioned to the table, "is for bad weather. Hardly anyone uses this."

The bathrooms all had marble countertops and floors, with gold faucets to complete the opulence. Mike showed me artwork by Keith Haring and pointed out fragile looking Lalique glass vases. It was like stepping into another world. I hadn't known a boat could be so luxurious.

"Everything is either velcroed to the wall or glued down so it won't break in bad weather."

He turned on his heel, his eyes narrowed. "You don't get seasick do you?"

Sea sick? How did I know? So far, I'd only seen the ocean from shore. I came from the Canadian Rocky Mountains where my closest experience to boating was in a kayak on the Bow River. "No, I'll be fine," I lied, hoping Mike wouldn't question me further.

—— VICTORIA ALLMAN ——

"You look like you'll get sick." His right eyebrow rose; he eyed me suspiciously. "I bet you will." He turned to finish the tour.

With my fists clenched in tight balls, I decided then and there I would never let this man see me sweat. He'd thrown out a challenge, and I was known to be stubborn. I hoped he'd hire me just so I could prove him wrong. Taking a deep breath, I followed.

Next on the tour was the galley. I didn't know what to expect, since this was my first boat tour, but surely this couldn't be the galley. The room was no more than eight feet by eight feet square. The two counters would barely hold a cutting board. The room contained two Meile ovens stacked on top of each other, a six-burner stovetop, and a stand-up fridge. I saw only one sink for dishes and six cupboards for equipment. In fact, the galley was so small both Mike and I couldn't stand inside at the same time. He had to move to the other side of the counter.

"This is where Christine, my wife, and our other stewardess, Yaz, make coffee," he explained. "They pick up the plates from you here." He pointed to one of the small counters that couldn't possibly hold more than four plates at a time.

While he spoke, I poked my head into each cupboard and wondered if all of this was normal. "Where is all the food kept?" I peered into cupboards, stuffed with pots and pans.

"There's little food on the boat at the moment. I fired our last chef a week ago, but around the corner is a corridor with one cupboard for you. Downstairs under the seats in the couch are two more storage spaces, and under the floor in the hallway is a spot for cans and drinks." He said this matter-of-factly, as if it was normal to scatter supplies all over the boat in every nook and cranny.

"Okay." I breathed deeply. I could handle that. I'd just have to be super organized, not my strong suit, but I could adapt. This was all part of the adventure. "Looks great." My voice held more enthusiasm than I felt.

"Down here is the crew mess and our cabins." Mike led me down a claustrophobic stairway that twisted at the bottom to reveal a living room, dining room, kitchen area with a table nook, a small sink, and two cupboards. A half refrigerator was tucked under the table, and over the table was a television. This was home for the crew. Off this communal area, he showed me three cabins: one for the girls, one for the boys, and one for Mike and Christine.

"Well, that's it," Mike said. "You share this room with Yaz."

"Does that mean I have the job?" I was a bit surprised we'd jumped to this stage of the interview already.

"Yeah, can you start right away?"

That was it. He needed me onboard and ready for the boat show the next day. I had no time to think about it; he needed an answer now.

I looked around the cramped surroundings one more time and thought about why I was there. "I can be here tomorrow with my bags."

"Okay, Yaz is on holiday, but she gets back tonight and can show you everything. We'll be showing the boat in the afternoon, so we'll need hors d'oeuvres for the people coming through, lunch for the crew, and dinner as well. You'll have to keep the galley spotless all day so we can show it off. This is a charter boat, and we're hoping to attract clients at the show." He thought for a moment, "Any questions?"

I gulped, "How many people for hors d'oeuvres?"

"About a hundred."

"And how many crew?"

"Six. Christine and I, Yaz, our deckhand, and the first mate."

"And there is no food onboard yet?"

"No, but I'll give you cash to go shopping."

"Maybe, I should start today." I needed more time to do all that and seriously wondered what I'd gotten myself into.

"Yeah? Great! Then you can cook dinner tonight as well. Welcome aboard."

And that was that. I was now chef aboard *Pari*. No test of my boating knowledge, no cooking trial, just a tour of the boat, an offer made, and a single afternoon to get ready for my debut.

During the next few hours, I quickly pulled a menu together, created a shopping list, and received directions to the closest grocery store.

Later, I explored my new galley, trying to find the right pot to use, where the whisks were kept, and how much I could physically do on the small countertops while making dinner and prepping for the next day.

Mike came by to check on me. "Can you cater a dinner party for the broker of the boat on Saturday?"

"Sure." What's one more meal, I thought.

He stopped in again. "A VIP will be onboard Sunday for a private tour. Can we serve him lunch?"

"Okay." I wasn't sure if I had the option to say no or not.

Christine came in the galley that afternoon to introduce herself, her smile calm and friendly. "Don't worry." She laughed and tucked a strand of long dark hair behind her ear. "Mike just gets wound up, it won't be all that crazy this weekend." Her voice soothed my nerves.

"It sounds busy." I confided my ever-growing nervousness.

"It'll mostly just be people looking. They'll come aboard with their broker and tour the boat with either Mike or myself. We'll answer their questions."

That didn't sound so bad.

"I'll offer something to nibble on to anyone who is really interested in chartering us," she continued, "but other than that, just keep the galley clean and smile a lot. In fact, that's the answer to most things in yachting: just keep smiling."

That night, I entered my new bedroom for the first time and looked around. Like the rest of the crew quarters, it was small. On the right, two bunks were staked, one on top of the other. I lifted my bag onto the bed Christine had said was mine. Above my bunk was one bookshelf. Under the bed I had one drawer for clothes and uniforms. I tried to hang some clothes, but the closet held no more than eight hangers. Four of them for Yaz, I supposed. This would be a different way to live. I prayed I would like my roommate and she me.

Exhausted from the day, I entered the bathroom (which I later learned is called a 'head'). Again, I was surprised by the space. The shower actually ran on top of the toilet—no room for a proper stall. A cabinet above the sink held three shelves. I washed my face and brushed my teeth, not sure where I was going to find room to put my toothbrush. I crawled into the lower bunk and turned out the light.

The cabin was literally underwater, with no porthole and no way for any natural light to get into the room. Once I turned out the light, the room plunged into complete darkness. Lying silent in my bunk, I could hear noises. Something hummed loudly.

The generator maybe?

Then I heard a creaking scream. What was that? The boat swayed gently beneath me. Weren't we tied to a dock? My mind raced. What was I doing here? I jumped when the air-conditioner clicked on. At least that noise I recognized. A rush of water through a pipe sent my heart racing. My throat felt dry.

And then suddenly, the door of the cabin flew open. Light flooded the room. I screamed.

"Who, the bloody hell, are you?" a proper English accent asked, "and why are you screaming?"

I held the comforter to my face. "You scared me." I lowered the blanket and smiled. "Are you Yaz?" Now that the light was on, I felt foolish.

"Man, what happened to the last chef? I go away for two weeks and everything changes." She threw her bags on the top bed and ran a hand through her short spiky hair. "I'm Yaz, sorry I scared you." She smiled. "I guess we'll be roomies."

My heart beat returned to normal. "Nice to meet you. Did you have a good vacation?"

It didn't take Yaz but a minute to launch into a full description of her last two weeks: who she'd been with, where she went, and how much fun she had. Shy, she was not. It turned out that the English accent was actually South African. She'd been onboard the boat for six months.

"Don't worry about a thing. I'll talk you through what you'll need to know for this weekend, and then we'll go out and I'll introduce you to everyone." Her smile was effervescent. "Sweetheart, you're going to love it. Yachting is addicting. It gets in your bones." Yaz climbed up onto her bunk.

I turned the lights out again, but, this time from the darkness, I heard, "We are going to have *so* much fun together."

Within minutes, I had a new friend who'd look out for me. I'd be okay in this new life.

Fresh or Not So Fresh

*M*y life story would sound so much more interesting if I could claim I grew up with an alcoholic mother, or in a small village in Cambodia dodging landmines. But the truth is, I led a completely ordinary life with two parents, a sister and friends at school. My teacher assigned homework, just like everybody else, and I went to the movies on Fridays. I spent most of my summer days outside playing and most of my nights reading. I cannot recall one extraordinary event in my childhood that stood out. That is until I met Lawrence.

At sixteen I went to work in a kitchen. While my friends were busy choosing universities to apply to, I was washing dishes at the *Next Wave*. It was there I got my first crack at real cooking. Lawrence and his wife Anita had traveled extensively, gathering ideas for their restaurant and were bursting with enthusiasm. They put all their energy into creating a sophisticated restaurant with a worldly air and an undercurrent of elegance.

Lawrence, a tall, slender man with the energy of a Ferrari, was in his thirties and manned the stoves each night. He cooked things I had never even heard of before: etouffées from New Orleans, mussels steamed in herbs and French wine, Jamaican jerk chicken, thin-crust pizzas topped with chicken and mangos, bruschetta rubbed with cold-pressed extra-virgin olive oil and raw garlic, and the creamiest crème brûlée coating your mouth with silk. Each night, exotic aromas wafted from his pans bubbling on the stove, through the kitchen's swinging doors, past the bar where polished wine glasses hung ready to be filled with wines from around the world, and into the subtle peach colored dining room.

Twice a week, Lawrence drove two hours into Toronto to the St. Lawrence Market to purchase fresh local products he couldn't find in our small town.

"Good food comes from great ingredients." He talked of food while we worked. "You start with a perfect tasting tomato, and it is *your* job as a chef not to screw it up." He believed the apple crisp he was teaching me to make should taste predominantly of apples instead of the fiery spice of cinnamon or over-sweet sugar. "Great tasting food is perfect when little has been done to transform it."

He made everything from scratch and experimented with new recipes using the fruits and vegetables he picked up at the market. Gone were the casseroles and spaghetti dinners I knew from home. In their place he created an ever-revolving kaleidoscope of Asian flavors, exotic seafoods, and intricate dishes.

On busy nights, I helped with the salad and dessert station, and on slow nights Lawrence would show me how to do some of the simpler kitchen tasks, like peeling peaches and chopping vegetables to precise sizes. He demonstrated how to wrap spring rolls without ripping their skin.

"Use a water bath when baking cheesecake," he said. "This way you avoid dry cracks on top."

Each night while he created his specialties, he talked of his travels through France, his culinary beliefs, and his love of food. "Here, taste this. It's a new marinade I'm trying for steak. I want it to taste fruity, like blackberries that just came into season. Can you taste it? What do you think?"

Even though I was just sixteen years old, he never thought of me as too young or too uneducated. He wanted my opinion. And in Lawrence's kitchen, I was discovering who I really wanted to be. Enamored with the exotic life he talked about, I decided I wanted to travel and explore the culinary world, just like Anita and Lawrence.

Now, ten years after my stint at the *Next Wave*, here I was aboard a yacht about to travel. I dreamt of going to local island markets every morning to buy fresh fish. I looked forward with excitement to exploring new cuisines. I imagined buying vegetables straight from Caribbean ladies who grew them, and creating menus on the spot at local markets using indigenous ingredients to create masterpieces of perfection for those I would serve.

My first trip on *Pari* would be to the Bahamas, a scattering of seven hundred islands and two thousand islets, stretching across one hundred thousand square miles of the Atlantic Ocean. This was the heart of pirating and privateering in the seventeenth century: Blackbeard with his fourteen wives, the nefarious Calico Jack, and the marauding Henry Morgan all lived and worked these islands. To me, it sounded like a dream. What better initiation could I get to experience island cooking? I quick-studied about conch fritters, Bahamian lobster on the grill, guava duff, pigeon peas and rice, and tender stew chicken. But as our departure date neared, my apprehension at being at sea was starting to outweigh my fantasies of tropical food and sandy beaches. And I still had no idea if I'd become seasick. Nonetheless, I was ready and excited.

The first glitch came when Mike told me we couldn't get fresh produce once in the Bahamas.

"We'll be anchored in the Exhumas." He laughed at my naiveté. "They're ninety miles away from the nearest store."

"No markets?" I heard my voice crack.

"Not even a convenient store." Mike walked away, shaking his head.

So, I'd have to provision the boat in Ft. Lauderdale and store everything onboard for the trip. There'd be no markets to peruse for inspiration. My mind galloped ahead; the trip was to be three weeks. How long could I store lettuce? How was I to keep fresh milk for so long? What would I do without raspberries after the first week?

Okay, I could handle this. Years ago, people went all winter without lettuce. I'd have to plan my meals accordingly—use the lettuce first, along with the berries and perishables. The last week would be squashes, cabbage, and potatoes. After writing and rewriting menus, I finally had it figured out and began provisioning. It was all so very new, trying to find the right shop to buy Maytag Blue Cheese, where the German deli was so I could buy specific rye bread, and which merchant had the best butchery. I had three days to stock my fridges and fill my shelves for our voyage.

Christine showed me how to secure the galley by tying everything down with special boaters blue tape and packing the fridges with bubble wrap so as not to break any bottles. Next, I locked all cupboards, taped egg cartons together, and wrapped kitchen towels around jars in the pantry so they wouldn't shatter. Crates were lashed with bungee cords, and all the equipment was moved from the counters to the floor. I had all my vegetables, meats, breads, cheeses, and dairy fastened in their seatbelts as we left port for my first sea voyage. I took one last look around the galley to make sure nothing would move and headed to the aft deck to enjoy the view.

Ian, our deckhand, was casting the heavy lines that tied us to the dock. He bent at the waist and pulled. Unclipping the radio from his belt, he spoke to Mike. "All lines are clear." Slowly we moved away from the dock. "Here we go!" Ian smiled at me. It was his first trip to sea as well.

We pulled out of the marina and turned to the left. We were heading out the Intracoastal Waterway. My mouth hung open as we passed the houses on the way to the ocean. Twelvebedroom, one-story ranch houses sprawled out on perfectly manicured emerald green lawns. Spanish-style, two-story mansions with marble columns and French glass doors lined the waterway. Elegant homes with bubbling fountains, lavish gardens, and infinity pools were built with no expense spared.

"That one looks like the Palace of Versailles," I said to Ian, who nodded and stared in awe. Every property we passed seemed grander and more elaborate than the last, each with a shiny white yacht or sleek and colorful cigarette boat docked nearby.

We produced very little wake as we cruised the channel. I was surprised at the calm that washed over me. Filling my lungs with fresh ocean air, I felt the tension and anxiety leave my body. I would not get seasick. I could do this.

I heard Mike on the radio requesting a bridge opening and watched as we lined up to go under the opening span. I felt like waving and throwing confetti as we passed the cars above. This was my first cruise.

I headed up to the pilothouse to show Mike I was doing well and feeling good, but all of the sudden we made a turn and started slamming. The ocean churned in front of us. Steel-colored waves formed much too close together and the wind picked up. Mike let out a squeal of delight. "Hold tight, this is going to get nasty."

Dark grey clouds blocked the horizon. The front was moving fast. *Pari* rode the short steep waves skyward only to drop at a 90-degree angle, bow first, off the face of the wave. Up and down she rode through the chop. The violent sea sent huge sheets of water up and over the pilothouse. *Pari* pitched at an unnatural angle, practically parallel to the turbulent sea thrashing around her. The waves had increased and were now ten-feet high in spots.

Returning to the galley, I braced myself against the counter and watched as cupboard doors I'd forgotten to tape swung open and shut with the movement of the boat. My head pounded and my stomach threatened to rebel against my enthusiasm. For a moment, doubt nagged that I might have trouble proving to Mike that I could handle being at sea. To make matters worse, he'd given me a copy of *The Perfect Storm* to read the week before. It was all I could think about now as we bounced from side to side.

But I refused to cave and admit defeat, especially not to Mike. I held my ground and made sandwiches for lunch while being thrown around the tiny galley, and sustained a dozen new bruises from slamming into the countertop repeatedly with every wave.

I gained a few points when I went to the pilothouse to sit watch with Mike during the evening. Although I struggled to keep my eyes open and my lunch down, I sat beside him for four hours, listening to his sea stories and watching for other boats. Mainly, my job was to ensure he had company and stayed awake. I'm not sure who was keeping whom alert, but when Yaz came to relieve my shift, I gladly went down to my bunk, a darker shade of green than hours before.

Fourteen hours later, when we finally dropped anchor, I was grateful the *Pari* hadn't met the same end as the fishing boat in *The Perfect Storm*. Feeling slightly better, I went to investigate the galley. I unlatched cupboards and ripped the tape from the boxes. Problems: we had three weeks to go, and the broccoli had already turned yellow, the green onions were sweating, which would turn them slimy by evening, and the box of oranges had shifted with the waves and squashed all my breads and hamburger buns.

Stay calm. After all, it wasn't the worst thing in the world. A competent chef could surely manage without broccoli and green onions. I love to bake bread, and I had lots of other vegetables.

After dinner, we were sitting on the aft deck, chatting. A cool breeze blew off the water, carrying the scent of salt and fish, and non-threatening waves lapped against the hull, creating a rhythmic ocean song. "Come on, Yaz," I pleaded. "Let's go for a swim." It was the night before a full moon, and the ocean was lit up like a stage.

"Not a chance in hell." Yaz had already curled up with a glass of wine and a book. She'd done this trip many times, but this was my first night at anchor; I wanted to experience it all. Quickly, I changed into my brand new bikini and dove off the swim platform into the glistening sea. At first blush, the water felt warm and refreshing, but almost immediately, I experienced a sharp stinging sensation from head to toe. It felt like I was zapped with a jolt of electricity. I surfaced screaming and thrashing, flailing my arms and trying to brush off what was attacking me. From the deck, Yaz and Mike howled with laughter.

"That's why you don't swim at night," Mike delighted in telling me. "You can't see the jellyfish."

* * * *

The next day brought sunshine and a soft breeze. I looked out the window in my galley to see radiant blue water as flat as the ice rinks I'd left behind in Canada. We were anchored off Hawksbill Cay, a small bump in the indigo plain, circled by natural sugar sand beaches. Palm trees on shore stuck out at crazy angles and sea birds soared above in a cloudless sky. The throbbing tropical sun reflected off the water. This was heaven. Not a thing to worry about.

Then the phone rang. The owners of the boat were delaying their trip by one week.

Panic time again. The vegetables would maybe last three weeks, if I was lucky, but definitely not four. And I didn't want to start off their holiday or my first job with old produce. Not a good start at all.

"No big deal." Mike threw an arm around my shoulder. "You can order a seaplane to re-provision and deliver." He said this as if it was an everyday occurrence.

"Fly food in? From where?"

"Miami." He looked at me like I was demented. *Where else, silly*, he seemed to say.

Christine explained. "Second rule of yachting. You do whatever is necessary to make the owners happy."

* * * *

Finally, my first night of cooking for the owners arrived. Admittedly, I was pretty cocky. With little knowledge as to how the generators and other things worked on the boat, food was something I did know, an area where I could excel and show off my talents. I carefully planned the meal I wanted to showcase. It would start with an architecturally stunning tower of sweet crabmeat and soft avocadoes, topped with tomatoes and cilantro and accented by just a hint of lime. Next, I would sear tender duck breasts to medium rare, slicing them thin and fanning them around a puree of butternut squash and carrot, lightly bathing the dish with a reduced raspberry and green peppercorn sauce. As a finale, I wanted a light and fresh dessert. The strawberries I had flown in were dark red and actually tasted like they'd just been picked off the vine. I would sweeten some whipped cream, just slightly, and fold the two together, wrapping the mixture in a golden crêpe and drizzle them with a rhubarb sauce. These were recipes I'd prepared thousands of times at restaurants and always received rave reviews. They weren't the Bahamian dishes I had envisioned, but I felt confident serving them to the guests as my first meal.

Christine stopped by the galley, and I discussed the menu with her. She assured me the owners loved crêpes and duck. "The kids are only three and five," she reminded me. I planned to prepare a simple pasta with butter and cheese for them.

I awoke early to start the preparations and bake bread for the evening. Along with this meal, I also cooked a separate meal for the crew: roast beef with sautéed mushrooms and Parmesan mashed potatoes for their heartier appetites. As the hour of the owners' arrival neared, we all showered and changed into our crisp white uniforms, the girls in skirts and the boys in shorts, all with stripes on our shoulders, like airplane pilots, to signify our positions on the boat.

As Mike and Ian took the small inflatable tender to meet their seaplane, I plated a snack of roasted chicken, pear and blue cheese pastries, and a welcome drink of fresh pineapple and banana smoothies for Yaz to serve as they stepped onboard. Christine, Yaz and I gathered on the aft deck, drinks in hand and smiles on our faces to greet the guests.

Mike expertly pulled the boat up to the swim platform and tied off the lines as the kids leaped out of the tender and tore up the stairs to our aft deck like a whirlwind.

"Hey, Yaz," the little boy greeted as he grabbed a glass from her tray, spilling on the first mate's newly scrubbed teak deck. He plopped his backpack in the center of the deck. "Can I play Nintendo?"

"Don't you want to meet the new crew?" she asked.

"Nah," the little boy replied and headed inside to play. In such a transient world as yachting, crew came and went; in his short life he'd already met many crew who were no longer there.

The owners and their little three-year-old girl ascended the stairs, all much more gracious then a precocious little boy. We were introduced, while trading a few words of small talk before they, too, disappeared inside to relax as Yaz unpacked for them.

They had traveled from Germany and would be tired and hungry, so I went to start dinner. Most things were already prepared and sat waiting in small individual dishes in the fridge to be assembled at the time of dinner, but I still had a few last minute herbs to chop and crêpes to cook. With my back turned to stir the squash and carrot mixture on the stove, the little boy came in, climbed up on my one free counter and announced in accented English, "I sit here and help you. This is my job." It was not a question. Before I had time to answer, his blond little doll of a sister appeared by my side, holding her arms up to be lifted beside her brother.

Exactly where was I going to plate dinner, now? I wondered. I picked up the child, cradling her on my hip as I looked around.

"Oh, I forgot to tell you." Yaz laughed. "These two little munchkins will be your new best friends in here if you let them."

Without any room to maneuver, I piled plates precariously in the corner on top of a basket of fragrant pineapples and mangoes and began to wonder how this was going to work. Having been around few children before, I was at a loss.

"Why don't you guys go sit down, and we'll serve you dinner." Christine gently guided the kids out of the tiny galley and onto the back deck, where she had set out candles and table settings. I was now free to plate my dinner.

I tasted the crabmeat for seasoning and added another squeeze of lime before piling it delicately into a ring mold. On top of the crab, I spooned an avocado mousse that felt light on the tongue, like whipped cream and then placed a finely diced yellow and red tomato salsa on top for color and texture. A drizzle of vibrant green cilantro oil around the outside of the plate finished the presentation. I wiped the rim of the plate free of fingerprints and nodded to Christine, who had just returned from pouring their wine. The plates were ready.

Christine carried the plates from the galley door and out to the aft deck. She was gone no more than a minute before she returned, plates in hand. "Victoria, they do not like avocado."

Okay, no problem. A few hiccups along the way were expected. I quickly deconstructed the perfect dish and placed the crabmeat in a small dish, surrounded by carrot sticks, celery, and pepper slices for a crudite with dip. Christine took platter out for them to munch on as I put the finishing touches on their main course.

After removing the duck breasts from the oven, I set them aside to rest so the juices would settle. Next, I sautéed wild rice with chopped shallots and spinach, and scooped my vegetable puree into the center of the gold rimmed plates. I sliced the duck breast to half the thickness of a pencil. It was cooked to perfection. I removed the simmering sauce from the stovetop and, smiling to myself, ladled the sauce around the meat. This would impress them.

Again, Christine took the plates to the aft deck and returned not a minute later, this time empty handed. But I wasn't off the hook yet. "They say the duck needs cranberry sauce."

Well, all right, to each his own, I thought, and grabbed a jar of Oceanspray. Had I known, I would have made fresh cranberry sauce for them but I was prepared for anything.

I cleaned the galley as best I could in the small cramped space and waited for the time to plate dessert. After twenty minutes Christine returned with the plates hardly touched. She didn't say anything and with my stomach in knots, I couldn't bring myself to ask. It wasn't as bad as the seventeenth-century majordomo who threw himself on his sword when the dinner he prepared for the King of France was a bust or more recently, the French chef who committed suicide after loosing a Michelin star, but still I felt gut-wrenched. Silently, I wrapped the strawberry cream in the crêpes and dressed them with the sauce. At least I knew from Christine that they liked crêpes.

Again she left the galley and instantly returned, plates in hand. "Can you make these crêpes hot with orange sauce and vanilla ice cream?" she asked, hardly able to look me in the eye.

Crêpes Suzzette? Ugh, I hadn't done that since chef school, and those recipes were packed in storage in Calgary. I quickly ran through my memory. I knew I had to caramelize sugar and add Grand Marnier, but I had no idea how much or what else. If I couldn't pull this dinner out of the disaster it was becoming, this would be a short trip.

As I sent Christine out to the firing squad again, I closed my eyes and prayed that I had it right. But this time, she came back smiling. "They love them and would like to speak with you." She quickly added, "Don't worry, they're happy."

I took off my apron and washed my hands, stalling for time while I gathered my wits. This was not the debut I'd hoped for.

Timidly, I approached the table, which was bathed in warm candlelight. "Good evening," I attempted with a weak smile.

They both smiled. I relaxed a little. "Victoria, that was a beautiful dinner, but we are European and eat differently. Can you make something more classical tomorrow?" the wife asked.

"Of course, do you have any favorites?" I stumbled, again buying time, as I racked my brain as to what they would like.

"No, we like everything."

That was no help.

"Okay, I'll have a new menu for you tomorrow," I answered retreating quickly to the safety of the galley. "Now what do I do?" I wailed.

"Welcome to yachting," Yaz said. "Don't worry, you'll get it."

"Just keep smiling," Christine chimed in.

* * * *

Luckily, these were the biggest problems I encountered on that first trip, although there were many things that I wasn't at all prepared for. After a few minor troubles, like not having the proper pan to make *tart tatin* (French apple tart) or not having known that they only drink skim milk and sorting out my initial produce dilemmas, I began to settle into a routine: Up at five o'clock to bake for the day, prepare breakfast for the kids and the crew, clean up, entertain the kids until the wife woke, arrange guest breakfast, clean up, start crew lunch, make the kids lunch, clean up, get the owners' lunch ready, clean up, bake afternoon nibbles, clean up, cook crew dinner, assemble the kids dinner, clean up, create the guests dinner and do a final cleaning of the galley.

There were many dinners where I just shut my eyes and prayed I'd remembered the right garnish for the consommé or had the sauce tasting the way I remembered it should. But as quirky as the owners were about what they liked to eat, they were equally as appreciative when they got what they wanted.

Once the trip was underway, Mike came into the galley one afternoon and said, "Hold dinner, we're going fishing," From that minute forward, freshness took on a whole new meaning. In a few short hours Mike and Ian had traveled to a reef outside the national park and gone spear fishing. Armed with only a spear, swim trunks, flippers and goggles, they dove off the back of the tender into schools of fish, coral, and sharks in search of grouper. Ian, an American city boy from Philadelphia had never been to the Bahamas. This was his first experience diving. Not only did he come back with fish for dinner, but also with wide eyes and an incredibly enthusiastic story about a shark he swore was following him around the reef. "It was the biggest shark I have ever seen." His brown eyes twinkled. "I thought we were going to be attacked. I mean we were in the water holding a dead fish, it was bleeding everywhere, and he was just circling us."

His big smile and passion for telling the story was great entertainment for the family and crew.

While I butchered the grouper on our aft deck, the sun sank over the horizon, leaving a sky the color of fire.

Now, I had fresh grouper caught barely an hour ago. This is what I thought yachting would be. I started thinking about how I might prepare it for dinner. Grouper are found in tropical waters throughout the world, but they are a specialty of the Bahamas. Mike and Ian had also brought back four large Bahamian lobsters, which they'd plucked from their hidden holes, and coral colored conch I'd make into chowder.

I decided the grouper should be served simply, with a little seasoning, lemon juice, and a tropical fruit salsa to bring out the freshness of the fish. The lobsters could use just a slight bit of acidity from lemon and a mix of fresh herbs. I decided it would be perfect served with an island recipe of red beans and rice and some of the green beans that I had stored. The conch chowder needed only a few onions, waxy potatoes, thyme, and milk to create a light soup that resonated with the fresh flavor of the sea. Of course, these light first courses should be followed by something sweet and equally as fresh. Pineapple marinated in rum and grilled with a caramel glaze, and topped with boat-made vanilla ice cream sounded good. I hoped this menu would please everyone but quickly decided fish and chips would be better for the kids, though. They had watched me butcher the fish, and I didn't want to freak them out by seeing dinner looking so "fishy" on their plates.

The grouper is a firm white meat. I hadn't tasted it before, but it reminded me of Halibut. I can't even begin to describe the difference between fish caught an hour ago and what I was used to seeing in landlocked Calgary. The closest I can come to an accurate description, is clean. It tastes of the sea, not of fish. Only the sharks ate fresher fish than we did that night.

When we cleaned up the galley that night, I looked at Yaz and smiled. "You were right. I'm addicted already. I don't think I've ever had so much fun working."

Yaz just smiled. "Sweetheart, you ain't seen nothing yet."

Crab and Avocado Tower

1 pound fresh lump crabmeat
1/4 cup plain Greek-style yogurt
2 tablespoons fresh orange juice
2 tablespoons olive oil
1/4 cup red onion, diced super fine
1 teaspoon sea salt
2 drops of hot sauce

2 avocadoes
1 teaspoon fresh lime juice
2 teaspoons sea salt
1 egg white
1 red tomato, chopped fine
1 yellow tomato, chopped fine
1/3 cup red onion, chopped fine
1 tablespoons cilantro, chopped fine
1/2 lime, squeezed juice
1 tablespoon olive oil
1 teaspoon sea salt
1 drop hot sauce

Combine first seven ingredients in a small bowl, taking care not to mash the crab too much. Taste for seasoning. Adjust amount of hot sauce if necessary. Set aside.

In a clean stainless bowl, whisk egg white until stiff. In another bowl mash avocado with lime and salt. Pass the avocado mix through a fine sieve to make sure there are no lumps. Gently fold together to create a light mousse. Taste for acidity. Adjust the amount of lime juice if necessary.

Note: avocado discolors after half an hour. Do this step right before serving. Combine remaining ingredients for a tomato salsa. Taste. In a stainless ring, build a tower of crabmeat 3/4 of the way up the side in the center of a plate. Top with avocado mousse. Spoon 3 piles of salsa around the outside of the tower. Garnish with cilantro.

As an alternate, mix all together and serve as a dip with crudite.

Bahamian Viagra

"**Y**ou be up there lovin' an' bumpin' an' grindin' tonight I tell you," Moe promised us with a flash of his gold front tooth that sparkled against his dark skin. A mischievous spark lit his eyes. "I take you for Bahamian hangover cure: conch salad. You be good as new by the time we get you home."

Ian groaned. "I'll try anything as long as it gets rid of this pounding in my head."

"No worries, man. It'll cure what ails you." Moe smiled knowingly. "You jus' eat that conch, and it'll feel you right. You know about conch don't you?"

Pari had been on Paradise Island for a week in the marina at the Atlantis Resort and Casino. We were in between trips with the owners, a time when the crew could explore the island and enjoy shorter days. Working eight to four Monday to Friday seemed like a vacation compared to the sixteen-hour days we'd put in with guests onboard. Each morning I went for a run to see the island, and most afternoons Yaz, Ian, and I ended up on the beach—at the beach bar drinking rum drinks out of coconuts.

The day before, we'd watched a nimble Bahamian youth, dressed only in ratty ripped shorts with a long machete tucked into the back, climb barefooted up the trunk of a palm tree. With a loud whack of the blade, he dislodged our coconuts, dropping them twenty feet to the beach below. I giggled as he climbed back down, hand over hand. He smiled a toothy grin at Yaz as he held a coconut in his left hand and swung the blade again for another loud whack. We heard the coconut crack as he pulled the top off to offer us the sweet water inside.

"Thank you sweetheart." Yaz flashed a smile that sent the shy youth retreating to his next customer. The bartender reached over the bar with a bottle of rum and poured a long shot into each of our coconuts. He floated a spoonful of chopped pineapple on top.

"Cheers." Yaz held her coconut high. "Now, this is the way to spend an afternoon." She adjusted her sunglasses, leaned back and looked out over the water.

"Just wait till tonight," Ian exclaimed, rubbing his hands together. "We are going to have us some fu-un."

* * * *

Atlantis sizzled. Slot machines rang out, screaming their winnings. Fast-handed dealers flicked cards onto the tables. Cocktail waitresses delivered gin and tonics and single malt scotches to highrollers. Throbbing dance music vibrated through the room.

This was the first casino I'd ever been in. It felt like I was in a James Bond movie. Women dressed in Hermes and Versace with ice cube-sized diamonds and gold dripping from their fingers were on the arms of powerful men in Armani, smoking Cuban cigars.

"Hit me." Ian tapped the first two fingers of his right hand on the table. He guarded his cards with his left. "Again."

This was a big night out for Ian, and he burned to get every last bit of fun out of the place. He drank numerous shots of rum and threw money away at the blackjack tables. He was out to experience it all. Me … I was feeling out of place. This was a long way from the country bars back home and quite different from the island bars we'd been visiting so far this trip. I decided to call it a night. When I left, Ian was dancing with a Bahamian beauty he'd been buying drinks for all night. He seemed determined to impress her, and it seemed his strategy was working. Laughing, Yaz and I left, knowing the outcome.

* * * *

I'd heard rumors that the Bahamians swear by the mighty conch as the be all and end all for hangovers, backaches, sore stomachs, hangnails, headaches and love troubles. But I didn't realize just how reverently they believed in its curative powers until Moe started talking.

VICTORIA ALLMAN

"For me see, it's best for lovin'. I use to eat it up everyday, and boy I had all the fun, if you know what I mean." Moe's laugh boomed. Ian winced. "Conch is better than that Viagra stuff you see on them TV's. Whew! I loved it. But den, after chil' number five, my wife, she say, no more." Moe seemed to be talking directly to Ian, now. "And that drink problem, it clear it all up. You go al' night wit dat rum, you eat conch salad for mornin' and you good as new."

It wasn't that Ian needed the Viagra aspect, per se, but his red, swollen, watery eyes and disheveled brown hair that stood up on one side, suggested the need for its magical cure for hangovers. Normally drop dead gorgeous, this morning he was sporting more of a homeless look. I'd found him in his cabin, passed out, yet still fully clothed. An overwhelming smell of rum emanated off him. This was no way to face Mike.

"Ian, wake up," I shouted, shaking him.

"Make it go away." He could barely focus. He was clearly in no shape to do anything, and if I wanted to avoid an explosion from Mike, I needed to take action.

Moe was the cabdriver who took me to the market each morning. Struggling to get Ian off the boat unnoticed, I called him. He was on his way to the daily domino game and agreed to take us to his secret spot.

Potters Cay was not far from the resort, just over and under the bridge. It hadn't escaped my attention that there IS a bridge to Paradise. Conch stalls lined both sides of the road. They looked like lemonade stands—of differentiating dilapidation. Each wooden stand was built with a concrete foundation, large sinks for washing the conch, and a counter where the proprietor made the salad. Moe directed us to Frankie's. "He's da best," he said, winking at me.

"You take good care of my friend here," Moe slapped Ian on the back and wandered off to watch the game of dominoes at the table beside us. It seemed to be the same perpetual game of dominos that was always underway. Twelve Bahamian men of all ages gathered around the table, slamming down their tiles. Some wore dress shirts and slacks, as if they just slipped out of the office; others sported ball caps and jeans with impressive gold rings and necklaces. Men with no teeth sucked on Kaliks, the local beer, while wrinkled old men with white curly hair shouted to the passing traffic. A few sat eating peanuts out of brown paper bags, waiting to rotate in.

Frankie organized his station in preparation for our medicinal meal. A native Bahamian, he had the dark skin and glowing smile we saw everywhere in the islands. He was mid-forty, as jovial and full of life as the local music. Without even asking, he knew why we'd come. He had Ian pegged the minute we sat down; everyone comes to Potters Cay for the same thing.

"Whew! Man, you need a Kalik, that'll feel you better." He reached in his cooler and pulled out two bottles. "You at that Atlantis las' night taking in the rum, maybe talkin' to some la-dies." He gyrated his hips and laughed.

Ian groaned. "Yeah, and now I'm here for the cure."

"You stand the heat?" Frankie raised an eyebrow.

"The hotter the better for me," Ian boasted.

"Good, good, you jus' sit back and let Frankie take care of you." With that he pulled two conchs out of the ocean behind him. He punctured the shell on the spiral, inserted his machete and cut the muscle. With expert precision, Frankie grabbed the meat from the open end of the shell and gently pulled. He sang us a Bahamian tune while dicing the meat. He neatly piled it into a heaping mound on the corner of his board and chopped onions, celery, and tomatoes with his long Indiana Jones-style knife.

A single Kalik beer umbrella sheltered us from the piercing sun. Normally, the fierce brightness is a welcome pleasure, but today the intensity sent daggers through an already fragile Ian. He moaned and dropped his head to the table. The heat of the day only exacerbated the smell of alcohol coming from his pores.

"You's always come to the big glitzy Atlantis with the music playin' and girls dancin'. You drink our fine rum, and come to Frankie the next day." Frankie squeezed three limes and an orange over the salad to marinate. He then pulled out the chili peppers; scotch bonnets, little bombs of heat as I have heard them called. "Jus' half for the lady, but for you man, you gotta have two." There was no room for argument in his voice. "We gonna sweat that stuff outta you."

He seasoned the mix with coarse sea salt and added another squeeze of lime, then opened another Kalik for Ian and handed us two heaping Styrofoam bowls. "This give you a stiff back my man. You be good just now." His eyes danced. "And tonight, you be real good." Frankie gyrated again.

We dove right in. Citrus spiked my tongue. The peppers hit but didn't overwhelm. There was the crunch of the celery, the softness of the tomatoes, and the unmistakable taste of the sea. It was sweet and hot and cooling all at the same time.

Concerned, I looked at Ian. He even had sweat coming out of his eyeballs and smelled more and more like last night's rum. The extra chilies in his concoction seemed to create a sweat lodge. He sat hunched over his bowl like he was at a prison mess table. Every few minutes he let out a shuddering sigh of exhaustion.

But a miracle was happening. Ten minutes earlier, he looked like death. But now, as he pushed away his empty bowl, he flashed me a big smile. Life returned to his eyes. Bahamian Viagra pulsed through his veins.

"Frankie, it worked," I said. "He's cured. Problem is, now he'll go out and do it all over."

"There are worse tings." Frankie gestured with a wave of his sword to his surroundings, "You can a'ways come back tomorrow. I fix you up again."

Tomorrow the sun would still be shining, the dominos game still going strong, and Frankie would still be chopping conch. I said, "Hold us a table."

Thank goodness, with a belly full of conch salad, and a few Kaliks sipped in the hot Bahamian sun, it was only a short walk back over the bridge to Paradise.

Frankie's Conch Salad

Conch is the beautiful coral and pink colored shellfish of the Caribbean. The white meat inside the shell is sweet, mild, and rubbery. To get to the meat, fishermen hammer a hole in the top of the shell near the center of the spiral, then they insert a knife and cut the muscle joining the meat to the shell. The meat is pulled out by hand and then scored or beaten with a mallet to tenderize it.

8 conchs, cleaned and scored or tenderized (it should come this way when
    you buy it, unless you are pulling it straight off the ocean floor)
2 stalks celery
1/2 white onion
1 green pepper
1 tomato
1/2 to 1 scotch bonnet, depending on your heat tolerance
1 orange
3 limes
1 teaspoon sea salt

Dice all vegetables to a 1/4 inch dice. Dice the conch as small as possible to avoid a chewy texture. Squeeze the citrus over the mix and season with salt. Taste and adjust the heat by adding more scotch bonnets. If you add more citrus, you will create a more piquant salad. Serve as a salad.

Serves 4

Norman's

*T*he smell of guava hung heavy in the air as I walked through the back door of Norman's. The pungent fruit filled the air with a sweet musk. The tropical produce and exotic spices on which Norman based his culinary creations melded together in the heat of the kitchen and lured me inside.

Our latest voyage to the Bahamas was over. When Pari entered the shipyard for a two-month paint job, my duties diminished to making sure plenty of pizzas and sandwich meat were available for crew lunches. At night, everyone scattered to various houses, girlfriends, and bars, so after cleaning up from lunch, I was off for the afternoon. Not one to sit around or lie on a beach for hours on end (my red hair and fair skin dictating otherwise) I volunteered my evenings at Norman's, my favorite restaurant in Miami.

I missed the heat of the kitchen, the adrenaline pumping through my veins just before dinner service as I watched the dining room fill with people. I missed the rush of not knowing what would happen on any given night, how many plates I would make, and wondering if I had enough sauce for the fish. I must confess I also craved the company and creativity of other chefs. I reminisced...

Knowing I couldn't stay at the Next Wave learning from Lawrence forever, I had headed west to Calgary, eventually becoming the sous-chef at River Cafe. Each night I stood in the open kitchen looking out at the birch wood tables and chairs. Apple-wood smoke gently drifted from the wood-fired ovens and grills.

The camaraderie of River's staff was what I loved most about my three years there.

"Ordering, two salmon, one chicken pasta, one rib-eye medium-rare," I would call to Dave, the man who'd stood beside me flaming pans and twirling pasta for the past four hundred nights.

"Right, duck for the peoples." He always answered the same way.

I didn't have to even look to know he was ready. We were a team and had danced this dance on many nights. I could hear his garlic sizzling beside me while I placed a rosemary and balsamic marinated dry-aged Alberta Beef rib-eye on the grill. Dave stepped behind me, reaching his long arm around to grab the barley for the risotto. I dodged under his six-foot frame to finish the plate and drizzled emerald green basil oil and canary yellow canola oil around the salmon. We wrapped around each other all night long, never once colliding.

"Next order, one venison and one arctic char."

"Right, duck for the peoples." And so our dance continued—until I packed my car and drove 3,500 miles to Lauderdale to join a boat.

I missed River. I enjoyed my own space on *Pari,* but now I needed the stimulation of a restaurant kitchen. I missed the immediacy of service and the familiarity with other chefs.

Norman greeted me like family. "Welcome to our kitchen." He smiled warmly. His demeanor and a slight graying of the temples gave him a scholarly air that enhanced his role of guiding the restaurant. "I want my food to challenge people," he said as we toured the kitchen. "I use unusual products most people have never tasted before. I don't want to scare anyone with these new flavors, so I build taste slowly through different courses and textures."

Norman Van Aken specialized in New World Cuisine, bringing together a culinary ethnic mix of Latin America, the Caribbean, and Asian cultures. He used Florida's local foods such as conch, plantains, mangoes, grouper, Key limes, and snapper. The restaurant earned accolades from prestigious sources including The James Beard Award, Wine Spectator's Award of Excellence, and New York Times' Best Restaurant in South Florida. With such a reputation, I was surprised to discover how easily I could talk with Norman. His charm immediately put me at ease.

"Where do you get these tomatoes?" I asked, hoping to source some of the same things in Lauderdale.

"Come in early tomorrow and we'll go to the farm in Homestead together.

I'll introduce you to Leorna, the woman who grows them for us." There were no secrets in his kitchen. "Everything begins with good ingredients." Norman echoed a statement I heard many times from Lawrence.

On my first night, I assisted Paula at the garde manger station, taking care of salads and cold appetizers. She introduced me to such local products as fresh hearts of palm (the inner tender portion of the stem of the cabbage palm tree that looks like white asparagus without the tip), bonito (a small variety of tuna), yucca (tropical tubers), and Key limes (a small, very tart variety of limes).

Norman came by half way through service to see how I was doing. "Always slice garlic with a sharp knife instead of chopping it. Pulverizing the clove leaves a bitter taste," he gently coached.

"Make sure you toast those spices before adding them to the marinade. That will release more flavor and aroma from them," Norman advised me a few nights later while watching me prepare the mojo, a popular Cuban marinade for a pork shoulder I was going to roast. He had the patience and tone of a father figure or favorite teacher encouraging rather than correcting me. I felt I was back in Lawrence's kitchen with his gentle nurturing.

Some chefs run their kitchens on fear. They intimidate. They scream. They throw things. Norman's fostering produced a better result than tirades.

* * * *

In the past, I worked briefly for a classically trained European chef. I was young and enthusiastic. He was not. Tired of sixteen-hour days, he stood at his stoves scowling night after night.

"What is this shit?" he screamed at me one evening.

I was totally confused. I'd seasoned the outside of the lamb rack with salt and pepper and then seared it on the grill, making diamonds on the top before finishing it in the oven. I tested its doneness the way he showed me the week before. I pulled it from the oven, allowing it to rest and develop a uniform pinkness throughout. I checked the order. The chit read one lamb rack medium-rare—that's what I thought I had in front of me. I couldn't understand his question.

"Lamb rack, chef," I squeaked.

"I can see that! I mean the bones. They look like shit. I can't serve them like this!"

The bones of the lamb had been scraped by the sous-chef that morning. They still had bits and pieces of fat and sinew running along the inside edge. With the heat of the grill, these pieces were now burned and shriveled, leaving the bones looking like the edges of a well-used pan.

"I ... I," I stammered.

I wasn't the one who butchered the lamb, but only last week I heard him screaming at an apprentice not to make excuses and blame others. "All I want to hear from you is 'Oui, chef'," he had screamed.

"I, I," he mocked. "You sound like a bloody broken record. Do them again. I'm not serving this shit." With that, he picked up the pan, threw it, and stormed off.

I could feel my face flush and my stomach tightened. My eyes burned hot; a single tear spilled down my cheek. Shit! I quickly wiped it away and turned from view. If the chef caught me crying it was all over.

Too late. Once the tears started, I couldn't stop them. They flowed silently down my face for the next hour while I worked, head down, facing the stoves. I tried laughing, but they wouldn't stop. I tried breathing deeply. They would not stop. I tried thinking of something else. They would not stop.

At that moment, this was not where I wanted to be or who I wanted to become.

* * * *

In the following weeks, I worked beside Norman's chefs at each station for two days. I rotated through every part of the kitchen, with every chef. I worked in the exhibition kitchen with its open counter top and two wood-fired ovens burning local citrus woods to flavor roasted duck and pork. I worked the stoves with Jeffrey Brana, where all main courses were produced.

Craig taught me to pan-fry yellow-tail snapper to a crisp golden brown while still maintaining a silky, moist texture inside. Brian introduced me to the management side of running the restaurant, actually giving me a copy of their handbook and recipes. And finally, I moved into the pastry kitchen where three different chefs baked breads and created desserts. I was dancing again.

I watched Norman listen to his kitchen team and respond to their information, ensuring every aspect of the restaurant fit his vision. He actually taught people instead of yelling at them.

The shouting from most notorious chefs ends up making them sound like asses. By comparison, this receptive climate translated into a calm, friendly kitchen, with a welcoming attitude of camaraderie, as I felt at the River. I was learning not only about food, but also how to manage people and create a productive environment. This culinary education was mostly lacking in stricter kitchens. Here at Norman's the cooks had no fear.

Their respect for Norman made them want to please him.

On my last evening I was invited to dine instead of work. Without a formal date, I invited Ian.

The restaurant glowed with soft lighting. Samba music played in the background as we passed under Spanish arches into the main dining room. The host seated us, placing menus designed especially for us into our hands: *Norman's Welcomes Victoria and Ian* they read. Ian nervously looked around as waiters worked unobtrusively, anticipating our every need. They kept our water glasses filled, never allowed to empty. Champagne was followed by selections of white and red wines from around the globe. The elegant ballet of service was flawless. Fresh baked breads arrived as our first course appeared in front of us. A bowl of creamy cracked conch chowder with toasted coconut started our meal.

Ian looked around sheepishly, then leaned over his plate and whispered, "Victoria, I've never had anything like this." He seemed almost embarrassed to admit it.

"Neither have I," I confessed. And it was true. Every dish proved distinctive and clear. The flavors of each course were perfectly balanced; subtle, yet full of flavor, nothing heavy or filling. Every spoonful tasted light and pure. The soup was followed by Vietnamese soft spring rolls with seared rare tuna and a peanut dipping sauce. Next came a fillet of Key West yellow-tail with asparagus spears and citrus butter.

I helped prepare each of these dishes in the previous weeks, but had yet to realize how intrinsically good they would taste as a part of the whole experience Norman created.

His signature dish was Down Island French Toast, which the waiter explained as he placed two plates in front of us. "Norman sears foie gras, marinated in a combination of vanilla, cointreau, cinnamon, and orange. He places it atop a bed of brioche to be baked, French toast-style. Surrounding that is a small dice of mango and papaya, and then sauced with a citrus caramel."

Ian and I dug in our forks. The French toast tasted soft and slightly sweet; the richness tempered by a hint of acidity. The taste lingered in my mouth.

Norman, himself, was a key factor in the success of the restaurant. He was there each night, overseeing plates as they left the kitchen. After service, he wandered through the dining room, asking each guest, "How was your evening?"

I stood to shake Norman's hand. "This was every bit the experience I knew it would be. Thank you so much."

"My pleasure." He leaned in and kissed my cheek. "Come again any time you need a dose of a restaurant kitchen."

After three weeks I said goodbye, having learned not only about tropical cooking and creating better tasting food, but also about the kind of chef and person I wanted to be. I decided then and there to cultivate the calm security Norman exuded. I wanted to be like Norman Van Aken.

Norman's Cracked Conch Chowder with Saffron, Coconut, and Oranges

This recipe's length may seem daunting, but it's Norman's most popular soup. The guests at the restaurant would riot in the streets if he took it off the menu.

Shellfish Broth:
1/4 cup olive oil
1 Scotch Bonnet, seeded and minced
6 shallots, thinly sliced
4 cloves garlic, thinly sliced
12 small clams, scrubbed
12 mussels, debearded and scrubbed
1 star anise
1 tablespoon roughly cracked black pepper
3 cups orange juice
2 teaspoons saffron
4 cups heavy cream
1 cup coconut milk

Vegetables:
6 new potatoes, diced
1/2 cup olive oil
1/4 cup smoked slab bacon, diced
4 cloves garlic, thinly sliced
1 poblano pepper, seeded and minced
1 ear corn, kernels removed
1/2 red onion, diced

~Continued on next page

2 large carrots, diced
1/2 fennel bulb, cored and diced
2 celery stalks, diced
1 red pepper, seeded and diced
1/4 cup roughly chopped cilantro leaves
2 bay leaves, broken
sea salt and pepper to taste

Conch:
3/4 pound cleaned and pounded conch
sea salt and pepper to taste
1/2 cup flour
1 pound panko crumbs
2 eggs, beaten
2 tablespoons half and half cream
3/4 cup peanut oil

To prepare the shellfish broth:
Heat the olive oil in a large, heavy-bottomed saucepan and sauté the chile, shallots, and garlic over medium-high heat for 1 minute, stirring them around. Add the clams, mussels, star anise and black pepper. Stir, add the orange juice and cover the pan.

As the clams and mussels open (after about 3 minutes), remove to a colander set over a bowl to catch the liquid. Take them out as they open, cover the pan again, and keep checking for more open ones. Discard any that do not open, cover the pan again, and keep checking for more open ones. Discard any that do not open after 10 minutes. Return the liquid caught in the bowl to the pan. After all the clams and mussels have been removed, uncover the pan and reduce the liquid until 1 cup remains, about 10 minutes.

Add the saffron, cream, and coconut milk. Bring to a boil, stirring occasionally; take care to prevent the mixture from boiling over. Reduce until the mixture just barely coats the back of a spoon, about 15 to 20 minutes. Turn off the heat and strain the mixture into a bowl. Discard the solids. Remove the clam and mussel meat from the shells and reserve.

To prepare the vegetables:
Bring a saucepan of lightly salted water to a boil, add the potatoes, and reduce the heat to a simmer. Cook for 8 to 10 minutes until they are underdone. Strain and set aside. In a large, heavy soup pan, heat the olive oil and sauté the bacon over medium-high heat until half cooked. Add the garlic and poblano pepper, and stir briefly. Add the corn, onion, carrots, fennel, celery, and bell pepper. Stir to coat. Add the cilantro, bay leaves, salt and pepper, Stir occasionally and cook until firm, about 8 minutes. Add the cooked potatoes, reserved saffron cream and the clam and mussel meat. Keep warm.

To prepare the conch:

Season it with salt and pepper. Place the flour and panko in separate plates, and whisk the eggs and half and half together in a bowl. Dredge the conch in the flour, then the egg wash, and finally the panko. Place on a large plate (layer with waxed paper or plastic, if you wish). Heat some of the peanut oil in a large skillet and sauté the conch over medium high heat in batches until nicely browned on both sides. Drain on paper towels and then chop them into pieces.

Ladle the soup into warm bowls and scatter the conch over the top.

You can substitute abalone for the conch in this recipe, or make the recipe without conch and garnish with cooked crabmeat or shrimp instead.

Optional garnish: orange sections, toasted coconut, or saffron threads.

Island Time

February has always been a month of the blues for me. Last year in Canada, I had wondered what to do with my extreme case of wanderlust. This year I planned to beat my low spirits by taking in a Blues Festival on Mustique, a small island in the West Indies.

The owners of *Pari* rent a seven-bedroom house every February on the island. Yaz and I were to fly down and meet them. She'd take care of the children, and I would cook. Three weeks on a secluded island in the Caribbean sunshine sounded like a good diversion from the blues.

I tried calling the butler of the house to ask some preliminary questions, "What equipment is in the kitchen? Where do I purchase food? What food is available?" The problem was, I couldn't get hold of the butler. For five straight days I called, and each day I was told Mr. Fitz wasn't available. One day it was a public holiday, the next it was siesta time, then he was serving lunch.

Finally, I was told, "Jus' a minute." Aha! He did exist.

The mysterious Mr. Fitz came on the line. "Good morning."

When I ran through my list of questions, he laughed whole-heartedly, a typical trait in the Caribbean. "Don't you worry. Everything is here on the island. You just ask me and I will get it for you."

I immediately felt myself slipping into a peaceful, relaxed mindset. This was going to be an easy working vacation.

Mike had warned me about the price and quality of the meat in the islands. "All provisions are shipped by boat. It's a slow boat from Miami that stops at each island along the way. By the time it gets to Mustique, it's all crap." No one ever accused Mike of holding back. "You'll have to carry all your meat with you on the plane or you'll be stuck with crappy chicken legs."

"On the plane? In my luggage?"

Mike rolled his eyes. "If you like, but coolers would probably work better." I'd pay for that naivetè later.

In the coming days I organized meals for the boat crew to eat while I was away, wrote menus, created shopping lists, planned and ordered. I combed Ft. Lauderdale for the bits and pieces I would need. Once everything was assembled, I began to pack away one hundred and fifty pounds of beef tenderloins, chicken breasts, veal, duck, crab, shrimp, and smoked salmon. I had everything delivered portioned and frozen in Styrofoam containers with ice packs to ensure it traveled safely and stayed frozen throughout the flights.

The day before my departure, I phoned the airline to confirm my flight and warn them of my intent to bring excess baggage; quite a lot of excess baggage. The woman on the other end of the phone recited the airline's script on flight time and baggage allowance. "One carry on and one seventy-pound bag," she droned in a robotic monotone.

"I have quite a bit of extra luggage. Can I pay an overage fee?"

Again she repeated the same phrase, not deviating at all from the script. "One carry on and one seventy-pound bag." Her tone of voice never changed.

Because of the smaller island planes to get to Mustique, I was only allowed one bag. One only! Not the three fifty-pound coolers I packed, plus my luggage, plus the owner's suitcases and their children's toys I would be bringing from the boat. After asking the woman repeatedly how I could solve my problem, I was told again and again that I could bring only one seventy-pound bag with me.

The situation was falling apart. I went to the captain.

Mike's laughed. "Do you really want to show up without any food?"

"No." I squeaked.

"Well then, you better think of something."

Sometimes he was no help at all. He must have seen the fear in my eyes. "Don't worry. I'll get you on that plane with all the meat."

Somehow I knew his answer to the problem would mean threatening the airline until I got on board with all the excess baggage, or bribing every person we came across. I wasn't overly impressed with either of these options, but they beat showing up empty handed and getting thrown to the wolves.

The following day, Mike and I left for the airport with one hundred and fifty-pounds of meat, one hundred pounds of luggage, and forty-pounds of toys, not knowing if any of it would actually be coming with me. To say I was scared would be an understatement.

Mike stood in line with his arms crossed. He braced himself, ready for a fight. Knowing his temper and flair for the dramatic, I decided the situation was up to me. Leaving Mike with the luggage, I swallowed hard and approached the man behind the counter. I put on my biggest and sweetest smile and innocently asked about my options.

"I really need to get this stuff to Mustique." I smiled wider. "My job depends on it."

The man looked at the pile of Styrofoam coolers on the cart behind me and shook his head in disbelief. I smiled sheepishly.

He nodded. "Just don't tell anyone who let all this stuff onboard."

"Thank you, so much. You just saved my job." I pulled out my wallet to pay the overage.

"Don't worry about that. Just have fun." Without even a fee, I was allowed onboard, excess baggage and all, proving once again my theory that a simple smile and kind words work wonders.

Relieved that Mike hadn't needed to scream at anyone, I said goodbye to him. Once onboard, I ordered a cocktail and I toasted the fact that I was on my way to the islands. After no less than three plane changes in Miami, Puerto Rico, and St. Martin, and multiple looks of disbelief from the baggage handlers at each stop, I arrived on the 1,400 acre postage stamp of an island.

Hot, heavy air enveloped me as I stepped from the small island-hopper that is common transport in the islands. I could hear the rhythm of ocean waves. The smell of tropical flowers filled the air. The dirt runway led from a rickety wooden shack into a jungle of lush green foliage.

I squinted in the bright sunlight. I spotted a dark-skinned man leaning against a golf cart-sized buggy. As I approached, he smiled. "Welcome to paradise," he said. "I'm Mr. Fitz."

It felt like I was being greeted by Tattoo. Mr. Fitz laughed the calm sweet laughter of someone who had found his happiness when he saw all my baggage being unloaded. He shook his head, and began loading it into his *moke*. "Come on, I will show you the house."

Frangipani, named after the small, lily-like flowers growing on the island, was a seven-bedroom villa overlooking *L'Ansecoy Bay*. The home featured mahogany floors and white sandstone walls. Flowing sheer curtains billowed in the breeze. The dark wooden furniture and brightly colored paintings played together in a true Caribbean way. Four acres of immaculate gardens surrounded the estate, with an Olympic-sized swimming pool overlooking the Caribbean Sea from high up on the hillside. The owners and Yaz wouldn't arrive until the next evening, so for a short time I had the house to myself.

As soon as I'd settled in my room, showered and changed, I was introduced to Irma, the cook at the house, who also exuded the carefree, joyful Caribbean spirit. Dressed in her Mother Hubbard flower-print dress she was singing when I met her. I instantly felt at ease in her kitchen.

"Child, you're gonna love it here," she exclaimed. She laughed when I asked about the vegetable order I'd requested earlier. "Everything arrive on Monday on da boat." Today was Friday.

I looked around the spotless kitchen. I had a hard time masking my shock at the cooking facilities. One of the two ovens was out of order. We had no propane for the barbecue, no fresh milk, no variety of cheeses and only a few vegetables. I had one papaya, twenty-four grapefruit, baking potatoes, and a large bowl of green tomatoes available to prepare the next day's dinner. Not quite the "everything you need" that Fitz had described on the phone. The meat had arrived with me, but there was nothing else.

Years ago I read *Don't Stop the Carnival,* a novel by Herman Wouk about life in the Caribbean. What I remember most is the author's portrayal of activities and business done at one pace: dead slow. At the time, I found this amusing and dreamed of such an idyllic lifestyle, never thinking I would one day be trying to work on "island time."

Fitz, still his friendly and helpful self, came to see how I was getting on. "It's not exactly what I'm used to," I said, not wanting to insult him.

He just laughed, "Don't worry."

Easy for him to say.

But it was Irma to the rescue. Having lived her whole life in the islands, she knew exactly how things worked. She roamed out the door to her garden, a tropical growth looking out over the cliff. Humming as she wandered the misshapen rows, she began picking. I smiled. We'd use what we had.

The gardener gathered coconuts from the yard. Irma sat in the garden, under the shade of a tree, hunched over a wooden board that resembled a huge cheese grater. Her large frame curved over the board as she put her whole weight into the job of extracting the thick sweet liquid. Homemade coconut milk. She scrunched her back up like a cat and extended out. No wonder she was such a strong woman.

Callaloo soup was the first thing she taught me. Callaloo is a hearty green leafy vegetable with a slight bitter taste, like strong spinach. Irma sautéed these heart-shaped leaves with carrots and onions and an herb called picky thyme from the garden.

Singing a hymn while she stirred the pot, she added chicken stock and the coconut milk. The final touch was a garnish of crabmeat that I'd brought from the States. It was smooth, slightly peppery on the tongue, and creamy at the same time. Irma had just saved me.

Over the next few weeks, with Irma's help, I learned such local dishes as pigeon peas and rice, banana fritters and pumpkin soup. She also taught me to marinate hearts of palm harvested from the inner top shoots of the cabbage palm trees that grew on the property for salads. On *Pari* I'd eaten fresh from the sea. Here in paradise, I would cook with nature's bounty fresh from the earth. Irma's patient sharing of technique and produce made me feel somehow more connected to the island, more at ease and self-reliant.

Still, the following weeks brought many challenges. Mustique's slow-motion existence was daunting. Fishermen sometimes brought only inedible barracuda to the market, and the delivery boat brought only half of my order. Extra guests were invited, arriving within minutes of a prepared dinner. Lobster was undercooked because I ran out of propane a second time, and one morning the kitchen was swarming with cockroaches. Life in the islands, I was told.

But there were also times when the owners left the house, and Yaz and I could go swimming in the pool. One afternoon we took the kids exploring on one of the seven beaches and saw Pierce Brosnon frolicking in the surf. I hiked over jagged boulders to a forgotten beach to watch the explosion of white foam produced by the pounding waves. I built sand cities with the children under the shade of a palm tree. And spent a night or two, floating on the water at Basil's with my tropical rum drinks, listening to the blues until the wee hours of the morning.

Basil's, a palm thatched bamboo bar, built on a wooden deck three-feet over the water, was the only place to go on the island aside from the two hotels. But with its ocean-breezes and dance floor under the stars, where else would one want to be?

Yaz felt at home in any location, but particularly in a Caribbean bar. On more than one occasion she had led me through a crazy night, and this night she was at the top of her game. She immediately struck up conversation with the bartender.

Leaning over her drink conspiratorially, she said, "So, tell me sweetheart, who's on the island this week?" Mustique had been the home to David Bowie, Mick Jaggar, and Princess Margaret. Hugh Grant was a regular.

The bartender looked around to see who was listening. "Tommy Hilfiger is at the other end of the bar."

"Ohh," Yaz leaned in even farther to get a better look.

"And Johnny Depp was in here two nights ago."

"I might just have to sit here until he returns." She smiled and ordered another drink. "There's no where else in the world I want to be than right here."

I agreed. Here I was, sitting at the bar, drinking rumrunners, laughing with my friend, listening to Ian Siegal perform 'One Bourbon' and watching stars dance on the water. February blues never felt so good.

Irma's Callaloo Soup

Callaloo Soup is a signature soup in the Grenadines but found throughout the islands. The soup's key ingredient is Callaloo, a spinach-like leaf from the dasheen plant. You can usually find it in Caribbean grocers but spinach is an acceptable substitute. Scotch bonnets are readily available in the Caribbean, but if you cannot find them you can substitute a habenero pepper.

1 tablespoon butter
2 tablespoons vegetable oil
1 large onion
1 carrot
3 cloves garlic
1 teaspoon sea salt
1 pound callaloo or 2 pounds spinach
1 scotch bonnet or habenero pepper
1 tablespoon fresh thyme sprigs
6 cups chicken stock
Sea salt and pepper
1 can coconut milk (450 ml)
1/2 pound crabmeat

Heat a heavy-bottomed soup pot over medium-high heat with butter and vegetable oil. When hot add onion, carrots, garlic and sea salt. Sauté for 5 minutes, stirring occasionally until softened. Add callaloo and sauté a further 2 minutes. Add scotch bonnet, thyme, and chicken stock. Simmer for 15 minutes. Puree in a blender and pass through a sieve. Season with salt and pepper. Add coconut milk. Heat just until warm being careful not to boil or the vibrant green color will turn grey. Add crabmeat and serve.

Serves 6

Buon Giorno Bella

I am guilty of a heinous culinary crime. For years my favorite food has been that of the Mediterranean. Anything with the warm summer flavors of sweet tomatoes and fragrant basil with the tang of black olives or the zing of salty capers won my heart. But I had never been there. I hadn't tasted authentic Mediterranean cuisine.

I'm embarrassed to admit that until *Pari* arrived in Europe for the summer, I thought tomatoes and basil were the flavor of the Mediterranean. I just assumed that sun-dried tomatoes and pine nuts were a prerequisite to every dish.

In the summer months, when hurricanes threaten the Caribbean and east coast, many yachts voyage across the Atlantic for the Mediterranean Sea. *Pari* was no exception. For three months in the summer we anchored off the island of Sardinia. Cala di Volpe, with its clear blue waters, white sand beaches, and terra-cotta villas dotting the hillsides is the Mediterranean getaway for the rich.

The fishermen in Cale di Volpe waited for the yachts to arrive each summer. Every morning as I started the day's baking, a tender would approach full of tuna, red snapper, sea bass, shrimp and lobster. The *pescatore* Vito, an Italian fisherman with dark hair slicked back off his aging face, bellowed to me. "Vitorea! Vitorea! Buon Giorno!" His thick accent brought me running—not only in anticipation, but also for fear he'd wake the whole boat.

"Buon giorno, bella," Vito sang out, his whole face lighting up as I approached the back of the boat.

"Buono giorno, Vito," I ventured, practicing the few words of Italian I had picked up. We exchanged kisses on the cheek. He was an olive-skinned wrinkle of a man who'd spent too much of his youth on a fishing boat in the hot sun. His hands were rough, his back slightly rounded, and his forearms bulged like Popeye's, but his eyes still sparkled with life. I would bet he could hold his own when trying to charm a young signorina.

I found Vito charming, but more for the load of freshly caught fish he delivered, some still flopping in the bottom of his boat. Each morning brought a lesson in the Italian language along with its seafood.

"Today, *Spigole*." Vito held up a silver-skinned fish for me to inspect. "Favorite here. On island." He prodded me with his rudimentary English.

"Si." I bought it to grill with olive oil, coarse sea salt and herbs. More familiar in Vito's boat was a varying array of *pescatrice* (monkfish), *tonno* (blue fin tuna), *muscolo* (mussels), *calamaro* (squid) and *vongola* (clams); all of which I bought throughout the summer.

My favorite discovery in the bottom of Vito's boat was his shrimp. I never thought I liked shrimp, having mainly experienced the frozen blocks of Tiger shrimp that were so popular with grocery stores at home. I long ago dismissed this popular seafood as being bland, rubbery and boring. I hadn't tried it in years. However, here in the middle of the Mediterranean, Vito changed my mind. One morning he arrived, excited and eager to sell me his *Gamberi Rosso*, a large, red-fleshed shrimp. He plunged his thick fist into a plastic tub and brought out a shrimp, fat as a cigar.

"Yes?" he asked expectantly. I was quite alarmed by the florescent purple vein running down its spine. But, Vito had yet to steer me wrong.

"Si." Later in the day, I sautéed them in olive oil and garlic for pasta. The taste was like no shrimp I had ever experienced. This sweet and tender meat was the way shrimp were suppose to taste.

The next morning, from the bottom of Vito's boat I selected the monkfish to roast that night.

"Benissimo," Vito cried, clapping his hands together with pride and approval like I had announced my winning of the Nobel Prize. Vito lovingly placed my fish on the back deck like a father placing his newborn down for a nap. "Grazi, Vitorea." He leaned out over his shaky boat to kiss my cheek. "Arrevederci." He sped off with the promise of more fish tomorrow.

The island of Sardinia is populated with shepherds and fishermen, so it is no surprise that seafood and pecorino cheese rule the table. Each week I went ashore to buy groceries. I stopped at a farmer's stand on the side of the road and picked up a wheel of *pecorino sardo*. I loved its rich flavor of the area. The sheep graze on the local myrtle and wild thyme, lending a unique taste to the ewe's milk. It seemed only fitting to serve it in the afternoons with juicy ripe pears, toasted walnuts, and a chilled glass of wine before the lighter dinner of fish that Vito provided.

In *caffes* I ordered strong black shots of espresso, not even close to resembling what I drank at home. "Vorrei un espresso per favore," I practiced the words. The robust coffee felt smooth in my mouth; the barista made a perfect pick-me-up for my foray to buy vegetables. The road twisted and turned over the jagged hills on my way to town.

At the market, shopkeepers accosted me with invitations to try one of their hand-kneaded breads. Made with durum wheat, the bread is dense and chewy and robust—much like the islanders themselves. "Due," I say holding up two fingers, forgetting the word for bread.

I gathered spicy charcuteries of pork made from the free-range pigs that fed on the same myrtle and thyme. "Buona flavor," the man tells me, combining English and Italian.

With a wink, a woman slipped a jar of fragrant honey into my sac as she packed the vegetables I'd selected. "You'll taste the flavor of the island in the honey." She spoke better English than my Italian. The food was simple yet flavorful, and I rushed back to *Pari* to set out the spread I'd procured.

Pari traveled back and forth from Sardinia to the mainland of France and Italy: Nice, Cannes, Monaco, St. Tropez, Genoa, Portofino, Livorno. Each region taught me something new. I discovered *cacciucco* in Livorno, a tomato based fish stew made with five different fish—one for each C in the name. In Sienna, I found *paneforte,* a very dense chewy fruitcake made with chocolate, dried fruits and nuts. Corsica provided warm chestnut honey that I drizzled over strong astringent cheeses. I experienced *panzanella salads* served with a glass of wine on a patio at a Tuscany and *Cassoulet,* the traditional peasant stew of duck, garlic sausage and white beans in Languedoc. Only on the Margarita pizzas and Capresi salads did I taste the tomato and basil combination I once associated with Mediterranean cooking.

* * * *

The owners of the boat lived onboard for the summer. This meant full sixteen-hour days, seven days a week. Ian awoke earlier than normal to arrange all the cushions outside and chamois the morning dew from the yacht. He then headed into the engine room to start his daily maintenance routines before devoting himself to the owner's needs of tender runs, water skiing, and swimming with the kids. At night he reversed the action and brought all the cushions inside to keep dry. He stayed up late to lock the doors after everyone went to bed.

I started my day even earlier, getting breakfast ready and cooking for ten people each day, as well as looking after the children and keeping them occupied in a small space. My nights went longer and longer as the owners relaxed and pushed the dinner hour back farther and farther. This was Italy, where eating dinner at ten or eleven at night was the norm. All day long the stewardesses had rooms to clean, laundry to do, and three meals a day to set and clean up after. We kept a hectic schedule.

With the extra hours involved with full-time guests, it wasn't long before we were worn out and dragging our heels. The crew needed more help. Knowing we needed a respite, Mike hired Chris, Ian's best friend, to join the boat for the summer. He came aboard smiling and pitched in wherever needed. Within day's of his arrival, we were all laughing and enjoying our jobs again.

* * * *

I ventured out to the bow one day to get a breath of fresh air, and there was Chris dangling the owner's son by the feet over the rail. "You better hope I'm strong enough to hold you," he said. "I could drop you."

"NO!" The boy squealed. "I tell father!" Both the parents were standing on the upper deck watching and smiling, the wife taking pictures.

"I don't think he can help you now, I'm the pirate king and you have to walk the plank." Chris pulled out a rope out and wrapped it around the little boy's legs. "You are my prisoner now."

"No! Victoria, help me!" he cried.

I folded my arms. "Not much I can do. Pirate Kings are too powerful for me."

The little girl came up behind me and held her arms out to be picked up. She, too, gave a high-pitched yell, "Let him go!"

Chris turned, an eyebrow raised, to glare at her. She yelped and hid behind my arm.

"Could you boil both of them in a pot for lunch?" Chris asked me.

—— VICTORIA ALLMAN ——

"No!"

They both screeched, laughing.

After that Chris was on babysitting detail and couldn't shake his two new best friends. It gave us all breathing room to catch up on some of the work that had to be done.

Finally, the owners went out to dinner, and we were given the night off. Someone had to stay onboard in case of emergencies, but Chris, Ian and I opted for some much needed time off the boat. As true American boys, Chris and Ian wanted to go for pizza. The three of us piled into the tender for the ride ashore, excited to step away from the boat and see something of the island.

Our plan was to meet up with another crew and then go out dancing to Sottovento, Sardinias' famous nightclub. The club didn't even start until after midnight and stayed lively until five or six in the morning, so we had time to explore the town of Porto Cervo.

The *Lady Linda* crew was already at the piazzetta when we arrived, and bottles of Sardinia's ruby red powerful *Cannonau di Sardegna* wine crowded the table. But my attention was focused on Patrick, their first mate. "Hey, it's about time you guys got here." He rose to shake hands with the guys and give me a kiss hello.

I blushed. "It's about time we were in the same place at the same time."

Patrick and I had met at the Lauderdale boat show eight months earlier and went on four or five dates before both boats left in different directions for the winter. While we were in the Bahamas, *Lady Linda* went to Mexico. Five months later, we were both in Lauderdale again for just one weekend before we both headed to the Mediterranean. But his boat went to Spain, and we cruised to France. This was the first time we'd been in the same port in three months and even then, it was only for the night.

When I first met Patrick, I thought he was sophisticated like a martini; but as I came to know him I realized that he was a Coke float. One minute I was impressed by his worldly knowledge, and a few seconds later I was laughing at his boyish antics.

On our second date, Patrick had taken me for sushi and ordered in Japanese. "Doumo arigato," he said after ordering us beers, a dozen different sushi, and miso soups in Japanese. He made the waitress giggle and run from the table. I sat astonished.

"Where did you learn to do that?"

"Too many years in Hawaii trying to impress girls." He had the quintessential blond hair, big smile and laid-back attitude of a surfer. Years of being in the sun had burned deep groves in his face, along with the obligatory sunglass marks. His broad chest from paddling out to the waves implied he might have been successful.

Our third date was to a go-kart track where he could hardly contain his excitement and played pinball games like a child. We hit balls in a batting cage and raced cars round and round a track. Our dates were never boring. I never knew if we'd be viewing an Impressionist painting at a museum or riding the roller coasters at Disneyland.

Pulling up chairs, we all exploded into stories of where we had been and what we'd seen so far. Patrick ordered more bottles of wine, and Chris, Ian and I ordered pizzas.

The bay was abloom with sailboats anchored for the night. They bobbed in the water. A mystical waxing moon hovered above their masts.

Our pizzas arrived. "Bon appetite," Ian said before digging in.

"That was last month, in France. You have to say "Buono appetito" now that we are in Italy," Chris corrected.

"Yeah, whatever." Ian was already chewing.

The thin-crusted pie was baked in a wood burning stone oven across the piazzetta. It had the telltale crispy burnt edges of such an oven. Half a dozen rounds of fresh mozzarella melted over a puddle of thin, yet sweet, tomato sauce. Four whole black olives, pits still inside, garnished the top. It shimmered with a healthy dose of olive oil poured over the top, resembling nothing like the three-inch-thick loaded supreme pizzas from home.

We drank, ate, and laughed talking long into the night. I nervously listened to stories and wondered where I stood with Patrick. Another bottle of wine was ordered, he leaned over my chair and whispered in my ear, "Let's take a walk."

I felt my temperature rise. I had trouble swallowing.

"Sure." I tried to stand on wobbly legs. I felt like a nervous teenager seeing Patrick again after such a long time. This was certainly a way to keep the newness of a relationship alive. It always felt like the first date. "We'll be back soon." I said to Chris.

Laughter and voices faded behind us as we left to stroll through the narrow, moonlit cobblestone streets. I breathed deeply, trying to steady my nerves. Patrick wore the same musky scent I remembered. It reminded me of the last time he held me close.

At first we didn't speak. I was too conscious of him walking beside me and couldn't think of anything to say. We started with small talk and finally felt comfortable enough to venture into something real.

"I was hoping we'd see you this summer," I said, cringing. Was that too dorky to say?

Patrick smiled and grabbed my hand. My throat caught. I laughed. That confirmed it, I was a dork. The moon rose higher in the night sky, flooding the dimly lit streets with its glow.

We roamed from one piazzetta to the next, past elite boutiques, lingering around each shop window, not wanting the end to come. Warm Mediterranean air filled with the scent of the sea blew through my hair. I felt like the heroine from the pages of a romantic tale.

I laughed at his stories of running through Rome, and the places he'd been that summer. I wished I'd been there with him. Finally, he pulled me into a doorway and ran his fingers through my hair, tilting my head back. He kissed me—a kiss I felt all over my body.

Eventually, Patrick had to leave. *Lady Linda* was picking up the owners the next day and he couldn't stay.

"I'll be in Lauderdale for the boat show in October," I said, hoping he'd pick up on my hint.

"I think the boat will be in the shipyard at that time, so I should be there too." It was the best we could do as crew. You never really could commit to anything. We were not the ones in control of our schedules.

He cupped my face in his hands and kissed me good-bye. For the first time that night I felt calm.

The long days of summer were dwindling fast. The children had to start school in Germany soon. The owners decided to sell *Pari* and just charter boats when the children had holidays.

After working together for three months straight in such a small living space, we were sad to see our lives together ending. But endings lend themselves to beginnings, and we were all excited to start our next adventures. Yaz had already moved on to another boat. Christine was pregnant, and she and Mike planned to move to Australia. Ian and Chris were planning a backpacking trip across Europe. I would join them for a few days and explore Paris. But mostly I was excited to head back to Lauderdale for another date with Patrick.

Shrimp and Haricot Vert Sauté

2 pounds haricot vert
1 tablespoon sea salt
1/2 cup olive oil
8 cloves garlic, chopped
2 pounds shrimp, peeled and deveined
1 teaspoon sea salt
1 teaspoon black pepper
1/2 red onion, diced finely
1 lemon, zested and juiced
1/4 cup chopped basil

Bring a large pot of water to a boil and add 1 tablespoon sea salt. Slice haricot verts in half on an angle. Boil in water for 4 minutes. Drain and place in ice water to retain bright green color. Drain and reserve.

Heat a heavy bottomed sauté-pan on high. Add 2 tablespoons olive oil and 2 cloves of garlic. Add 1/4 of the shrimp and season with some of the salt and pepper. Sauté 2 minutes on each side until they are just cooked through, the flesh will turn from opaque to white. Be careful not to overcook them or they will turn tough and chewy. Scrape the pan into a large salad bowl with a rubber spatula and repeat process working in batches for the rest of the shrimp.

Add 2 tablespoons olive oil to pan and sauté the red onion for 1 minute until soft. Add reserved haricot vert and sauté for 2 minutes to warm. Scrape into salad bowl. Toss all with lemon juice zest and basil. Taste for seasoning and acidity.

Serve warm as a salad with crusty bread to dip in the residual lemon vinaigrette. Any leftovers make a great salad the next day.

Serves 6

A Night in Provence

*T*raveling alone can often be a blessing in disguise. A lone-traveler, if open-minded and receptive, can experience all the pleasures of local hospitality and atmosphere better than a group of any size. People are more willing to speak to a person alone and conversation flows more naturally than with a collection of people.

This is what happened to me as I left St. Tropez for a few days of travel through France before flying home. I was headed to Paris to meet Chris and Ian, but first I wanted to stop in a few towns along the way to see France—something I had no time to do while working. At the bus station the dark-haired girl in front of me was struggling with the language.

"Just me. Un! No one else. Pas de personne," she enunciated.

"Oui, deux personnes pour Marseilles." The ticket agent held up two tickets for her to see.

"Non, Un! Me only. Une autre personne is gone." She waved her hands like an umpire calling a player safe.

"Deux billets pour Marseilles?" the man questioned.

The girl sighed. Her shoulders slumped forward. "Oui, deux." She had two pre-paid tickets and was trying to sell one back to the agent, who was having none of it.

"I'll buy the other from you," I offered. I wanted to go to Marseilles anyway.

"Really? That would be great." She brightened and grabbed both tickets back from the sour agent with a thanks-for-nothing smile. "Hi, I'm Linda." She shifted her backpack to her other shoulder and stuck her hand out. "My boyfriend and I have been traveling through France for the last month. He was supposed to take this bus with me to visit my family, but just this morning he decided to go to Spain instead." She rolled her eyes. "You just saved me forty dollars."

We rode along the high coastal roads along the Cotes d'Azur of the French Rivièra, enjoying the panoramic views of the Mediterranean Sea. We spoke of her travels that summer, the food she'd experienced, the challenge of not speaking French, and how hard it was traveling with a man who was quickly becoming an ex-boyfriend.

"I envy you," she said. "You can do exactly what you want to do, see what you want to see and go where you want to go."

"Well, that's one way of looking at it." I hated to disappoint her. "Lately, I'm starting to think I would love to have someone to share all of this with."

"Ugh!" She may have had trouble with her boyfriend, but the two of us found we shared the same desire to see the culture of the places we were visiting. "There has to be some guy out there who is interested in the things we are," she lamented.

I thought of how much Patrick and I had in common, but kept that tidbit to myself.

We passed rolling foothills with fields of lavender blooming purple flowers, and rows of sunflowers lined up like soldiers, rotating to face the sun. Three hundred days of sun a year create a perfect canvas for the colors of Provence, land of the sun. Again, I thought of Patrick and how I wish he'd been sitting beside me, but timing worked against us. I had time to travel while he was busy working. Last month he had a week to travel, but I was in full swing with guests on the boat.

The day, awash with sunlight that coated the olive trees in gold, cast a glow over us as we stepped off the bus in the bustling old world port city. As I considered where to head, my new friend Linda spoke up, "Hey, my sister is expecting two anyway. Would you like to stay with us tonight?"

I planned to stop in Marseilles only long enough to taste the *bouillabaisse* that the region is famous for before traveling on to Lyon. But Linda was offering an evening in an authentic Provençal home. This was an opportunity I couldn't refuse.

Linda's sister Marybeth, a short wisp of a woman, so unlike the tall anorexic women of the French Rivièra, was waiting for Linda at the station. She, too, insisted I stay with them. "I hope you don't mind coming to the market with me to pick up a few things for dinner?" How could I have a problem with that?

But first it was lunchtime. We wandered through town toward the waterfront, stopping to get a history lesson from Marybeth, who had married a French man and lived there the past twelve years. Having heard of my quest for a bowl of *bouillabaisse*, Marybeth directed us to an outdoor patio on the quay. We sat at a rickety wooden table beside two crusty French fishermen, still dressed in yellow overalls and rubber boots. They sat hunched over steaming bowls of soup, slurping loudly. This had to be the place for fish soup.

A round, robust woman with thick fingers and her hair pulled back by a scarf placed baskets of warm baguettes before us. She spoke a few words of French to Marybeth. There was no menu. No options. Three large shallow bowls of fish soup appeared. The same woman plunked bowls of rust colored *rouille,* shaved gruyere cheese and toasted croutons rubbed with garlic cloves, in the center of the table. She scattered a handful of thick heavy soupspoons before us.

"I think I like this dish so much because it is a great excuse to eat garlic and bread." Marybeth picked up one of the crouton rounds and spread a generous amount of the *rouille* over the top. She floated the prepared bread in the saffron and tomato broth. She pinched a teaspoon of cheese with her fingers and sprinkled it on top of the suspended bread that was now soft, having soaked up the flavorful liquid of the soup. "Sometimes you don't even get any chunks of fish in the soup. There is just the liquid to soak up."

Watching closely, I mimicked her routine. In lifting the round soupspoon to my lips, I inhaled the powerful aroma of saffron, fish, and garlic. The raw piquant burning of garlic mixed with rich olive oil and roasted red pepper puree of the *rouille* created an explosion of flavor in my mouth. The taste of fish danced on my tongue and brought a smile to my face. This is what I had traveled here to taste. I wanted to reach over and hug the fishermen at the next table for their long hard labor in the sun.

After a filling and satisfying meal, our afternoon progressed to the local markets in the port. Marybeth picked out the freshest seasonal vegetables from tables laden with grey-green bulbs of baby artichokes still on the stalk. Purplish black elongated eggplants known as auburgines sat beside long stalks of leeks, with mud from the fields still clinging to their roots. Piles of wild mushrooms gathered from the nearby woods were heaped in a wooden basket.

"I love this time of year." Marybeth picked up a long braid of garlic from the table in front of her. She moved the garlic just under her nose and breathed in deeply. "The summer vegetables are still on the tables, and the first of the fall root vegetables start to appear." She handed the garlic braid to the market woman, nodding in approval.

We passed tables piled high with over twenty different olives. Black wrinkled olives cured in salt sat next to pale green ones mixed with snipped herbs and whole cloves of garlic. Others floated in brine or were chopped to a fine paste to be used as a spread on crackers. Marybeth popped a youthful fat green olive with smooth skin into her mouth as she perused the selection.

Strolling farther down the street we entered *La Poissonnierie*. The fishmonger explained that being late in the day, the usual stocks of *dorade royal* (sea bream), *loup de mer* (sea bass), monkfish and rockfish were depleted. After looking over trays of sardines, lined up like cigarettes in a package, anchovies, and tiny mussels in a pile, Marybeth decided on the bright red-fleshed loin from a bluefin tuna, *thon rouge*, still moist and plump looking.

The next stop was the *boulangerie* for fresh baked baguettes and then around the corner for cheeses. The people of Provence prefer to shop daily instead of stockpiling their refrigerators with a weekly shop. The market was bustling with people, all searching for that night's meal.

We piled into Marybeth's tiny Peugeot and drove out into the country, where we passed stands of umbrella pines that cast shade over the green-black grapevines along one side of the road. Silver-grey olive groves lined the other. We pulled into the long driveway of her stonewalled farmhouse, the thick walls covered in ivy.

Inside, Marybeth began poking through the dark wood cabinets. Warm yellow tiles in her kitchen provided a welcoming invitation. The home had high ceilings, large rooms filled with fruit wood antique furniture, dark wood shutters on the windows, and the vivid country prints of Provence. Burnt terra cotta tiles covered the floors and herb baskets lined the windows.

Marybeth chatted as she worked. "Bernard is from this area and when we were dating he brought me by this house. I just fell in love." She chopped rosemary on a thick olive wood chopping block. The task sent a woodsy aroma through the kitchen. "We walked around the town, and I knew this is where I wanted to live."

The afternoon passed in a blur of cooking, talking, and tasting. Preparation was intermingled with frequent trips to the sun-soaked pool to swim, followed by a relaxing glass of rosé on the terrace under the shade of a cypress tree. There was no rush, no set hour for dinner, no stress. We marinated tuna, snipped herbs from the gardens, stewed the ratatouille, and bathed and spun the lettuce.

The smell of the lavender wafted through the open shutters as a gentle breeze blew in from the garden. It was all so civilized. A sense of loving life, relaxation permeating the afternoon.

Bernard, a tall slender man in his early forties, arrived home around seven, signaling the time had come to switch from the afternoons rosé to the Muscat de Beumes-de-Venise, a rich, amber-colored wine that balances sweetness and acidity. "This wine is usually served as a dessert wine after the meal," Bernard explained in a French accent. "But it is actually the perfect aperitif, and often we enjoy it at the beginning of the evening."

Using her stone mortar and pestle, Marybeth pounded black olives and capers into a paste. The resulting pungent *tapenade* was set out in Provençal pottery, along with more of the heady *rouille*, and fresh anchovies to be placed on bite-size pancakes.

Bernard was right, the taste of honey and apricots cut through the salty avalanche of flavors and ignited my hunger. Talk turned to food and wine and how they are an integral part of life here.

"We have eaten this way our whole lives in France." He spread tapenade on bread. "Food is so much more apart of our life than in Western cultures. Here you eat and drink to enjoy yourself and the people around you. Not because it is a necessity, but because it is a pleasure. Food is the way the family interacts with each other," he continued. "We make an effort to never miss a meal. Dinner is a time to bond."

"Tonight's dinner is very indicative of Provençe," Marybeth added. " This is our usual meal on a typical night here."

The distinctive cuisine of Provençe is formed from its location. The proximity to the sea allows for an abundance of seafood, while the hillside and steep mountains provide the perfect conditions for growing olives and raising sheep. Orange and lemon groves, vineyards, and vegetable gardens fill the fertile spaces in between. The cuisine is light and one of the healthiest in the world. Provençe's ample sunshine supplies the area with warm weather, as well as aromatic herbs and vegetables such as tomatoes, zucchini, peppers, basil, and oregano. Use any combination of these ingredients with a large amount of garlic and you have the harmonious bold flavors and base of Provençal cooking.

Since the night was warm, with only a slight breeze, we set the table outside at the outdoor kitchen/dining room that overlooked the gardens. Marybeth started our dinner by tossing the greens first in olive oil to protect the tender leaves, then adding sea salt for seasoning. Finally, she squeezed a splash of fresh lemon juice over top. She then adorned the top of the baby greens with *foie gras de canard*, smoked duck breast, and cherry tomatoes. Bernard poured *Loupiac*, a sweet Bordeaux that's lighter than a *Sauternes*, and which paired perfectly with the rich *foie gras*.

"Salut," we toasted. "To family and new friends."

Next came the tuna, marinated in olive oil and rosemary. Marybeth grilled the steaks to medium rare over grapevines on her outdoor grill. Musky smoke filled the air. She served the fish on a puddle of ratatouille, a Provençal stew of eggplant, red peppers, zucchini, onions, and thyme laced with olive oil and black pepper. For this we returned to a rosé, *Coteaux D'Aix en Provençe*, a light dry wine of the area.

Slowly, we worked our way through the courses while the crescent moon rose higher in the night sky. The cheese course consisted of flavorful French cheeses: a soft textured goat cheese from the area, a ripe and runny brie, and the creamy *St. Marcellin*.

Bandol now came out, a full-bodied red wine made from Mourvedré grapes. The taste was intense and spicy.

"Aren't you an accountant?" I asked Bernard.

"Mmm." He had his nose buried in the bowl of his wine glass. He inhaled deeply.

"How do you know so much about wines?"

He looked up startled. "I am French."

Marybeth knew that wasn't enough of an answer. "Bernard grew up in Lyon, arguably the culinary capital of France. He has been exposed to great food and wines his whole life."

Bernard nodded. "I am not out of the ordinary here. It is our way of life." It all seemed very natural to him, this dinner experience wasn't a special event, like it was to me. Here, children eat what the adults eat and drink what the adults drink. I looked to his children. Emily, seven years old, dined on the goose liver *foie gras,* and Thebour, at two years old, was busy "gumming" the strong blue *Roquefort* cheese like it was a candy bar. This certainly was a different childhood experience from that in North America where the children would be having hamburgers and French fries in front of the television.

My night in Provence finished with a stroll through the garden to pick fresh raspberries, purple ripe figs, and almonds from the tree. There is something intrinsically fresh and natural about picking your food straight from the source moments before consumption.

Looking out at the view from the house, my glass of wine in hand, I realized I could not have planned this evening by reading any guidebook or consulting a travel agent. The friendliness and hospitality gained by a chance acquaintance on a bus trip along the coast of France is something I will always remember. And to my growing list of close friends, I added three more names.

Marybeth's Provencal Ratatouille

I can only hope that this dish tastes half as good as it did under the stars on a warm summer evening in Marseilles with new found friends.

1/3 cup olive oil
4 cloves garlic
1 red onion
1 green pepper
1 red pepper
1 yellow pepper
1 zucchini
1 yellow crookneck squash
1/2 eggplant
1 teaspoon sea salt
1 teaspoon black pepper
4 tomatoes
3 tablespoons red wine vinegar
1 tablespoon thyme
2 bay leaves
Sea salt and pepper

Dice all vegetables into a small 1-inch dice. Sauté onions and garlic in olive oil for 2 minutes over medium heat until soft. Add peppers and sauté for 2 minutes. Add zucchini, squash, and eggplant. Sauté another 5 minutes. Season with sea salt and pepper. Add tomatoes, red wine vinegar, thyme and bay leaves. Combine rest and stew for 20 minutes over low heat. Season with more vinegar, salt and pepper if necessary and serve with Grilled Tuna. Also great with grilled chicken, tossed in pasta as a sauce or served as a vegetable.

Serves 8

Fatty French Fare

Some things are better left not known. The amount of butter and fat that goes into French food is one of those things. I had been naive to this fact earlier in the evening but by dessert I was all too aware. I'm the one who ordered the crêpes Suzette.

Earlier in the day, we were innocents, wandering the streets of Paris. Chris, Ian and I walked from the Latin Quarter to Notre Dame, along the Quai d'Orsay, over the Seine and up the Champs Élysées to the chaotic roundabout of the Arc de Triomphe and back again to the artistic history of Montmartre. An autumn sun cast its fiery orange glow over the city as we strolled past ubiquitous cafes and the stone sides of buildings. We followed a twisted maze through narrow cobbled passageways, being pulled forward to explore more and drink it all in.

My thighs burned as we climbed the hills of the boulevards passing nearly identical, six-storey buildings covered in ivy, their shutters thrown open to absorb the last few warm days before a winter chill filled the air. The sun edged lower in the sky, and our stomachs began their plea for nourishment.

"I'm starved," Ian said, as if this was shocking news. His wide shoulders like those of a linebacker and muscular arms indicate his need for constant nourishment. We all may have been pushing thirty, but he had the appetite of a teenager. The craziness of our summer aboard *Pari* was only a week behind us, but it felt like a lifetime ago.

"The restaurant should be around the next corner," Chris directed. Our wanderings had the ultimate goal of a French bistro for dinner. We had been given directions by a couple next to us at lunch. They had dined at *Chez Francis* every time they traveled to Paris. They raved about the food and praised the couple who ran the place. That was testament enough for us. We followed their instructions and headed uphill for dinner.

We were in the highest point of Paris, perched along its steep flanks with the lights of the city laid out at our feet. We stumbled, too weary to put one more foot in front of the other. Then ahead, on the corner of the street above a doorway hung the sign, *Chez Francis*. Bushes obscured a small patio from view, but a warm orange glow flooded out of the windows, inviting us in. A dark set of stairs led down into the dining room. An older French woman dressed in a Mother Hubbard frock greeted us. Rolls of fat rippled out from the sleeves to her pudgy elbows and down her legs to thick ankles stuffed into hospital shoes. "Bonne Soirée, mes amis."

I had been practicing my French all day and was glad to have another opportunity to speak. "Nous voudrions une table pour trios, s'il vous plait." That much French I could handle.

"Oui, oui." She led us outside to a table on the terrace.

The menu read like one of my chef school textbooks. This was a traditional French Bistro. Boeuf Bourgoin and coq au vin graced the pages of the menu in front of me. My stomach growled like a confronted wolf protecting her cub.

The voluptuous woman returned with a basket of crusty baguettes and the sweet French butter I had been falling in love with since we arrived in France. We ordered wine, then I translated the French menu for Chris and Ian. My knowledge of French menu items is much better than my grasp of the French language.

The woman looked pleased with our selections. She leaned her ample bosom over the table to collect menus and spoke rapid-fire French—something about her husband being the chef was all I could pick up. I smiled brightly in response and hoped she wouldn't call on me to further this conversation.

The bells of Sacré-Cour tolled, their haunting metal clang filled the night air. Indigo twilight settled over us. No sooner had I taken another sip of wine than a pot of foie gras pate arrived for the center of the table.

"This is a popular French starter," I told Chris and Ian. "Foie Gras is the fattened goose liver."

———— VICTORIA ALLMAN ————

"Is this the thing that is force fed with a tube until its liver explodes?" Chris wrinkled his forehead into a contorted display of disbelief and disgust.

"Not quite explodes but yeah, it is fed four times a day until the liver expands to about ten times its normal size," I corrected, hoping not to insult either Chris or our host by discussing the treatment of the goose.

"I'd like to be fed four times a day." Ian reached for his knife. "My God, that is good." He could care less about the ethical repercussions of what we were eating. And he was right. It was delicious. Rich, smooth and decadent, no matter what our personal beliefs, we devoured the dish.

My first course seemed light enough upon ordering, it was vegetables after all but with its arrival it screamed fat. In front of me was a plate of sautéed mushrooms in a puff pastry case. The earthy smell of mushrooms wafted up off the plate and attacked my senses. I gathered my red hair off my face and lowered my head to breathe in the aroma. Woodsy sexual smells assaulted me. My salivary glands began to water.

One bite was all I needed to know this was perfection on a plate. The mushrooms were sauced with a veal glaze that shimmered with mounted butter. The pastry rose to a teetering height, the layers of butter expanded by the heat of the oven. The rich feel of that first bite accentuated the luxury I was ingesting. I quickly calculated three tablespoons of butter on my plate alone.

I slathered more butter on a piece of bread and washed it down with another glass of Rhône.

Chris reached for a baguette as well to dunk into the melted garlic butter his escargot swam in. Nine pools of sunlight yellow liquid glimmered on his plate ready to be absorbed by the bread. "This is so good, here Victoria, taste this." He held out a piece for me.

My main course was cassoulet, another traditional French dish. Duck legs had been slowly poached in duck fat for hours until they literally fell off the bone in tender pieces. This rich meat is then mixed with white beans, fatty sausage, carrots, onions, garlic and tomatoes. A healthy dose of melted duck fat is poured over the mixture, and it is topped with breadcrumbs before baking. The husband would have spent hours watching over the slow baking bubbling dish. I ate slowly, enthusiastically relishing each bite.

Dessert is where I thought I could make up for all the fat we had consumed. I knew I could not eat a creamy dish of crème brûlée or a rich chocolate torte. Ian had already unbuttoned his pants and Chris was moaning with delight.

Crêpes Suzette seemed like the logical selection. Paper-thin batter with an orange sauce. It was the healthy choice.

The woman wheeled over a rickety wooden cart with a one-burner gas flame station. This was her dish to execute. She lit the flame of the burner to start the show. On the cart in front of her was a half-pound of butter. She scooped out three tablespoons and with the flick of her wrist, the butter hit the frying pan with a plop. Instantly it began to melt as the woman spooned sugar into the pan. The sauce spattered and spit. Without even blinking from the hiss and sizzle, the woman expertly tilted the pan to one side and drizzled Grand Marnier from an open bottle. Phoomp! The alcohol exploded into flame and danced orange and blue across the surface. Not even a flinch from the woman.

She picked up two oranges and sliced them in half, squeezing the juice from each in her strong grip. Next, is what started the arteries in my heart constricting before my first bite. The woman turned back to the mound of pale creamy butter and dolloped an additional two tablespoons into the liquid. She extinguished the flame of the burner and swirled the frying pan to melt the butter slowly, thus thickening the sauce. My thoughts of a healthy ending to the meal vanished as the woman soaked two crêpes in the sauce and folded them onto a plate. She poured the drippings from the pan over the crêpes and, as the piece de la resistance, scooped a small perfectly round snow-white ball of vanilla ice cream into the center of the plate. "Bon Appetit!" She wheeled the rickety cart across the patio to its home in the corner.

Everything that the woman had put in the pan, every last tablespoon of butter was on the plate in front of me. It called to me. It sang out in richness. It was all for me. A vision of my face on the woman's body floated in the back of my mind. Ah, what the hell, I thought as I lifted my fork from the table. It was still a long walk home.

Crêpes Suzette

I could not in good conscience showcase a recipe with as much butter in it as witnessed that night. This is a much healthier version.

Crepe Batter:
1 cup milk
3/4 teaspoon sugar
1 tablespoon butter
1/2 cup flour
2 eggs

Heat the milk, butter and sugar over medium heat until the butter melts. Let rest 5 minutes to cool and whisk in rest of ingredients. Whisk until smooth. Let stand 1 hour to rest.

Heat an 8 inch nonstick frying pan over medium heat. Add 2 tablespoons of batter and rotate the pan to evenly distribute the batter around the bottom of the pan. The thinner the layer of batter the better. Set the pan back on the burner and heat for 30 seconds. With a rubber spatula flip the crêpe upside down. Cook for another 20 seconds and remove from pan. Repeat with the rest of the batter. You may need to adjust your burner heat so as not to burn the crêpes. You are looking for an even golden brown color.

Sauce:
4 oranges, segmented and juiced
1/4 cup sugar
1 tablespoon butter
1 tablespoon Orange Juice Concentrate
1/4 cup Grand Marnier
2 tablespoons butter

In a nonstick frying pan over medium high heat melt sugar and butter. Simmer, stirring lightly until it starts to turn golden brown. Immediately remove from the heat. The sugar is extremely hot at this point, so stand back as you add the Grand Marnier, it will start to hiss and spit. Carefully add orange juice and concentrate. When the liquid settles down add orange segments and butter, swirling the pan continuously to thicken the sauce.

Use tongs to add crêpes to the pan one at a time to coat in sauce. Fold each crêpe into four to create a triangle. Pour extra sauce over crêpes and serve with vanilla ice cream.

Makes 6 servings

Jumping Ship

*I*t was time to start looking for a new boat. I returned from Europe and, with confidence, headed to Lauderdale. This time I knew something about boats and about what I wanted. This time I could actually be picky and select the right job for me.

Patrick was also in town for a few days. It had been three months since we had seen each other in Sardinia. "I just pulled into town last night," I said when I called. I bit my lip and shut my eyes hoping for the response I wanted.

"Great, what do you think about going to the Keys this weekend? We can kayak and dive in Key Largo, maybe go sailing?"

I let out the breath I'd been holding. "That sounds great." I smiled like a little girl on Christmas morning. I danced a little jig and jumped up and down. I was glad he couldn't see how goofy I was acting. We'd had little time to talk all summer and, with so much time passing between dates, I was never sure what had happened in his life. I dreaded the day I would call and hear that he had met someone else. But, today was not that day. We spent the weekend in Key Largo, kayaking through the mangroves and sailing the peacock blue waters. Yet once again, we had to part ways as *Lady Linda* left for the Bahamas, and I started my search for a new job.

It didn't take me long to find *Blue Moon*. I spoke with the same crew agency I had used to find *Pari*. "We have a Feadship looking for a chef. It's a great job for you. It's one hundred and sixty-five feet. It's bigger than *Pari* and a better quality boat. It's only six months old, practically brand new," the agent assured me.

I called Patrick, using this as an excuse to talk to him again. "What is a Feadship?" I asked.

"It's like the Mercedes Benz of the sea. I know that boat. It's a great program. You should take it."

I spoke with their captain, Emile. He had been with the owners for seven years and two different boats, as had his girlfriend, Marisa. "We'll be traveling through the Caribbean to Jamaica and the Cayman Islands for the winter. We spend the summer in Chicago and the spring in Savannah." Emile's South African accent reminded me of Yaz. I instantly felt comfortable. "Most of the crew have been here since we launched."

"The owners are adventurous eaters that love light and fresh flavors." Marisa added. No more struggling over unfamiliar recipes. These would be people I could cook for.

It didn't take me long to accept their offer and agree to join *Blue Moon*.

Emile was one hundred and eighty degrees different from Mike. He was tall and thin, studious looking in his designer rimless glasses and goatee. Instead of controlling everything, like Mike had done, he broke the boat into different departments—galley, stews, deck, and engineering—and had each department run by its senior crewmember. They then reported back to him. He had a business degree from University and ran the boat like a management company. A successful company. He was CEO of the owners thirty-five million dollar company, *Blue Moon*.

I was the only crew that would be in the galley, so I was to manage the whole operation. Executive chef and chief dishwasher. Marisa and I would work together to make sure the meals ran smoothly and guests were happy.

Blue Moon itself was also one hundred and eighty degrees away from *Pari*. It was one of the floating palaces I had encountered that first day on the dock. It had snow-white paint, polished steel rails that you could see your reflection in, and tinted windows. There were three decks of teak, a Jacuzzi, and a classic wooden gentleman's boat for cruising.

I had progressed from a crew of six to a crew of ten. "This is Shannon." Marisa toured me through the boat and introduced me to a jet-black haired girl with the most piercing dark eyes and lush long lashes I had ever seen.

Her face lit up in a welcoming smile. "Hello," she said.

Immediately, I detected her Canadian accent. I smiled back. "Saskatchewan?" I questioned.

"Saskatoon," she nodded.

A little piece of home so far away.

I also graduated to a considerably larger and more functional galley. Space and equipment I had previously only dreamed of were presented to me to work with: steam ovens, induction stoves, marble countertops and stainless steel backdrops. I would no longer be limited in the food I wanted to create because of a lack of space or not having the right equipment.

The galley was one of the best I had seen on a boat. It was brand new with top-of-the line equipment. Windows along the port side provided an unbelievable view for me to enjoy. A large steam oven would keep meats and fish moist and a six-burner stovetop sat next to it, in which two burners were induction heat, meaning instant heat where a large pot of water could come to a boil within five minutes. It would be perfect for last minute requests from guests. There was also a secondary conventional oven and a deep fryer, as well as a large flattop griddle for pancakes and a broiler for browning the tops of crème brûlée. I ran my fingers over black marble countertops and watched my reflection in the polished stainless steel refrigerator. The cabinets were finished with a warm caramel-colored wood. All drastically different from *Pari*.

The cupboards contained every gadget imaginable: KitchenAids for baking, Cuisinarts for chopping, tart pans, and ramekins for desserts, an ice cream maker, a pasta maker, and a sausage maker. Copper pots and Teflon coated pans of every size and shape were stacked in neatly organized rows. An olive pitter, a lemon zester, melon ballers, oyster knives, ice-carving picks, and lobster crackers were concealed in drawers. It was a Williams-Sonoma salesperson's dream.

"This is amazing," I said to Marisa.

"Just wait, there's even more."

She led me downstairs to the pantry, full of six different types of flour for each individual baking need. Shelves displayed French green lentils, truffle oil, squid ink pasta, semi-dried tomatoes, black olive paste, Vietnamese fish sauce, toasted sesame oil, dark chocolate buttons, Spanish olive oils, and one hundred-year old balsamic vinegars. Anything that I might need while guests are on board.

There was a large walk-in fridge on the main level next to the galley that could contain enough food for a two-week trip without reprovisioning. Next to that was a walk-in freezer with stainless steel shelves.

This was the boat for me.

* * * *

I had been onboard for two months when we took our first trip to Key West. Instead of getting thrown into it like what happened on the *Pari*, I had time to get to know the galley and the crew before our first trip. Shannon and I were becoming great friends. Emile and I shared many common interests, like music and traveling. Marisa and I bounced our love of food and wine off each other. Her ideas and knowledge challenged my cooking and inspired it to a new level. I loved this new adventure. And even better … shortly after I was hired, an opening came available for a deckhand. I called Chris, who joined the boat in Lauderdale. Not long after that, he called Ian for the second engineer position. I was surrounded by friends, new and old.

I had been working eight to six, getting to know the new galley and cooking lunch and dinner for the crew. Every morning, I made fresh fruit salad and granola for ten o'clock tea break. Mondays and Thursdays I went to the market. On Tuesdays, I baked a cake or dessert as a mid-afternoon treat. Thursdays, I prepared a hot breakfast for everyone with platters of scrambled eggs, crispy bacon, home-made grain toast, seared mushrooms and roasted tomatoes. Fridays, I cooked all day long to fill the fridge with food for the weekend.

In between cooking, I found myself scrubbing the walk-in floor, taking inventory, writing out menus, cleaning out the cupboard and shopping for the upcoming trip. We were headed to Key West for Christmas and then down to the Caribbean for the next four months.

"You'll want to buy all the meat and specialty products here." Marisa echoed Mike's warning about the quality of food in the Caribbean. "The freezer will fit enough food for six months if you plan properly."

I spent days making lists. I measured the freezer and estimated just how much space six months of food would take. I phoned Niman Ranch in California and placed a twenty-two thousand dollar meat order to be FedExed the next day. It took me the better part of the day to organize organic fillets, lamb racks and pork tenderloins so I knew where they were and could grab them easily. I looked around the freezer and realized there was still space left.

Next, I called up to Boston and placed a fish order. Even with the ocean all around us, I could not rely on the crew to have enough time to catch me fish every night for dinner. I would visit local fish markets as much as I could, but if we were traveling or anchored in a bay somewhere I wanted a back up.

Once that was all put away, I had just enough room for an array of ice-creams for the crew. I would make homemade, or rather boat-made, for guests, but I could never keep up with the amount ten crew could go through.

On one of my first nights on board we had all gathered in the crew mess to watch a movie on the big screen TV. We changed into pajamas and brought out our comforters to lie on the couch. Couples and non-couples weaved in and out of each other, curling around the person beside them to get comfortable. Just before Austin Powers filled the screen, Pierre got up and went over to the crew fridge. "Who wants ice-cream?"

Suddenly, blankets were flying and crew bolted up from their reclined positions. In a flurry, Chris pulled out bowls and placed cartons on the table. Spoons clattered. Voices shouted requests. "Ow!" Someone stepped on Shannon's foot in an attempt to jockey for a better position. Emile knocked over the chocolate syrup creating a thick dark pool on the table. Marisa swatted him. Within fifteen minutes everyone was back to lying down, some groaning in delight. Six different cartons sat empty on the counter, crushed and dripping melted ice-cream. I would need to do a lot more shopping.

As the trips departure date grew closer, I spent every morning in grocery stores, pushing three or four full carts up and down the aisles. I stuffed the back of the rental car with as much as possible, mentally making a list for the next day as I tried to shut the trunk. It takes a lot of food, time and money to feed ten hungry crewmembers and the eight guests that would arrive the next week.

The fiasco of my first meal on *Pari* had happened over a year ago. Although still fresh in my mind, I had many successful meals since then and had learned much about cooking for others. I wasn't as nervous with these new owners but put just as much thought and preparation into the meal. On the first day of the trip, I started at six in the morning. I baked two different breads for the day; one for each meal. I made a light and fruity dessert for lunch but wanted something more extravagant for dinner. I decided on a decadent white chocolate margarita mousse. I made a platter of almond cookies and mixed a tart shell to bake later for hors d'oeurves. After cleaning up the dirty pans and spilled flour, I cut fresh fruit for salad and cooked bacon for breakfast.

"Good morning." Marisa was up and ready to start serving the guests.

She would lead the service with Shannon's help, while our third stewardess, Jacqueline, cleaned the guest rooms and started the laundry. By eight-thirty I had started working on crew lunch.

We had many different nationalities, tastes and appetites on board, so I planned to make a number of different things for the crew to satisfy everyone's desires. One day I might make a hot lunch of grilled chicken and pesto pizzas, the next, a shrimp, feta and tomato pasta, or caramelized onion and Brie cheese omelets.

On this day, I chopped vegetables for a minestrone soup, tossed a tomato and basil salad and mixed tuna with capers, black olives and red onions for sandwiches.

While I was making crew lunch Marisa took the guests order for breakfast. She also spoke with them about their daily plans and preferences for lunch, presenting them with the menu I had written. "They like the menu. There will only be six for diner tonight. Lunch is at one."

Guest's lunches are always a challenge. I want them to feel like they were special, so a quick sandwich would not do. More often than not, the guests had been out in the sun and would like something light and cool. I prepped an elaborate lobster tail salad; next I blanched and refreshed crisp green beans and wrapped them in prosciutto. I poached sweet fingerling potatoes in saffron and pureed a fragrant fresh basil vinaigrette. I tried to make this meal interesting and flavorful but not as formal as dinner. Usually, the guests dine outside in a casual atmosphere to soak up as much of the day's sun as possible. They might also be coming or going from different activities and lunch was often delayed while someone went shopping or jet skiing, so I had to be flexible with the menu and the timing.

This meal went off without a hitch. Marisa brought the plates back empty. "It's a winner. Mrs. asks that you make that again another day."

After lunch, I thoroughly cleaned the galley, then took a shower and changed, ready to start the second part of my day. I began with dinner for the crew. I have a lot of opinions on what crew should eat. I always want to give them something hot with lots of vegetables and a salad. Because I cook everyday for the crew, I try not to repeat meals too often. I like to experiment with a number of different foods and ethnic combinations, and I am constantly reading cooking magazines and books to find new ideas and recipes to test. I can go up to thirty-five weeks of lunch and dinner without making the same meal twice.

That afternoon, I skinned red snapper and sliced bok choy for a green Thai curry. The smell of freshly grated ginger bit at my senses. A pot of jasmine rice steamed on the stove while I tossed a green mango and pork salad. Before I had even finished pouring it all into serving bowls, Chris popped his head into the galley. "Smells great."

"Almost ready."

Ian stuck his head over Chris's shoulder. "Yum, I'm starving."

"What a surprise." Chris mocked.

"Can I help carry it down?" Ian asked. They circled like sharks eager to help if it meant dinner would arrive earlier. I loved the fact that our easy-going friendship had been transported to *Blue Moon*.

With one more burst of energy, I again cleaned the galley and started dinner for the owners. Depending on the number of guests and who they were, dinner consisted of three courses. This is where the full luxury of the boat and having a personal chef pays off. All meals were served by Marisa. She dressed elegantly in pleated black pants, a white blouse, and black bowtie, with her dark Spanish hair swept into a French curl. She had spent the past hour arranging flowers and decorating the table in different colors and themes with an artistic flourish.

I plated each course on our Bulgari china.

Marisa began the evening by announcing that dinner was served. She then lit the candles, poured water, inquired about wine selections, and distributed home-baked bread.

Once the guests had their wine, I sent out the appetizer: seared scallops with a fine herb potato salad and champagne sauce.

While the guests were eating, I once again cleaned the galley and got ready for the main course. Since the appetizer was seafood, I picked a meat dish to follow. I roasted beef tenderloin to medium-rare and had it resting on the stove. I sautéed leeks with garlic until they were soft. Next, I poured a flavored chicken stock in the pan to make a sauce and seared an exotic mushroom variety of chanterelles and porcinis to scatter around the plate. Marisa whisked the plates away like a ballet timed to silent music. She returned with another approving smile. "They are loving it." She was very supportive and nurturing.

I didn't believe in serving just a piece of cake or scoop of ice cream for dessert. Instead, I created complex desserts, complete with sauce and garnishes. Something crunchy, or something smooth for texture. Over the years I had collected a large number of dessert recipes that always went out with a flourish. Bing cherry clafouti with vanilla rum cream and caramelized cherries; bittersweet chocolate soufflés with a cinnamon caramel sauce; port-poached peaches stuffed with mascarpone ice cream.

The guests were treated to the best that we could provide. No effort was too much, no corner was cut, no detail overlooked. For *Blue Moon's* guests, the night ended with espressos, cognacs, truffles, and the stars overhead.

On a good night I could usually have the galley floors washed, the dishes done, counters cleaned and food put away by eleven o'clock. The galley was then shut down. With any luck I'd just enough energy left to read a little, write a few e-mails or watch an episode of *The Sopranos* before falling into my bunk for the night. This schedule would be repeated for the next ten days.

On the last day, the lunch I prepared was packed into catering bags to be served on their private plane home. The crew gathered on the aft deck, dressed in our white uniforms with bars on our shoulders to signify rank. We stood in a row to say goodbye.

"The food was wonderful," Mrs. said to me kissing me on both cheeks. Mr. rubbed his stomach and smiled brightly.

Chris carried the luggage that Shannon and Jacqueline had packed. Ian helped Mr. and Mrs. down the dock. Emile drove them to the airport to see them safely off. The rest of us stood smiling and waving as they retreated.

"I'll set up lunch on the sun deck," I said once they were out of view.

"I'll mix some drinks," Marisa volunteered.

"We'll put the jet-skis in the water," Chris said.

It was now our time to relax and enjoy the new island we had only seen from the deck for the past ten days.

Fish On

*E*verything I knew about Key West I had read from Hemmingway. He wrote many of his great American novels there, drank and fished there, living his larger than life existence. He had created an inspiring sense of place and aroused my desire to experience exactly what he described. I wanted to go deep-sea fishing and battle a great fish like Santiago in *The Old Man and the Sea*. The Keys are home to more game fish records than any other area in the world. The waters are full of bonefish, tarpon, dolphin, tuna and grouper. We had two days off before we traveled again, and I was convinced that I would go out and bring home dinner.

While the rest of the crew slept off their hangover from the night before, I headed out to Charter Boat Row, to look for a guide. I wanted an old sea dog who knew the waters and where the fish were hiding. Walking the docks allowed me time to pick just the boat I was searching for. Jack looked like he stepped right off the page of a Hemmingway novel. Slightly scrawny with at least two days growth scratching his face, he exuded the feel of Key West through his slow gate and southern drawl. "You can fish with me," was all he said as he climbed up to the tuna tower to pull the boat off the dock.

His sport fish boat was set to go out onto the ocean. The other four clients were experienced deep-sea fishermen. They were interchangeable with identical dark hair, stocky broad shoulders and thick Jersey accents.

"What's a nice little girl like you doin' here?" one asked, amused.

"Mountains in Canada? You even seen the ocean before?" another asked.

"Honey, you just work on your tan, and we'll do the fishing," the next chimed in.

"Don't worry, sweetheart. I'll grab the line if it starts to run." I don't think he meant to be funny. In his own macho way, he was being chivalrous. Fuming, I secretly vowed to show them exactly what I could do. I just prayed I wouldn't make a fool out of myself and prove their misjudgments right. After all, this was my first deep-sea fishing excursion.

The Rolling Stones belted out *Start Me Up* over the rumble of the powerful engines as we headed out to sea. I could barely hear Mick's voice. *Ride like the wind at double speed. I'll take you places that you've never, never seen.*

Jack was a man of few words, but he had a keen sense of the water and shortly picked up a group of birds ahead. "Birds starboard," he yelled as he swung the boat to the right.

The scruffy mate in a blood-stained t-shirt let the lines out, and we watched the lures dance in the foamy wake.

"I'm circling back to check out the birds," Jack shouted down to us.

"They're diving the surface of the water," Beef Jersey explained to me. "That means there are larger fish below them driving smaller fish to the surface."

I was enjoying the whole scene when Jack started yelling, "Fish on, fish on." In awe, I watched as my line began to run.

"It's your rod," the mate scoffed at me as Jack switched the boat into neutral. With a violent twitch, the tip of the rod in the holder in front of me bent like a bow. The reel whirled, letting out the spool with an alarming buzz saw sound. It hissed like a hose that had snapped and was spewing steam. I grabbed it from the holster and placed it on my thigh to anchor it. I held on and adjusted my stance as the tension increased on the line.

"Reel in, reel in," Jack shouted at me. I looked down at the reel that was spinning and began winding the handle.

"No, no, let it run now," one of the unshaven meatheads chastised as he reached in front of me to adjust the drag on the rod.

"I got it," I seethed.

I knew they were all chomping at the bit to take the rod away from me and do it themselves. But there is a code of respect on the water, and this was my rod, my fish, and my fight. I let it run awhile before starting to wind the reel and pull the fish back to the boat. I knew I had to tire the fish out before he exhausted me. I had seen this done before and remembered Hemingway's writings about hours of struggling with large game fish.

I shifted the rod and bent my knees slightly, flexing to absorb the pounding of the waves. I pulled the rod tip up towards the sky, bringing the fish in closer. I dropped the rod, parallel to the deck, reeling in the slack. I repeated this procedure three or four times. The muscles in my arms shook.

You make a grown man cry.

"There it is, reel it in now," Jack shouted from above. As the fish got closer to the boat, I could see flashes of color and the blunt nose of a mahi-mahi head. A blur of silver and blue lit up the water as the fish saw the boat and panicked. He leaped effortlessly, flashing iridescent green stripes.

I hesitated, watching the show. Adrenaline surged through my veins. I felt just like Hemmingway. The fish gathered a reserve of strength and ran with the line. I leaned back and reeled once more. The fish finally appeared behind the boat once more. The mate leaned over the side and gaffed the beast. It bucked and flopped wildly as he hurled it onto the deck at my feet.

I looked down at my conquest. He was beautiful. He was mine

"Not bad," the loudest guy mumbled.

"Beginner's luck," another conceded.

* * * *

Back in the galley, I picked up my filleting knife, testing its sharpness against my thumb. I looked into the fish's eyes. "Thank you," I said in homage. I ran the knife down its pectoral fin, separating the bones from the flesh.

My mind raced through recipe options. Mexican? Asian? Caribbean? I didn't want to insult my fish with just any old preparation. This meal was going to be a memorial to its life. To the fight he gave.

I cut thick meaty fillets for the crew. The scent of cilantro filled the air as I puréed cilantro and cashew nuts to crust the top. I danced around the galley. I steamed coconut rice and diced mangoes for a salsa. The work flew by.

This was no ordinary crew dinner. This wasn't food I picked up at the market. This was *my* dinner. *My* fish. The delicious smell of the sea emanated from the oven.

The men from Jersey may not have been forthcoming with praise for my fishing skills, but they would have loved the dinner I had just brought home.

After all, that's what fishing is all about. The meal it provides. And tonight, I provided the meal for *Blue Moon*.

She's a mean, mean machine.

Herb and Cashew Paste for Mahi-Mahi

6 fillets of 6 oz mahi-mahi
1 teaspoon sea salt
1/2 teaspoon black pepper

Sprinkle salt and pepper over all sides of mahi-mahi and place on a cookie sheet.

Paste:
1/4 cup cashews
1/3 cup cilantro, stems removed
4 cloves garlic
2 green onions, cut in quarters
1 teaspoon ground white pepper
1 teaspoon cumin
2 tablespoons white vinegar
2 tablespoons honey
2 tablespoons olive oil
1 teaspoon sea salt

Place all ingredients in a food processor and puree for 2 minutes until a rough paste is produced. Spoon on top of fish, creating a 1/2 inch thick topping. Preheat oven to 350 and bake fish for 15 minutes, until flesh is firm. Place on top of rice and serve with mango salsa

Mango Salsa

1 ripe mango
2 tomatoes
1/2 red onion
1/2 habenero pepper
1/4 cup chopped cilantro leaves
2 limes, juiced
1 teaspoon sea salt

Dice mango, tomato and red onion to uniform 1/2 inch small size. Chop habenero as small as possible to evenly distribute heat. Mix all together and serve with fish or as a dip with chips.

—— VICTORIA ALLMAN ——

Coconut Rice

Coconut milk is readily available in cans throughout North America but in the islands where fresh coconuts readily fall from the trees, it is made fresh. Grate 2 cups of fresh coconut meat and boil with 2 cups of water. Puree in a blender, let stand for 15 minutes and strain.

1 cup coconut milk
2 cups water
1 teaspoon sea salt
2 cups long grain rice

Place coconut milk, water and salt in a heavy-bottomed saucepot. Bring to a boil and reduce heat to low. Stir in rice. Cover with a lid and simmer until liquid has evaporated (approx. 20 minutes). Remove from heat and let sit with lid on for 5 minutes. Flake with a fork and serve.

Serves 6

Cayman Conscience?

*M*y friends call me a tree hugging liberal; I take it as a compliment. I recycle. I turned a corner of my mother's backyard into a compost heap. I fast in recognition of world famine. I have adopted foster children from third world countries and whales on the brink of extinction.

Ever since my first trip to the farmers market with Lawrence, I have turned my focus to food—eating and cooking in a way that supports sustainable agriculture. This means always using local products, which in turn supports local farmers and local economies. Wherever possible, I try to eat and cook organic foods that do not harm the environment, and I choose my food conscientiously. I boycotted swordfish when stocks were low. I refuse to buy baby veal that is raised in boxes to ensure tender meat and sought alternatives to the endangered Beluga caviar. This is why I found myself in a quandary while in the Cayman Islands.

As a chef, I'm always curious to sample the local fare. While *Blue Moon* was in the Caymans I wanted to taste the local dishes featuring turtle meat. But turtles are endangered. In good faith, I could not possibly add to the declining number. I struggled between my desire to taste and my environmental beliefs. Could I eat turtle meat? Could I be here and miss this opportunity?

At one time, the Cayman Islands and surrounding waters were full of green sea turtles. Historically, Cayman Islanders survived on their turtle populations as a source of food and income, selling the meat to sailors. It was perfect for ships, as the turtles could be kept alive onboard until needed and were a great alternative to the usual meal of fish.

For many years, turtling was the prime industry for the people of the Cayman Islands, which ultimately led to the loss of turtle populations. By the 1900s stocks were so depleted that today, these once numerous creatures are all but gone. Turtles are now protected, and efforts are being made to restore the population but the fact is, it is a rare sight to see one of these magnificent creatures in the wild.

There is a ban on turtle hunting in many countries. Yet, in the Caymans turtles are raised for meat on a turtle farm, then sold and served in stews, soups, and as pan-fried steaks. Wild stocks are not hindered in any way. You would think my conscience would be relieved with this knowledge. But I was still torn. It would be hypocritical to fight to save a species and then turn around and eat one for pure pleasure. To make matters worse, I was getting a lot of ribbing from my friends, who had all heard my views (okay, lectures) on the environment and our roles in preserving it.

"Ms. Greenpeace here is going to kill a defenseless animal?" Emile's voice dripped with incredulousness at lunch one day.

"Canadians club those cute little baby seals, but that is not enough for Victoria. She's moving on to turtles." Chris laughed.

Could I justify eating turtle meat to myself, but also convey to others that as a chef it was my job? Eating turtle meat was not any different from eating cow meat or chicken meat, yet I would never eat rhino or elephant. I knew there was a distinction, but my ethical lines were becoming increasingly blurred.

The Gods were clearly playing with my head during this trip. Earlier in the week, Chris and I dove the coral reefs that surround the island. The Cayman Islands were formed by volcanic activities under the ocean creating a submerged mountain range, complete with cliffs, drop-offs, and caverns. Over the years coral and tropical fish have made these underwater mountains home, developing some of the best diving and underwater viewing in the Caribbean.

We had been diving every day since the owner left and had come across gigantic golden barrel sponges, black coral, lavender sea whips, sea foam green sea fans, vase sponges, tube sponges and brick colored branching coral as well as grouper, lobster, starfish, and queen angels.

Early one morning, Chris and I were exploring the sheer wall that makes Cayman famous for diving. Suspended in indigo, we floated past wide expanses of hard coral. I was mesmerized by the vibrant colors. Patches of bright yellow, fiery red, and deep purple circled in front of our eyes. Bright stoplight colored parrotfish swam past our masks. Gem-like speckles of the midnight blue damselfish flashed like a disco ball. The large black eyes of red and silver squirrelfish followed our movement, preening like peacocks, their yellow dorsal fins extended like a fan. I caught a glimpse of the streaming tip of a turquoise triggerfish's tail as he darted out of sight. The visibility was clear, and we could see almost a hundred feet in front of us.

Chris was leading the dive since I was looking around too much to be of any help navigating. We were nearly out of time and at the turn-around point when Chris suddenly stopped, waving to get my attention and pointing upwards.

Caught in the rays of sunlight striking the surface were two turtles. Their front flippers propelled them forward effortlessly as they soared past. They must have been old. Covered in a green slime that looked like moss, the creatures seemed ancient. Their hard dome shells emitted protruding necks. We stayed glued to our spot and watched as these peaceful animals glided above, unconcerned with us and oblivious to our awe. I wanted to reach out and touch them, they were that close, but the rule of diving is to observe, not interfere.

Chris and I watched, wide-eyed and smiling behind our regulators, both giving the thumbs up sign, signifying our delight instead of our need to ascend. We made eye contact and Chris pointed at himself and then me and then the turtles. He flicked his fingers in a scissoring motion to tell me that we were going to follow them. We set off after them, but try as we might we could not catch up. They were too fast. We were left in their wake, watching as they swam out of sight.

How could I eat turtle meat now?

Confused, I decided to journey to the island's Turtle Farm in West Bay to learn more about the turtles. Started in 1968, the Cayman Island Turtle Farm is home to more than sixteen thousand green sea turtles ranging from six ounces to six hundred pounds. It is both a commercial enterprise raising turtles for local consumption and a sanctuary successfully operating a breed/release program, introducing fifteen hundred turtles back into the wild a year.

"The conservation program at the farm is the only one of its kind in the world for green sea turtles," my guide told me. "After being hatched from eggs, the turtles are raised for one year before forty percent of the stronger turtles are tagged and released by professional divers who swim them out to sea, giving them a head start and better rate of survival."

"They make it?" I asked.

"The survival rate of these farm-raised turtles is higher than turtles born in the wild where they are prey for birds, animals, marine life, and poachers." The man nodded. The farm's commitment to conservation ensures the continuation of the species as well as contributing to ongoing research. To date, over thirty thousand sea turtles have been released.

"And these wild ones aren't the ones in restaurants?"

"No," he said. "They're ones from the farm. Just liked farmed chickens and cows."

The farm is expensive and difficult to fund. This is where the commercial side comes into play. The other sixty percent of the turtles are raised to four years of age and sold for food. This commercial arm supplies local restaurants and shops with more than one hundred thousand pounds of meat to prepare their national dishes. The farm diminishes the need for locals to hunt turtles in the wild, further protecting existing populations. The program wouldn't be financially viable without this local market.

Armed with these new facts and reassured that I would not be depleting the world's population of wild sea turtles but actually helping them, I was ready to make my decision, or so I thought. But once again I chastised myself. How could I spend the day learning about these magnificent creatures of the sea and then sit down to dine on them?

Ultimately, my chef's curiosity won, and I went seeking turtle steaks at The Wharf, a seafood restaurant on the western side of the island. Located just north of the main town of Georgetown, the Wharf is decorated sailor-style in blue and white, with a large verandah looking out over seven-miles of beach and the nearby sea.

I had trouble convincing Chris, or anyone else, to try turtle meat, so I was dining alone on the deck outside. The February night was warm, and a full moon filled the sky over the bay. A guitarist strummed soft Caribbean music from a stool in the corner. Strains of Bob Marley filled the air, *Stir it up; little darlin'. Stir it up.* The smell of bougainvillea wafted over the verandah with the breeze. I took a sip of my wine and opened the menu. This was it. Right there on the menu were Turtle Steaks in an Island Sauce.

—— VICTORIA ALLMAN ——

"I am in the Caymans. I want to try the Caymanian cuisine." I handed the menu to the waiter. "I want the turtle steak."

"Good choice," he told me with a wink. "You won't be disappointed."

I pondered my choice once more as I waited. A dining companion tonight would have eased the tension I felt about my choice. Emile's words rang in my ears—*Ms. Greenpeace, Ms. Greenpeace.*

I watched the waiter carry one lone dish across the deck. The time had come. "Bon appetite."

The waiter placed the dish in front of me. The meat, from the flipper, was cut into a thin scaloppini. It was presumably seasoned with a little sea salt and pepper and pan-fried. Ripe tomatoes, celery and green pepper were added to make a sauce. It was served with the island staple of rice and peas and fried plantains. I took another gulp of wine for courage and lifted the fork to my mouth. It had the color of well-cooked pork. I shut my eyes and chewed. It was slightly chewy. A beefy flavor filled my mouth, both delicate yet distinct in flavor. I opened my eyes. A smile danced across my lips. It was delicious.

I ate only the one meal of turtle. But I decided that there was a valid reason for turtle being a national dish, something every visitor must indulge in—once. It was truly a culinary experience I will always remember. Tree-hugging Liberal or not.

Pan-fried Chicken Thighs with Island Sauce

As legal turtle meat is still a rare commodity, I have changed this recipe to chicken thighs, which is much more common in the islands. The sauce is fragrant and could be served with tuna or pork as well. The chicken in this recipe is falling off the bone tender.

1/4 cup vegetable oil
8 skinless chicken thighs
1 teaspoon sea salt
1/2 teaspoon black pepper
1/2 teaspoon allspice
4 cloves garlic
1 large onion
1 green peppers
5 tomatoes
1/2 scotch bonnet or habernero
1 teaspoon sea salt
1 cup chicken stock
1 tablespoon thyme sprigs
1/4 cup chopped cilantro
1 tablespoon fresh squeezed lime juice

Chop the onions, peppers, and tomatoes into small dice. Thinly slice the garlic. Chop the thyme roughly. Mix 1 teaspoon sea salt, pepper and allspice and sprinkle evenly over chicken thighs. Heat a heavy-bottomed stockpot on high heat. When hot add vegetable oil and 4 of the chicken thighs. Brown for 1 minute on each side and remove from pan. Repeat with other 4 thighs. Turn the burner to medium-high heat and sauté the onions, peppers and garlic for 5 minutes until soft. Add the tomatoes, scotch bonnet, sea salt, chicken stock, and thyme. Bring to a simmer and add chicken back into pan. Simmer over medium-low heat, uncovered for 30 minutes until the chicken is tender and falling off the bone. Stir in cilantro and limejuice and taste for seasoning. Serve with Pigeon Peas and Rice.

Serves 4

Pigeon Peas and Rice

Pigeon Peas are brown oval beans, nutty and earthy in flavor, that are found in the Caribbean, originating from Africa. Caribbean markets sell them but they can be substituted with Red Kidney Beans

1 cup pigeon peas or red kidney beans
2 cans coconut milk (400 ml)
1-1/2 cups chicken stock
2 cloves garlic
2 sprig thyme
2 cups rice
1-1/2 cups chicken stock
1/2 teaspoon sea salt
1/2 teaspoon black pepper

Soak beans overnight in 4 times the amount of water. Drain and place in a large heavy bottomed pot with the coconut milk and 1-1/2 cups chicken stock. Simmer on medium high heat until tender (approx 45 minutes) with the garlic and thyme. When soft, season with salt and pepper. Add the extra 1-1/2 cups chicken stock and rice and bring back to a simmer. Turn the burner to medium low and cover the pot. Cook for 15 minutes until liquid has evaporated. Serve with curries, stewed chicken, or pork.

Just Another Day

*A*nchored off the emerald island of St. John, a small island in the middle of the US Virgin Islands, was where I stole a moment of luxury. I was busy cleaning up after lunch. My phone rang and I walked out to the bow to speak briefly with Patrick. He rarely called, so I was happy to hear from him. The view from the bow was of undulating green tropical hills that make up the nine thousand acres of virgin forest in the island's national park. Shadows fell across the dips in the hills creating a tie-dyed color of green.

As we talked, a lone kayaker paddled by, rhythmically breaking the water with a muted swish-swish-swish. I looked out over the water that mutated from navy in the deep water where we were anchored, to blue-green, to aquamarine closer to shore. It moved, lapping in soft waves and lined the white sand beaches that folded into the forest beyond. The triangular shapes of sailboats in the distance speckled the ocean from here to the neighboring island of St. Thomas. It was a balmy tropical kind of day, and a hot sultry breeze blew.

Hanging up the phone, I couldn't resist the call of the ocean. I could taste the salt from the warm trade wind on my lips. The bright sun illuminated everything in marigold. The bow of the boat was bathed in this orange glow.

A warm puff of air blew over me, tempting me to forget about cleaning the galley. A plunge into the inviting water would feel so good. I looked around to see if anyone was watching, and decided to do just that. I climbed up on the rail, teetering while trying to find my balance. I stood straight, closed my eyes, bent my knees and jumped into the abyss. The rush of the air whipped through my long red hair sending it up on end like Pipi Longstocking. Graceful, I am not. Flailing my arms for balance, I entered the water from twenty feet above, feet first, with a splash and the whoosh of salty water rushing past me. The momentum of my descent slowed, and I began kicking to the surface. Smiling, I broke the surface of the water. Those twenty seconds of pure pleasure would be enough to keep me smiling all day.

I climbed up the swim ladder and grabbed a towel from the guest basket. Wrapping the plush fabric around me, I tiptoed down the deck and past questioning looks from my crewmates.

"What happened?" Ian asked.

Chris just smiled. "It's about time you got out of the galley."

I returned to my cabin for a dry uniform and resumed my daily tasks as if nothing had happened. Just another day in paradise.

Caribbean Spiced Pork

1 bunch green onions, chopped rough
1/2 bunch fresh cilantro
1/2 white onion, chopped rough
1-1/2 tablespoons dark rum
1-1/2 tablespoons apple cider vinegar
2 teaspoons soy sauce
1 tablespoon vegetable oil
1 teaspoon sea salt
1 tablespoon fresh thyme
1 teaspoon brown sugar
1 inch piece fresh ginger, grated
1/2 teaspoon allspice
1/4 teaspoon nutmeg
1/4 teaspoon cinnamon
4 cloves garlic
1/2 scotch bonnet chili
1 lime, juiced
3 pork tenderloins, cleaned and cut in half

~Continued on next page

——— VICTORIA ALLMAN ———

Put all but pork into a cuisinart. Puree to rough paste. Rub over pork tenderloins and marinate 3-24 hours. Remove from marinade. Grill on BBQ until cooked through or roast in oven on a baking tray at 400 for 20 minutes—until internal temperature reaches 160. Let rest 5 minutes to allow juices to settle. Slice.

Serve with Coconut Squash Sauce and Pigeon Peas and Rice.

Coconut Squash Sauce

2 tablespoons vegetable oil
1 white onion, sliced
4 cloves garlic
2 pounds butternut squash, peeled, seeded and diced
1/2 scotch bonnet chili
2 cups chicken stock
1 tablespoon fresh thyme
1 teaspoon sea salt
1 can (400 ml) coconut milk
1 tablespoon apple cider vinegar

In a heavy bottomed saucepot sauté vegetable oil, onion and garlic for 5 minutes until golden. Add butternut squash, scotch bonnet, chicken stock, thyme and sea salt. Simmer over medium heat for 20 minutes. Add coconut milk and simmer 5 more minutes. Add apple cider vinegar. Puree in a blender. Pass through a sieve to strain. Taste for seasoning.

Serves 6

Chocolate Lime Rum Cake

Sauce:
1 cup sugar
1-1/2 tablespoons lime juice
1/4 cup dark rum
2 tablespoons water

Cake:
3/4 pound bittersweet chocolate
3 sticks butter
2/3 cup dark rum
2 cups milk
2 cups sugar
3-1/2 cups all-purpose flour
1-1/2 teaspoons baking soda
3 eggs
1-1/2 teaspoons vanilla

~Continued on next page

Pre-heat oven to 325. Grease one loaf pan.

For the sauce:
   In a heavy bottomed small sauce pot boil sugar and lime juice. This will change from a clear color, progressing to golden brown. This is called caramelizing sugar. The liquid is extremely hot at this point. Do not touch. Caramelization happens quickly when it starts so watch the pan and remove from heat once a golden color appears . Carefully add rum and water. The liquid will sputter and spit so stand back. Return to heat and simmer 30 seconds until the sauce is smooth. Set aside.

For the cake:
   In a bowl over simmering water, melt chocolate and butter. Remove from heat. Beat in rum, milk and sugar. Beat in dry ingredients 1/2 a cup at a time, incorporating until smooth. Beat in eggs and vanilla. Pour into loaf pan. Bake for 1 hour, rotating the pan after half an hour. Check doneness by inserting a skewer. If it comes out clean the cake is finished.
   Use the same skewer to poke holes through the cake top to the bottom of the dish every centimeter. If the sauce has thickened with cooling, return to heat for 1 minute. Spoon sauce evenly over the cake. It will run down the skewer holes to keep cake moist. Cool and slice.

Makes 1 cake, 12 slices

A Home in the Islands

"**Y**ou can not find love in the bottom of a bottle!" the preacher cried from the stage.

"Hallelujah," the whole church responded.

"It is not there! Jesus Christ is not in that bottle!" he raised one fist over his head, bending slightly at the waist and doing a little touchdown dance. "Do you hear what I am saying?" He looked wildly at the congregation.

"We hear you," everyone responded.

The woman in front of me had her eyes closed and was swaying back and forth, crying out, "I hear you, I hear you, oh my Lord, I hear you." She shook her head like she was having a one-on-one conversation.

The preacher leapt into the crowd and grabbed a young black man dressed in a crisp white shirt and bright blue tie. "There is no salvation in that bottle, my brother."

"I know that," the man responded, thrusting his fist in the air in triumph.

"Amen," the women of the congregation sang out.

It was Easter Sunday, and Jacqueline and I were attending a Baptist church service in St. Thomas. *Blue Moon* had been in the Virgin Islands for a month, and we were starting to feel like we had moved past the tourist stage and become residents. Marilyn, a local woman I had gotten to know on the island, invited us to Easter service. She worked at the market where I bought our fresh vegetables and milk.

Every morning this large woman with skin the color of melted chocolate and dressed in over-sized t-shirts and black spandex tights, would sing out "Good morning to you," as I came through the doors. She would stick by my side, helping me with my groceries, asking what I used this or that for, telling me what was good and just generally gossiping until I walked out the door again. "God Bless you today," she would call before hurrying to her next customer.

Two weeks before Easter, Marilyn began inquiring about my plans for the day. When I replied I had none, she quickly told me what I would do. "I will pick you up at nine here in the parking lot, and you will come to church with me," she said. "You can not be alone on Easter, with no family."

When I returned to *Blue Moon* and told everyone what I was going to do, Jacqueline asked to come along.

When Marilyn pulled into the parking lot in her maroon box-like car, she had transformed from the woman I met every morning. Sitting behind the wheel was a woman on a mission. She wore a purple polyester skirt and matching jacket with fabric-covered buttons the size of silver dollars. A matching purple hat adorned with tulle and fabric flowers sat on her head like an island version of Jacqueline Kennedy. "Well girls, now don't you look a picture," she cried, clasping her hands together beneath her chin.

Jacqueline wore a long, flowing peach colored dress with baby doll scallop sleeves, with her fine brown hair pinned from her face with tiny butterfly clips.

I had on a silk powder blue dress that gradually deepened to navy blue by the knee length hem. My hair had been straightened, and I even wore a touch of mascara. This was a long way from our normal uniform of white polo tops and khaki shorts.

We both piled into Marilyn's car and set off over the pothole-strewn roads to the center of the island. The one room white church sat in an open field, with goats grazing on the grass in the back yard. Dozens of cars parked on the front lawn and along the roadside. We had to park a hundred yards away and walk to the church. Marilyn usually sang in the church choir but was sitting out today since she had company and wanted to make sure Jacqueline and I were okay.

We stopped and chatted with every person we passed. Marilyn introduced us as friends of hers who incredibly had nowhere to go on Easter. "These here girls were goin' be all alone on that big boat," she revealed. "They are here as my guests." She preened like a peacock.

"Welcome," they all responded to us.

"George, how's your foot feeling today?" she asked one man who walked with a limp.

"Henry, I missed you at choir practice last week," she said to another.

"Denise, how's your mamma feeling after her operation?" She knew everyone.

The temperature was pushing eighty-five degrees already, and sweat trickled down my back by the time we made it to the door of the church. But it was clear we would find no reprieve from the oppressive heat. Inside, over a hundred people were dressed in suits and their Sunday best dresses. They piled into pews and milled about at the back of the church. Extra folding chairs were set along each aisle and in rows in back for the additional people today's sermon would bring.

"Easter and Christmas are our best days," Marilyn said proudly.

It was a miracle we found three chairs. As we passed women in big colorful hats and men with their hats in their hands, we were introduced to each and every one of them.

"This here is Victoria and Jacqueline. They visitin' the islands with no family to be with today." Marilyn repeated.

"Well, they are welcome here," we heard with every handshake.

The loud, haunting groan of an organ filled the room, and people quieted. The choir, dressed in heavy maroon robes, began singing the first hymn as they filed in through a side door, then climbed onto a stage at the front of the church. They swayed back and forth and belted out the song with searing vocal intensity. The whole room filled with the sound. It built stronger and stronger as the choruses went on. By the last lines, I could feel the music vibrate in my chest. As soon as the hymn ended, we took our seats. A spindly black man with hollow sunken cheeks jumped up on stage.

"There is no more glorious a day than this!" he called out.

"Amen!" the congregation responded.

"There was no more glorious a day in history," he called again.

"Amen," the congregation replied louder and clearer.

"Today is the day our Lord showed us his love." He lowered his head.

Suddenly, it was Marilyn's voice I heard sing, "Thank you, O Lord." She had a deep voice as soulful as Nina Simone's. She repeated the words again with more smoke and gravel in her delivery "Thank you, my Lord."

The preacher went on with an omni-potent voice, shouting, screaming, begging and crying. The audience responded spontaneously with Amen's and Hallelujah's. Jacqueline and I were the only ones who didn't follow the responses, but we certainly felt them.

The boisterous choir sang six more deep, moving songs of redemption, with the audience dancing and swaying along, before the preacher changed from reading scriptures to his sermon of the day. He had already been jumping around the stage, animated with each declaration from his Bible, but now he took on the fever of a man possessed. With dramatic booms of his voice and added thrusts of his fist, he gave an emotional delivery of his message: I would not find love in the bottom of the bottle.

Jacqueline leaned over to me. "Do you think he's talking about us?"

"It sure feels like it," I responded.

Marilyn's raw voice sang out a few more Amen's for good measure. The power in her voice made my skin goose pimple as I sat in the heavy heat, regretting my decision to wear silk. Dark pools of sweat were already showing through the material. I didn't want anyone to mistake my sweat for an admission of guilt. I didn't think I found love in the bottom of a bottle.

Just as I thought the preacher was going to start physically shaking people with his passionate pleas, a new sound came from the back of the church. It wasn't the soprano of a choir member or the vibration of the tambourine, but the bleating of a goat that had wandered in from the backyard to see what all the fuss was about. Three of the men in the back chairs jumped to action and shooed him out. But he broke the heavy spell.

The choir finished off the day with a few more songs, and we stood to sing and clap our hands once more before we all filed out the open back doors, where the smell of johnnycakes and fried chicken filled the air. Set up along the side of the yard were large picnic tables piled high with a potluck Easter spread. Bowls of creamy macaroni salad, goat stewed in tomato, rice and peas, golden fried chicken, string beans, coleslaw, fried fish, potato salad, chicken curry, buttery corn on the cob, barbecued ribs dripping with sauce and sliced tomatoes sat waiting the parishioners.

"Child, we can't let you two leave without a good Easter dinner," Marilyn said.

Beaming with pride, she led us through the line and made sure we didn't miss a thing.

"You have to try Virginia's johnnycakes. They are the best, because she still fries them in lard," she whispered conspiratorially. "And here, this is banana pudding made from the tree in Estelle's back yard."

As belle of the ball, Marilyn worked that church yard like a pro, stopping to talk to everyone, never forgetting anyone's name or what was happening in their household that week. Just as we were finishing our plates, the preacher came over to us. He looked more like Sammy Davis Jr. up close than I noticed inside the church. We shook hands and Marilyn repeated her nowhere-to-go story.

The man grabbed my hand, looked deep in my eyes, and said, "You always have a home here."

Marilyn sang out one last Hallelujah that carried over the wind for the whole yard to hear. We moved on to the next group of people to say our goodbyes.

By the end of the afternoon, we'd heard all of the island gossip, had been accepted in the church, and were invited back anytime. We now had a home for Easter and every Sunday, thereafter.

Caribbean Chicken Curry

2 pounds chicken thighs, cut to 2 inch dice
10 cloves garlic
2 teaspoons sea salt
1 teaspoon white pepper
1/2 teaspoon allspice
1/4 cup vegetable oil
2 medium onions
2 inch piece ginger, grated
1 green pepper, cut into 2 inch dice
2 sweet potatoes, cut into 2 inch dice
3 carrots, cut in1 inch lengths
2 cups chicken stock
2 teaspoons tomato paste
1/2 scotch bonnet chili
1 teaspoon dried thyme
1 teaspoon dried oregano
2 teaspoons salt
1 tablespoon paprika
1 teaspoon cloves
2 tablespoons cumin
1 teaspoon dry mustard
1 tablespoon turmeric
2 tomatoes, diced
1 can (400 ml) coconut milk
1/3 cup fresh cilantro, chopped
1 cup cashews
1 lime juiced

Mix together chicken thighs, garlic, salt, pepper, and allspice. Heat a heavy bottomed frying pan over medium heat. Working in three batches sear chicken in vegetable oil for 3 minutes. Remove from pan and place into a large soup pot. Sauté onion for 3 minutes until soft. Place all ingredients from ginger to tomatoes in soup pot. Bring to a boil.

Reduce to medium heat and simmer for 30 minutes. Add coconut milk and simmer an additional 15 minutes. Taste for seasoning. Add more of the scotch bonnet if you like hotter curry. Add cilantro, cashews and lime juice. Serve over steamed rice with mango chutney and fresh grated coconut

Serves 6

Johnnycakes

1 cup flour
1/2 cup cornmeal
3/4 teaspoon sea salt
2 teaspoons baking powder
1 tablespoon sugar
2 tablespoons shortening
2 tablespoons soft butter
1/2 cup water
2 egg whites
1/4 cup vegetable oil
1/4 cup shortening

Mix flour, cornmeal, sea salt, baking powder, and sugar. Rub shortening and butter into the mix with your hands until it is uniformly distributed. Whip egg whites to stiff peaks. Gently fold water and egg whites into flour mixture.

In a heavy bottomed frying pan heat 2 tablespoons shortening and 2 tablespoons vegetable oil over medium high heat. Carefully spoon 4 johnnycakes into the oil (2 tablespoons of batter each). Fry for 2 minutes until golden brown, flip and repeat on other side. If the pan is too hot your cakes will turn dark brown. Too cool and the dough will soak up all the fat and become soggy. The right temperature will produce a golden brown Johnnycake.

Remove from pan and place on paper towel to soak up extra grease. Repeat with next 4 johnnycakes.

Makes 12 cakes

Fire!

*W*arm smells of my oatmeal, white chocolate, and cranberry cookies filled the galley, signaling to me they were almost done. I looked at the clock on the wall to check: 2:04, I still had another minute to go. That is when the lights went out. I wiped the flour from my hands onto my apron as I crossed the room to call Mase, our engineer, and let him know that we had blown a breaker.

"Mase, the lights just tripped in the galley." In the five seconds it took me to relay the short sentence, the scene had already changed dramatically. "...And I smell smoke."

"On my way," Mase blurted out. The engine room was in the stern of the boat, down a level and through two doors but it couldn't have been more than ten seconds before I heard his Bluntstones thumping down the passageway. His eyes darted around the room. "Is everything off in here?" His first instinct was a galley fire, but I still had forty-five seconds before the cookies were done.

Turning off the oven, I replied, "Yeah, all off. It's not in here."

But Mase was already headed for the next room. "Grab the fire extinguisher," he yelled back over his shoulder.

"Got it." I ran behind him through the galley to the main salon, following the smell of smoke.

"It's in here, look over there." Mase pointed to the adjoining dining room.

"No, nothing," I shouted.

"What about the entertainment system?"

"No, it's fine."

Mase looked up and saw the problem; smoke was streaming out of the gold light fixture above the couch. "It's in the ceiling," he exclaimed as if in awe. He stood a moment staring at the ceiling contemplating the task before us. In an instant, he snapped into action, jumping onto the white couch and prying the fixture out of the ceiling with his screwdriver.

"Wait, I'll get a towel," I said, in a ridiculous effort to save dirty footprints on the satin smooth material. Ignoring me, Mase dropped the hot fixture, as thick grey smoked billowed out of the fist sized hole in the ceiling.

"Give me the extinguisher," Mase yelled. "Go get more!"

Racing back through the galley to the next extinguisher in the hall, I caught a glimpse of Julie, our new stewardess, heading past. "Go get the boys immediately!" I screamed at her.

Momentarily, caught off guard by my uncharacteristic tone, she opened her mouth to reply. But, seeing me rip the fire extinguisher from the wall, not taking the time to unbuckle it from its harness, she turned on her heel and bolted to get help. All of us had completed yearly fire training and medical classes, but neither of us thought to pull the fire alarm that was mounted on the wall just inches from the phone.

Running back into the salon, again I removed my shoes so as not to damage the carpet. That was what we were trained to do. We wore gloves while cleaning, we removed our shoes before entering carpeted areas, and we put down cloths to avoid scratching the beautiful wood. We were conditioned to protect the boat and even in this emergency situation, I was following procedure. The smoke that had been filling the room exploded into flame and shot out of the hole in the ceiling like a blowtorch firing up. Pieces of burning ash fell onto the sofa that I had tried to preserve from footprints and sizzled deep into the cushion. One piece caught Mase as it fell, lighting his pants on fire. I pointed and aimed the fully charged extinguisher in my hands at him. I hit him with a blast before he even knew what was happening.

The room was filled with a soupy fog of smoke now, and I was having trouble seeing; my eyes burned and I blinked furiously to clear my vision. I dashed frantically back and forth from fixture to fixture as Mase jumped across the sofa to the coffee table, prying the line of lights out of the ceiling as I hit them with a blast of the extinguisher. We had a little assembly line going, Mase leading, me following, but it was not fast enough to control the racing flames. Strangling smoke penetrated the air, and I began to cough as I tried in vain to move artwork and cushions out of Mase's way. Strangely, I was not worried or panicked and barely noticed that I was choking in the limited air. I had been trained to fight a fire and calmness had taken over. I was just following directions and orders.

Suddenly the aft doors opened and in came Ian and Chris in their fire suits. Dressed in silver aluminum jackets, helmets, breathing apparatus, and overall rubber boots, they looked like a Hazmat team more than my handsome young friends. Julie had alerted them to the situation, and they were quick to respond. Hoses and fire axe in hand they streamed into the smoky room.

Blue Moon is worth over thirty-five million dollars, and the four of us had spent the last two years preserving that value, so just as I had tried to put down drop clothes before fighting the fire, Chris hesitated a moment before proceeding. He looked at the axe in his hand and then at the handcrafted ceiling above. As he looked back at the axe and steadied it I could almost see him cringing through his mask as he swung, embedding the sharp edge of the blade in the wood. Destruction had begun, and he yanked hard to pull down the overhead and threw it to the custom-woven wool carpet below where it continued to smolder, giving us more exposure to fight the fire. With this new burst of oxygen, the flames swelled like waves across the whole ceiling, glowing bright blue and carrot orange. Mesmerized, I just stood and stared as I breathed in and began coughing uncontrollably. Mase looked at me and grabbed my hand.

"Come on Victoria. We need to get out." He protectively led me through the open doors into the fierce sunlight. Squinting from the change in light I saw that everyone had gathered to watch and wait as Chris and Ian battled the fire. We were tied to the dock in St. Barth's so there was no danger of sinking, but my friends were still inside. We had worked together on *Pari,* and they had followed me to *Blue Moon.* We had been living, working and traveling together for the past three years. I trusted fully that they knew what they were doing and would be walking out the same doors I just had. I went over to Julie, Chris's girlfriend and put my arm around her. Quietly we both just stood there watching those doors.

Outside, we were surrounded by the tranquility of the island. The afternoon sunlight bathed us in orange. Birds sang. Sapphire blue water lapped gently against the hull. But inside the guys were fighting their way through the grey cloud of smoke.

Julie and I turned as sirens approached and horns honked signaling the arrival of the island's fire department. Men in suits poured out of the truck. They bombarded the boat, pushing past Julie and I. They assembled their gear. Just then we heard a loud crash. The aft door slid open. Smoke poured out of the opening. Ian and Chris stepped out of the doors and into our sight. Removing their helmets they smiled. The fire was out. My friends were safe. The danger was over.

Cranberry, White Chocolate Oatmeal Cookies

Every afternoon at 3:00, without fail, Mase would brew himself a cup of tea and sit down for a cookie. It was a civilized break in the chaotic life as crew, and I cherished those few minutes to talk with my friends. Throughout the years, Mase sampled many of my cookies but these were his favorites. They are the cookies I was baking when he and I battled the fire.

1 cup butter
3/4 cup sugar
1/2 cup brown sugar
2 eggs
1 teaspoon vanilla
2 cups flour
2 cups oats
1 teaspoon cinnamon
1 teaspoon baking soda
1/2 teaspoon baking powder
1 cup white chocolate chips
1 cup dried cranberries

Preheat oven to 350. Combine sugar, brown sugar, and butter in a large bowl, beat with a mixer at medium speed until well blended. Add eggs and vanilla; beat well. Add flour, oatmeal, cinnamon, baking powder and baking soda and mix gently. Add cranberries and white chocolate and mix until combined. Shape into golf ball size rounds and slightly flatten into a disk. Place evenly on a cookie sheet that has been lined with grease-proof paper. Bake at 350 for 10 minutes, taking care to rotate pans in the oven half way through so as not to burn one side of the cookie. Remove and cool.

Makes 24 cookies

Welcome to Middle Earth

I grew up as a tomboy, the closest thing my father had to a son. And my love of cooking, while certainly stemming from a maternal need to take care of people, had deposited me into a male-dominated profession. So it wasn't surprising that instead of spending my vacation relaxing on a beach, I chose to spend my spring vacation in the Adirondacks rafting, camping, and fly-fishing.

I had been missing rugged and immediate nature. Spending the past four years on a yacht in the Caribbean was a little too perfect and pristine a version of nature for me. I longed to swim in a river, sleep on the ground, and cook over an open flame. While *Blue Moon* was being repaired from the fire damage, I had the opportunity to do some exploring on land.

My love of the Canadian Rockies is deep and unending. They are in my blood. I return to them any chance I get. But for this trip, I wanted to experience another mountain range so I picked the Adirondacks in northern New York State. Six million acres of gentle hills, mirror-smooth lakes, fast moving streams, and trout-filled rivers—all encompassed by the largest state park in America. Guided trips through this area, offered any combination of kayaking, horseback riding, hang-gliding, fishing and camping.

The moment I read *Middle Earth Expeditions* blurb in Lonely Planet, I knew they were who I wanted to camp with. Named after JRR Tolkien's stories, Middle Earth brought pictures to my mind of embarking on a journey in discovery of one's self. The philosophy was simple: adventure and intimacy are vital tools for human well-being.

Wayne, the owner and guide for Middle Earth Expeditions, promised pristine forests, fields of wild flowers, crystal clear and unpolluted waters full of trout, and the call of the loon in the early morning mist. What more did I need? I packed my gear and drove north from Savannah to the Hudson River, and then on through cedar and sugar maples, and past old-growth hemlock forests. A hawk soared in and out of sight overhead. I knew I was in for a completely relaxing three-day trip as soon as my cell phone clicked out of range.

When hiring a guide, you want someone with experience, who knows the region well and can direct you to the best possible spots. Many times I go by the recommendation of others. This time I was going solely with the *Lord of The Rings* connection. The moment I met Wayne, I knew I'd made the right choice. He looked as if he stepped right out of the pages of the story: larger than a Hobbit but just as hairy. He had a bushy, mountain man beard and long dark hair.

"Welcome to my middle earth." He opened his arms wide and tilted his head back to soak up the rays of the sun. At that point he looked more like Moses parting the Red Sea than a hobbit. Wayne seemed rugged and weather-worn and young and boyish all at the same time.

"Are you ready to conquer the river?" he asked.

"I'm ready."

"I just need to pack a few more things." He turned to his mountain of gear and began fiddling with a strap. Maybe this wasn't going to be so relaxing after all, with just two of us to inflate the raft, pack tents, coolers, stoves, lanterns, pots, fishing gear, guitars, and tables and chairs. We spent most of the morning just getting organized. Not only was I going to learn to fly-fish, I was going to learn to camp—in style. Wayne had more luxury items packed than any camping trip I'd ever been on. Instead of the requisite marshmallows for s'mores, he had packed beautifully baked pies and pastries from a local bakery.

He showed me every food item. "I have basil and chervil for the trout. Is that what you use?"

It wasn't, but I wanted to see the way he cooked trout. He had more experience than I with campfire cooking.

I think I made him nervous. Cooking for a chef could be daunting. He didn't realize yet how grateful I am whenever someone else takes the lead. This was my vacation, and I was going to enjoy having Wayne cook for me.

By mid-day we were packed and ready to start our first run at Class IV rapids. We launched the raft, jumped in, and began to make our way to the campsite. The Hudson River offers some of the most challenging and exciting white-water in the Northeast. The spring mountain melt-off leads to an exhilarating initial charge down the river. As we headed toward our first set of rapids, the sound and sight of rushing water surrounding us made me glad I had decided to hire an experienced guide.

"Left, left! Paddle hard!" Wayne shouted from the back of the raft. "Now back paddle. You got it." Wayne's confident manner made me feel safe as we faced the class IV's ahead. We aimed for the first rapid as he steered to line the raft up for entry. "Here we go!" He screamed.

The front of the raft, where I was sitting, dipped low under the first wave of white foam, sending cold water up and over my body. I shook my head and yelped as we raced forward. We bounced off the boulder in the center and spun to the right like the teacup ride at Disney. Wayne dug in to straighten us for the next set of rapids that were fast approaching. Another wave soaked the rest of me. This time we spun to the left and exited the rapid backwards.

I couldn't stop giggling. "That was awesome"

He grinned at me. "That's nothing! Just wait!" Wayne shook his long hair like a sheepdog after a bath. His smile grew wider. He loved it here. Every turn of the river brought another yelp of enthusiasm. I was in good hands.

Wayne kept the raft on course through the rapids and eddies we encountered. He sat in the back, steering the raft, and letting the rushing water work as our propeller. The river rocks were exposed in areas, creating challenging shoots. We spun one direction and then the next, but always ended up facing the right direction and position for the next set of rapids. I didn't even need to see them to know they were approaching. Suddenly, the water would get choppy. The sound of water running over rocks roared louder. The current picked up and waves crashed over the raft, submerging the bow completely.

Wayne paddled furiously and pulled the boat into position before we entered the rough, tumbling waters of our descent. It was like looking into the glass door of a washing machine. All the while Wayne displayed a wide, come-and-get-me smile, hollering with each crashing wave. I couldn't help but get caught up in the excitement. A few "whoops" escaped my lips.

Our journey took us from the rapids into narrow stretches of river that widened into quiet ponds. Buds of spring were visible on the foliage lining the riverbanks. Small wild flowers coming into bloom emerged along the shore. This was where Wayne brought out the fly fishing rods for my first lesson. After a quick demonstration, he pointed me toward the eddies right behind a series of large rocks in the rapids. "This is where the fish like to sit waiting for food to get swept past them with the running water," He told me. "White-water is the least fished area of a river and will often hold the biggest fish."

I was hoping we'd land trout for dinner. I envisioned fresh-caught fish sizzling over the glowing embers of a fire. Wayne demonstrated the motion of the rod a few times and then handed it to me. I mimicked his fluid movement. Smack! The line hit with a vibration, plunging below the water.

"Not so jerky. You don't need strength to throw it. Just momentum." He demonstrated with a wave of his arm. I reeled it back in and tried again. This time the line played out, but the fly stayed in the raft, hooked to a rope on the floor. Wayne showed me again how to move my arm.

"Like this?" I asked. He nodded encouragingly. Again, I came up empty. The fish were just not cooperating. Apparently, they didn't think a little lemon, parsley and a hot fire was such a good idea.

After an uneventful afternoon of fishing, we picked a site to set up camp. Rapids to our right provided the sound of running water. The rocks and cliffs straight across the river with white cedar trees lining the cliff face gave us a stunning view. A shallow eddy around the corner was available for a cold early spring swim. The woods stretched out behind us for miles of walking trails. We were the first to camp the site that year, so there was plenty of firewood available.

While Wayne set up the outdoor kitchen, I contemplated typical gender roles and realized I often thumb my nose at them. He brought coolers filled with steaks, salad, potatoes, and whole-grain breads. He began dinner while I collected firewood and pitched the tents. It felt good to focus on my chores in the fresh air without an ounce of responsibility. Someone else was in charge of dinner.

A higher level of creature comforts come with rafting, as opposed to hiking, kayaking, or climbing, where your carrying capacity is limited. From our large, spacious raft, Wayne pulled bottles of wine, wine glasses, tables and chairs and lanterns for our evening meal. Soon, the fire had burned to hot coals and the steaks were marinating in herbs and olive oil. I finished foraging for wild strawberries the deer and bears had missed.

After dinner, I had just enough energy for a few campfire songs on the guitar. Wayne strummed renditions of Dylan and the Eagles. *I had a job in the great north woods, working as a cook for a spell.* I sang along. I drank one more glass of wine as I watched the moon rise, read a few chapters of my book, and headed straight to my tent to fall asleep against the backdrop of nature's song.

I arose early the second day with a new sense of determination. I *was* going to be successful. I *was* going to catch a trout for dinner.

Fly-fishing is a passion in the Adirondacks—a thinking-man's sport of patience. You have to master the casting technique and read the water to determine where the fish are and what they're feeding on. The idea is to choose a dry fly resembling what the fish typically eat and present it to them in a realistic way, fooling them into thinking it's a real fly they want to eat, and thus, become hooked. The weaving motion of the fly rod is meditative and captivating; the line glistening in the air and the soft arrival of the fly on the water. Fly-fishing is distinguished from other forms of fishing by its grace and beauty. Of course my casting technique looked more like bad disco dancing than Brad Pitt's *A River Run's Through It* character.

During my first hour, I successfully hooked the raft, the net, and an overhead tree branch. I seemed more likely to hook my own ear than a fish at this point. Thankfully, Wayne was still asleep and not a witness to my disgrace. I could throw a net farther than I was placing the fly, and would probably have more success. I've had silly ideas before in my life, but learning to fly-fish was quickly topping the list. But just as I was about to turn in my waders, I tried one final cast exactly how Wayne had taught me. I placed the fly right into the eddy behind the midstream boulder where the fish sheltered from the currents and could save their energy to strike at flies.

And that's where my trout was, waiting for me to perfect my cast. Before I knew what was happening, he had the fly, and I was setting the hook. I reeled him in and lowered the net for my first fly-fishing victory.

He was beautiful: brown scales with slight red spots along his spine; twelve inches of pure mountain brown trout. He was mine. We were going to eat fish tonight. Suddenly, I was the hot rod on the river.

Triumphantly, I turned from the river back to the campsite just in time to see three white-tailed deer venturing into our camp. They were thin after the long winter, but tall and proud. Timid at first, yet bold enough to hold eye contact and walk through camp in search of berries. They barely took notice of me and showed little surprise that we were even there. They blended into the woods and rocks, yet stood out with such beauty and strength, mesmerizing me with the deep pools of their innocent eyes and trusting natures.

With these three visitors, along with the mallards flying overhead, a beaver swimming past, and all the trout in the river, this was quite a busy little spot. And the best part of all, we were alone.

That afternoon, the roles reversed again. I gathered fresh fiddleheads from the riverbank and picked fresh wintergreen for the asparagus. Wayne chilled the Sauvignon Blanc in the river and boiled brown rice. He placed a cast iron pan on the burning embers of the fire to heat. He sprinkled sea salt and ground fresh pepper over the whole fish. He stuffed basil and garlic inside its belly for flavor. The pan spat oil and hissed as he placed the fish in the center. He used a flat whisk to ensure it did not stick to the bottom. "Is this right?" he asked again.

"This is your kitchen." I indicated the forest around us. "You're the chef tonight."

I'm not sure whether it was the thrill of finally catching the trout, the trout itself, the setting, or the simple fact that I was on an adventure immersed in nature that made this a great meal. I loved the clean and clear flavors. The trout was moist and delicate, the crisp asparagus still had a snap and a bite from the wintergreen, the fiddleheads added an earthy quality, and the rice had a nutty, chewy texture that rounded out the meal.

"Can I ask you something personal?" Wayne sat by the firelight, strumming his guitar. I sat, leaning back in my camp chair, my Birkenstocks warming by the fire.

"Sure, ask away." I had more than an inkling what would come out of his mouth next. I had known this question would come up at some point in the trip.

"Why are you doing this? Why are you traveling alone?"

This was a question that I faced every time I made plans to travel. Everyone I met, my friends, and especially my parents, couldn't understand what I was doing. Sometimes I didn't even understand. It wasn't that I was anti-social. It was just that I preferred having time by myself.

"I like traveling alone." I stared into the glowing coals. "I get to go exactly where I want to go, do exactly what I want to do, and see exactly what I want to see. I think I get a better sense of a place by myself than I would if I was constantly in conversation with someone." That was the short, quick answer that usually satisfied people's curiosity. The long answer included my theory that traveling is a personal act. To travel with someone involves opening yourself up and showing your true self to another. They see you in all states; in times of frustration, confusion, and even stupidity. I was just not ready to trust someone with those aspects of myself. I was still trying to invent myself, be the person I wanted to be, lead the life I wanted to lead before I showed myself to another.

My short answer wasn't enough for Wayne. "What about a boyfriend or someone to share these experiences with?"

And there it was. The boyfriend question. I had boyfriends. I dated. I was going to meet Patrick in New York City for two days after this trip. But my new lifestyle of traveling for twelve months a year wasn't conducive to a long term relationship. It's hard to keep a boyfriend when you keep sailing out of port and can never say when—or even if—you'll come back.

But Wayne wanted a deeper answer. "For a lot of years, I waited until I met someone to start traveling," I started to explain. "But my list of things I wanted to do kept getting longer, and the time I had to do them in kept getting shorter. A couple of years ago, I decided I wouldn't wait any longer. If I wanted to go to Ireland, I'd go to Ireland. If I wanted to go backcountry skiing, then I'd go backcountry skiing. No more waiting for someone else to show up and lead me." I took another sip of wine and stared into the dancing flames. "I date, but so far no one has signed on for the journey."

"Hmm, I like that. Pretty gutsy." And that was it. My explanation for being on the river, rafting after the first break of spring with a man I had hired to guide me was complete. Wayne's way of life and his viewpoint meant that he understood what I was about. He lived life by his own rules as well.

I sat there by the firelight that night for a long time. I could do these things. I liked doing these things. It might not be everyone's idea of a perfect life or travel situation, but it was mine. I had such rich experiences, meeting interesting people, exploring new places. Maybe one day I'd have someone to share these experiences with but for the moment, I liked being by myself and running my own game.

As we prepared to raft out the following day, osprey flew overhead to lead us home. The river ran swiftly for another few miles to our dropout point, and the sun beat down, burning off the cool night air. We hit another four rapids in quick succession, managing to stay dry in the raft before turning the corner to see Wayne's truck parked on the shore. My time on the river was over. The trout were safe for another day.

Passion at the CIA

A strange thing about being aboard a boat is that I cook for the same ten people every day. No one eats at the same restaurant, three meals a day, everyday of the year, but here onboard a boat, the crew has no choice, they are my captive audience. Once underway, there is no restaurant down the street if they don't like what I serve. I had cooked for Chris and Ian for over four years, and now Emile for three. They were at my mercy in terms of what they eat.

It is an awesome responsibility in terms of their health. If these guys eat poorly, it is my fault. If they have high cholesterol, it is my fault. If they develop clogged arteries, it is my fault. With this in mind, I really wanted to make sure I was providing the healthiest meals possible for my friends and crewmates.

Blue Moon was still in the shipyard restoring the damage from the fire, so I decided to take a few classes. There was only one place I wanted to go: *The Culinary Institute of America*. With Lawrence's encouragement, I had attended culinary school at the *Stratford Chef School* in Canada. Ever since then, I had read and fantasized about the Culinary Institute, in Upper New York State. It is the premiere school for chefs worldwide. It is like going to Harvard but instead of reading Shakespeare and Tolstoy, you study chocolate and grilling procedures. The CIA, as it is commonly referred to, was the best in the country. It produces many of the top chefs in the field today. My opportunity to see this magnificent faculty firsthand came when I registered for one of their continuing education classes. *Healthy Cooking Techniques* was a week-long class covering basic nutritional guidelines, how to analyze, modify and develop healthy recipes, healthy cooking techniques, and planning alternative healthy menus. I was excited to learn something new but even more excited to just be at the school.

I drove to the school on a warm spring day and rolled down my windows to breathe in the air. Cherry and dogwood blooms lined the roads. I meandered along the Hudson River to the small town setting just outside Poughkeepsie. Stone fences, Victorian cottages, and extravagant mansions led me through romantic scenery that suggested another era. I imagined Jay Gatsby playing host to summer parties, with ladies in white gloves holding parasols and watching the men play croquet. These days, the road is dotted with roadside produce stands, inns, bed and breakfasts, dairy farms, and horseback riding stables, all adding to the quiet charm of the Hudson Valley. It was the perfect Sunday afternoon drive in the country.

The Culinary Institute's one hundred and fifty-acre campus is on the banks of the Hudson River. The classic old stone and brick buildings were built in the late nineteenth century as St. Andrew-on-Hudson, a Jesuit Seminary. The original character of the buildings is still evident in the stained glass windows and the beautiful stonework of the main halls. Images of Oxford University permeated my mind.

I arrived late and immediately fell asleep on my dorm bunk. The next morning, I awoke early, refreshed and eager. I wound my way through the corridors and past stainless steel kitchens lined with counters and multiple stoves. The desks were prep tables in the center of the room. Each had half a dozen white cutting boards set on top. Pots were stacked high along one wall. Pans hung from the ceiling. Room after room was filled with cooking equipment. Finally, I found the kitchen I was supposed to be in. It was identical to the eight I just passed.

I was early but not the only student there. I smiled and placed my knives on a cutting board beside a man that looked to be about my age. We were dressed in identical starched white chef's jackets, pressed pants and polished black shoes. The only difference in our looks was his clear blue eyes that shone like Murano glass. We both wore a tall paper hat on our heads. But while I struggled to keep mine from tilting askew with my ponytail, his crew cut allowed his hat to stand straight and tall.

—— VICTORIA ALLMAN ——

"I'm Victoria." I reached out my hand.

He pointed to his name stenciled on his jacket just above the cooking medals he displayed. "René."

There were six people in the class, a cross section of students representing the broad spectrum of cooks. René was a CIA alumni and gold medal winner at the Culinary Olympics in Germany. He was now engaged in a culinary career through the army. Another man owned a restaurant in Rochester and was trying to keep up with the demands of his clientele. There was also a hospital dietitian, a private house chef, a sous-chef at a health spa and me, chef on a private yacht. Our diverse backgrounds would lead to varying points of view born out of our unique experiences regarding what healthy cooking is and how it applies to each of our particular situations. Is it fad dieting? Is it substituting real food with engineered modified products? Is it a vegetarian lifestyle? Is it weighing every morsel and calculating every aspect of your life? None of these really reflected what I thought of as healthy. I still believed in good tasting natural food.

Classes began at seven in the morning with a lecture by Chef David Smyth, an associate professor in culinary arts. He wasn't the typical older, heavy-set chef who could not tie his apron around his waist. Instead, he was in his early fifties with the physique of a long distance runner. He instilled confidence that there was another way to prepare food rather than using pounds of butter and liters of cream. He began the morning by discussing cooking techniques, the importance of buying fresh quality foods and current nutritional trends. We spoke of ways to eliminate unnecessary fat without compromising flavor and discussed ways to make healthy foods desirable—exactly what I wanted to learn. Some of the points were common sense, things that any health conscious person would know: eat lots of fruits and vegetables, choose lean cuts of meat, minimize the fat intake and cook with a wide variety of food. But this was a class on how to make healthy cooking taste good so we talked of ways to make easy changes to our cooking without sacrificing taste.

"Start by choosing a healthier cooking method," Chef Smyth instructed. "Steam vegetables instead of frying in butter. Sauté in broth and wine instead of oils, and roast foods in an oven instead of pan-frying."

"Make flavorful vegetable sauces instead of heavy cream sauces," he continued. "Use a non-stick pan to minimize the amount of oil needed."

Some of his suggestions, I already practiced. Official healthy cooking was not far from what I did naturally. I preferred roasted butternut squash sauces to creamy alfredos. I thought steamed asparagus was crisper than boiled limp stalks.

After our morning discussion, we proceeded to the practical side of the class. This is where we put all the newfound knowledge into practice. We broke into teams of two and were given three hours to produce a three-course meal, using recipes from the school's *Techniques of Healthy Cooking* textbook as guidelines.

I was partnered with René. He and I had the most formal culinary training. With guidance from Chef Smythe, we began reviewing the menu and recipes and made a game plan. René was a chef instructor in the army and had a lot of experience at taking charge. With all the mannerisms of a drill sergeant, he quickly and efficiently divided up the tasks at hand.

"I will handle the main course, I have done this dish a thousand times before. It is a guaranteed hit. You can do the dessert and the vegetables. We have three hours, you better start now." René exuded confidence with each word. "We will make ostrich with a variety of whole-grains and a cheesecake with ricotta and cottage cheese. I'm sure you can handle that. Ask me if you have any questions." I bit my tongue and shook my head. "Oh, and you can come up with a salad or something." This was going to be a long afternoon.

Without even a chance to reply, René began butchering the ostrich, marinating it in orange juice and fresh herbs to add a depth of flavor. He seared it to caramelize the outside and build even more flavor. He had good technique and did exactly what I would have done. It was hard to fault him, but I couldn't help but put my shackles up at his attitude. I didn't feel like arguing with him. Years of being in kitchens with egotistical men had taught me that fighting back just made them stronger. I smiled to myself and began on our dessert. To add more fruits to our day's meal I suggested to René that we change the sauce accompanying the cheesecake to fresh ripe spring berries poached in port and cinnamon.

He agreed and liked the idea. "Yeah, and maybe some toasted almond praline chopped into the crust for texture." At least we thought alike.

I cleaned the baby vegetables for our main course and assembled the ingredients for a salad of golden Bosc pears, toasted walnuts and braised leeks in balsamic vinegar. I reduced the vinegar to lose the sharpness of the acid. This allowed us to omit the use of oil in the dressing. René was busy assembling a medley of different whole grains for cooking with a *mirepoix*—a small dice of onion, carrot and celery, when he again began to speak of his attributes.

"This dish is one that I cook for the dignitaries who come through the base. I'm always head chef for the generals and VIP's. I create meals for all their functions. I love using ostrich or game. Everyone else cooks beef tenderloin and salmon. Boring, boring, boring." He was boasting, but it was actually interesting. He spoke of all the different functions the army hosted. I always had the view army cooks only served gruel, but here was someone who, under all his macho bragging, was actually a CIA graduate and a fantastic cook. He was on the Army's Culinary Olympic Team and ran a training program for army chefs. After awhile, he began asking me a lot of questions about what I did and what it was like to be a chef on a boat. As the afternoon wore on, we discussed how our lives had taken different paths since leaving chef school. If I looked beyond the bravado, he had some incredible experiences and knowledge of food to share. We had a lot in common and similar views on food and cooking: we just had different ways of presenting ourselves. It had been a long time since I encountered someone with so much enthusiasm for food, and I was becoming very intrigued and impressed.

We clicked and worked well together. René's army training fit with my belief in doing things properly and to the best of my ability. Neither of us believed in shortcuts and both had strong work and kitchen ethics. We fed off of each other and pushed one another to the next level. I liked being around someone so passionate, even if he could get a little overwhelming at times.

The best aspect of going to chef school is in grading your work. After presenting the meals, everyone is required to taste all the creations and discuss their merits. Of course, it is a well-known fact it is easier to taste good food with a glass of wine in your hand. This only added to the sacrifices we had to make in the pursuit of knowledge. I have heard scary rumors about starving university students eating only ramen noodles for weeks on end. Luckily, that does not apply to chef school students.

Each group plated their three courses and presented them to Chef Smythe, along with a written report on calories, fats, protein, and sodium in each dish. We all stood around a central workbench, forks in hand, discussing each of the dishes, what worked and what didn't. We then tasted each plate to see if the healthy techniques actually translated to great tasting food.

When it came time for René and I to produce our dishes, I was confident and pleased. We had taken three simple courses and created a complex, interesting meal full of flavor, contrasting textures, and unique ingredients. This was no celery stalk, low-fat Jell-O lunch. This was real food.

Of course René stepped up to croon about the dish. "It is light and healthy but damn tasty. I guarantee you'll love it."

An approving smile spread across Chef Smyth face as we set the dishes in front. And with the first bite our efforts were rewarded. "The salad is a perfect balance of sweet and bitter. There is the crunch of the walnuts and the softness of the leeks." He smiled at me. "Good work, Victoria."

While it's easy to give the facts and details of being at the school, it is more difficult to describe the essence of the CIA. This is a place where students are surrounded by a shared passion for food. A passion demonstrated not only by the instructors, but also by the students and visitors. Everyone is there for one purpose only: to enjoy food and everything about food. The main goal of the school is to instill this passion and a commitment to excellence in each and every student. There is a definite energy and enthusiasm emanating from everyone immersed in the program, and it is impossible not to be excited when surrounded by such a deep degree of drive and dedication to quality.

As the days went by, I became more and more impressed with the CIA's stance on healthy cooking being high-quality food first and foremost. I learned how to cook healthy, as well as how to cook fundamentally good food. I was told to select ingredients with care, to prepare them with the aim of preserving their best possible flavor through careful preparation and cooking techniques. Fresh ingredients were championed. Skill-based cooking was taught as opposed to bad cooking with unhealthy products.

By the week's end, I had had a sensory overload of excitement, fantastic food, exceeding amounts of knowledge and a new friend who was as passionate about food as I was. This was more than a course on healthy cooking. This was a recharging of my love of food, fueled by those around me. It was impossible to be here and not to pick up the excitement in the air. I was on a food high. I walked away with a renewed love of food.

———— VICTORIA ALLMAN ————

Under the Southern
Stars of Africa

I slept under the southern sky of Africa. It was the dead of night and Scorpio, Sirius, and the Southern Cross shone brightly overhead. The stars, close and luminous in the nearly moonless sky splattered overhead like a Jackson Pollack painting. I could hear the distant call of lions roaring and the incessant chatter of monkeys in the trees. Snuggled deep inside my sleeping bag at the Ngala Private Game Reserve, I was camping in the true wilderness, set to experience the wilds of this expansive country.

Africa appealed to me. I wanted to see the exotic animals, hear the bellow of the mighty lion and witness the stealth of a hunt. I wanted to see an epic sunset over the plains with its great explosion of color. I wanted to experience the hot searing sun and feel apart of a world so extremely different from yachting.

Emile and Marisa married in Paarl, South Africa's wine country. I had been there for the wedding and stayed for a month. I kayaked the Orange River and camped on its banks. I climbed Table Mountain and repelled down its face. I mountain biked the Garden Route, overlooking the Indian Ocean. I rafted the Zambezi River. It was an adventure driven vacation. My last experience was to go on safari.

That night, not long after exhaustion forced me to sleep, I heard a noise outside the tent. I looked at my watch—five-thirty in the morning. Ugh! And I thought I was on vacation. I peeked outside. This wasn't the sound of an elephant in camp or hyenas sniffing around for food. This was Jimmy, our camp-hand, coming to fill my shower bag and wake me for the morning safari walk.

Days start early on safari. This was the best time to view game. They gathered at watering holes or scouted breakfast before the heat drove them to cover.

I dressed and joined the others around the campfire. Last night's landscape of stars were barely fading from the sky. Yet there we were, ready to go on our first hike beyond camp in hopes of discovering elephants, giraffes, lions and hippopotamus.

"Everyone ready?" our chipper guide, Gavin asked.

Low moans and whimpers of consent echoed around the campfire.

"Right, then. Off we go."

This was what the Ngala Walking Safari was all about—eight guests, a ranger, and a tracker all setting out on foot across the bushveld and savannahs to see Africa. We were in search of the *big five* (lions, elephants, leopards, rhinoceroses and buffalos) and any other indigenous animals we might find. Many of us had only seen those animals in zoos or by watching documentaries. This was our chance to glimpse the grand beasts up close. Many African safaris are conducted from the safety and comfort of Land Rovers, but Ngala's unique approach to safari limited the impact vehicles had on the ecosystem and allowed everyone a chance to explore and learn.

We left the comfort of camp in the grey light of dawn to be begin our search in the Timbavati riverbed. The Ngala Reserve is one of the richest wildlife regions in Africa, encompassing fourteen thousand hectares surrounding the Timbavati River. Timbavati means ever-flowing river. Strangely enough, the so-called riverbed we walked in was dry. We walked along the sand. Ever-flowing? That was the Africa I was beginning to know—constant change, constant contradiction. What was once a flowing river was now a path of dry sand.

Not long after striking out from camp, Ranger Gavin, a young Africaander from English descent and our native tracker, Abednigo, showed us both elephant and buffalo tracks in the sand.

"See the indents, just here." He pointed to the dusty sand. "They're headed east." To me they looked like normal scratches. I would not have hesitated or noticed them, but to Gavin and Abednigo they were signs. Thousands of marks and indentations in the sand surrounded us. The guides easily identified the different tracks and assessed how old they were.

Gavin, a twenty-something fair-haired man had studied biology in Cape Town; this was his field study experience. With his Johannesburg accent, he described what we were seeing. "These buffalo will travel long distances in search of water. They travel in large groups and create many prints in the sand." He had the knowledge of a scholar and seemed to recite facts verbatim from texts.

Abednigo, graced with strong cheekbones and a flat chocolate colored face, had not been to university to learn about these animals: he had grown up in the area and had been tracking since he was a boy. His father was a tracker; so was his grandfather. His dark eyes seemed to pierce through the bushes.

"We head this way," Abednigo whispered. With an inherent trust that he could pinpoint a tsetse in the vast amount of space before us, we followed the tracks in single file, as quietly as possible, our cameras at the ready.

It wasn't long before Gavin stopped us dead in our tracks with a signal of his hands. We had come across the herd of water buffalo traversing the dry riverbed and heading towards a nearby watering hole. He whispered quietly to each of us, "This is a herd of about seven hundred."

Buffalo are extremely dangerous animals if startled, and since we were on foot we didn't want to start a stampede. "Walk quietly and keep your eyes on me for a signal. I'll let you know when to move and in which direction," he said.

We silently obeyed and followed the two guides closely. This was no time for any hotshot cowboy rebellions. We just wanted to observe and retreat without interrupting anything.

We hiked to the rise over the riverbed where we could observe the animals from relative safety. The immense herd moved slowly below us. They ambled sluggishly along the riverbed and into the distance, heads low looking for fresh grass to eat. Flies buzzed around them as they kicked up clouds of dirt.

Because these were not the most exciting game the bushveld had to offer, we only sat observing them for fifteen minutes or so before moving on. We took out our binoculars to search for a mother cheetah and her cub.

"They've been seen here every morning this week." Gavin was convinced we could find her. Tracking light agile cheetahs seemed much more difficult to me than the larger and heavier water buffalo, but Abednigo had been tracking for more than twenty years.

"We find her." He had no trouble reading the signs and brought us to a hill overlooking the den where the feline and her cub played under a cover of grass. The mother, the color of marmalade with dark spots along her flank, had a shiny well-groomed coat like that of my mother's tabby cat. She even had the same walk, swaying her hind quarters back and forth as she sauntered toward her cub that was running circles around an invisible play toy. As the mother approached, she stretched out a large powerful paw and gently scooped the cub up to nuzzle under her chin. We studied the lethal and cunning animal and the innocent playfulness of her cub, and felt awe at this display of a rare and graceful, yet powerful, animal in an intimate embrace with her offspring. Everyone was full of questions for Gavin.

"How old is the cub?" one guest inquired.

"How many are in Ngala?" another wanted to know.

"How big is she?" a third asked before Gavin could even answer.

"What does she eat?" The first guest forgot his previous question.

"Who eats *her*?"

Our group shot off questions faster than throwing punches at a sparring bag. Another perk of being part of the safari was the instant biology lesson we were all given in each situation by our ranger and tracker. Gavin provided a wealth of information and he recited facts and stories while everyone shot reel after reel of film. Finally, the most important question was asked.

"What's for lunch?" This was the land of hunting and survival of the fittest. We did not want to miss the next meal.

After such a powerful morning, I found it hard to imagine anything else could happen to enhance the experience. Ngala, however, knew how. Upon returning to camp, I discovered the best thing about camping in Africa—the *braai*. *Braai* is South African for barbecue and one of the favored forms of cooking. Whether one is camping or having friends over in the backyard, a *braai* is an informal way of entertaining with earthy simplicity. This is a food culture based on meats and game that descended from the early days of settlers, who led a nomadic lifestyle as hunters and trekkers and took advantage of native South African resources like impala, springbok, ostrich and warthog. What better way to cook their bounty than over wood gathered from the area, to give the food a distinct outdoor flavor?

Our campsite had been transformed since early morning light into a five-star outdoor dining room. They had placed a dark mahogany table under the umbrella of an acacia tree. It was set with bamboo woven table mats, hunter green napkins, heavy white plates, bold wine glasses and chunky silverware. The aroma of food cooking in the fresh air was overwhelming.

The *braai* was lit and soon the coals emitted an amber glow. The smell of lunch permeated the air as Henri, our camp cook kept busy grilling warthog, corn on the cob, and tomatoes. A number of salads had been set out on the buffet. In the coals of the fire pot bread baked. This was unlike any camping I'd ever experienced before. It was so *civilized*.

After an energetic and exciting morning, our group didn't linger long before digging in. We eagerly dished up the best smelling and most incredible tasting camp food. The corn was sweet and smoky from the acacia wood that burned underneath. The bread, warm from the fire, was rich with a cake-like texture. And the warthog! So tender, succulent and moist from its diet of savannah grasses. It had a rich and sugary taste, a stronger flavor than its cousin, the domesticated pig. It may be ugly and scary but it sure was tasty.

The searing heat of the African climate was too much for the animals and delicate visitors alike. The hottest part of the day was spent napping—whether under a rock, in the shade of a tree, or in the luxury of a camp tent. The land around us became deserted while we baked in the sun.

After a quick nap, our group gathered again for another trek. Since it was our first day on the safari, and everyone was lethargic from an afternoon spent sleeping, Gavin and Abedigno knew we needed more excitement to pick us up. They arranged Land Rovers for us to cover more ground in the dwindling light of day. They didn't like using the vehicles, but since it was our first day, we needed a good teaser to keep us all enthused.

We set out in the comfort of Land Rovers. Not far from camp we turned north to follow a trail Abednigo had picked up.

"We are tracking white rhinoceroses," Gavin told our group. He drove the Land Rover while Abednigo sat on the hood, legs dangling over the grill. He studied the land ahead, signaling to Gavin to turn left or right. A few feet back, we passed a large mud pit. Ahead was a trail of muddy broken branches.

Rhinos are very shy in nature and were all but extinct in the area until recently when conservation efforts and enforced poaching laws combined to reintroduce the animals to the bushveld. I felt very lucky that we were able to find any sign of one at all. Mind you, considering rhinos also weigh up to five thousand pounds, how could we not find the one we were tracking?

"Rhino's travel similar paths everyday to mark territory and stick close to water." Gavin explained. Both he and Abednigo felt that we were in close vicinity due to the direction, shape, and size of the tracks we were following.

I had invited Patrick to join me on this trip, but he couldn't get away. I was traveling alone again. His one request was for me to take a picture of a rhino. He was captivated by them. He felt they were modern day dinosaurs and worried they would be poached to extinction before he got a chance to see one. I had my camera ready.

Gavin stopped the Land Rover near a stand of thorny bushes. Both men got out to study the ground. The stillness of the area enveloped us with a blanket of heat. The only sounds I could hear were the rustling of the long grasses in the dry wind. Then I heard it, the sound of something chewing, something *large* chewing. My breath lodged in my throat. Gavin returned to the vehicle. He raised a finger to his lips to silence us. He inched the truck forward through the bushes.

In the clearing stood three rhinos, within sixty feet of me. Their heads dipped to graze on the dry grass. The sheer size and presence of the white rhino bulls in the clearing was overwhelming. I stared transfixed.

Our sudden intrusion into their domain was met by—nothing. They took absolutely no notice of us and continued to graze. We were down-wind of them and apparently no cause for alarm. This extremely thrilling situation for us wasn't even a cause to stop chewing for them.

A group of rhinos are called a crash, and looking around at all the mud and destruction of trees I understood why.

Not one of us spoke. We sat under the vast, pale-blue sky, lit by the sun. White cumulus clouds moved quickly overhead as an arid hot wind blew. It suddenly dawned on me how small a part of nature we humans really are. This was the same sun that shined on me at home, but there was something different about it in Africa. There seemed a different light about the place; a different feel. Mother nature has a way of dealing out healthy doses of respect for her land without a single word.

Gavin slowly backed the truck out of the clearing. We traveled home in silence. We were nearly to camp when I realized I still clutched my camera and hadn't taken one shot. This was something Patrick would have to experience himself.

Back at camp, Henri prepared Sundowners with fresh squeezed juice, Grand Marnier, and Amaretto. Cold Castle beers were on ice and bowls of *biltong* (dried jerky) were set out to nibble on. These were enjoyed while watching a view of the wild orange sunset.

Our camp was perched on the edge of a wide-open expanse of savannah, shaded by a stand of acacia trees, whose tall lean trunks and umbrella-like canopies created ideal shade from the blazing sun. Stretching endlessly in front of us, as far as the eye could see was Africa.

As the sun descended, the sky took on a deeper radiance. A warm golden glow fell over our camp and the mighty land before us. No matter where I looked, the camp was lit with a serene light. Crimson reds and blazing oranges turned the sky the color of fire. As the light faded, it ran through the colors in a crayon box: oranges, reds, yellows, purples, until we were left with a black sky that slowly showered with thousands of stars. Southern stars.

Dozens of hurricane lanterns hung from the trees like our own private stars and illuminated our intimate dinner. "To Gavin and Abedingo." We toasted our guides and the promise of a fantastic meal. We excitedly discussed the day's events. While everyone was busy telling stories and comparing where they were from, I wandered over to the fire. I went to investigate what Henri was cooking.

"Tonight we feast on impala," he said. "It's a lean meat so it's perfect with the high heat of the fire. It only needs a short while on the flame or it will dry out. Medium-rare is perfect." He marinated the impala in rosemary, olive oil, chutney, garlic, onions, and peppercorns to moisten the meat. He handed me a piece to try. The sweet and savory aspects of the marinade perfectly complimented the gaminess of the impala.

Henri served the evening meal with vegetable kebabs of zucchini, mushrooms, and tomatoes, rice, pot bread, and a pumpkin *potjie*—a stew of lamb, onions, garlic, and pumpkin cooked long and slow over slow-burning coals.

"Potjie is an Afrikaanders dish that is cooked in a cast iron pot. It is great for camp cooking like this. I just have to brown the meat and onion, add the rest of the ingredients in layers, and leave it to simmer away over the fire while I prepare the rest of the meal." The cauldron-like pot sat in the center of the table wafting mouth-watering smells through the barren air.

Bottles of South African Pinotage, the local grape that's a cross between Pinot Noir and Cinsaut accompanied the meal. We toasted the knowledge of our guides, our good fortune of observing the elephants, rhinos and cheetahs, and the tasty food that sat before us.

My first day in the African bush ended as it started: under the southern sky with Scorpio, Sirius and the Southern Cross shining brightly overhead. Exhausted from the day's excitement I retired early to my tent. Five thirty would come again soon. The days are full while on safari in Africa, as are the nights. While I drifted off to sleep I could hear the distant call of a lion cutting through the darkness. I dreamt of Africa.

Pumpkin Potjie

8 slices bacon, diced
2 onions, chopped to a 1-inch dice
2/4 cup vegetable oil
4 pounds lamb leg, cut to 1-inch cubes
1/4 cup flour
1 teaspoon sea salt
1 teaspoon black pepper
2 tablespoons garlic, chopped
2 tomatoes, diced to 2-inch cubes
4 bay leaves
2 tablespoons fresh thyme
1/4 cup Mrs. Balls Original Chutney
2 cups chicken stock
6 carrots, sliced to 1/2-inch thickness
4 cups butternut squash, diced to 1-inch cubes
1 teaspoon sea salt

Heat a seasoned cast iron skillet on high. Add bacon and sauté until brown and starting to crisp. Add onions and sauté for 4 minutes until soft. Remove from the pot and add 2 tablespoons vegetable oil. Sauté 1 tablespoon garlic for 1 minute until golden. Meanwhile, toss together lamb, flour, sea salt, and pepper. Place half of the lamb in the skillet and sear, stirring occasionally to brown all sides for 5 minutes. Remove from pan and add to bacon and onions. Repeat process with remaining vegetable oil, garlic, and lamb. Add reserved bacon, onions, lamb, tomatoes, bay leaves, thyme, and chutney. Stir and top with chicken stock. Place lid on skillet and reduce the heat to medium-low so the liquid will just simmer. Simmer for 1-1/2 hours. Do not stir. Mix butternut squash and carrots with 1 teaspoon sea salt and stir into stew. Simmer for an additional 20 minutes.
Taste for seasoning and serve with crusty bread and rice.

Makes 6 servings

Savannah Shrimpin'

Whenever I'm traveling, I always make a concerted effort to meet the local people, to share meals and conversation with them. It is my way of soaking up culture. In France, I stayed with Marybeth and Bernard and dined in the slow, easy pace of the Mediterranean. In the Virgin Islands, I went to an Easter Sunday brunch with Marilyn, who introduced me to island pot-luck cooking.

I can imagine no better way to get to know a place than through its food and its people. So, during *Blue Moon's* six-month stay in Savannah, I took the opportunity to learn about Southern cooking and culture, not to mention a few ways of having fun.

If you've read *Midnight in the Garden of Good and Evil* by John Berendt, you already know how the "old money" in Savannah loves a good party. High society balls run throughout the year with women in diamonds and long white gloves. Men dress in tuxedoes and tails, chauffeur driven cars line the streets and orchestras entertain the guests. But there is another kind of Savannah party that is equally rich in pleasure. Savannah residents love getting together outdoors. Why not, in such a beautiful setting? In summer and early fall, when shrimp are in season, people gather for a low-country boil. Late fall and winter brings oyster roasts. With Georgia's favorable weather, you can host a southern BBQ at any time of the year.

Jacqueline grew up in Savannah and instantly became social director for our multi-national crew of ten, most of whom seldom knew anyone in the ports we traveled. A Southern belle herself, with brown flowing hair, dimples, and strong traces of a Southern drawl, she wasted no time in setting up our social calendar. Within days, we were invited to an oyster roast. Savannah is not called the *Host City of the South* for nothing.

It was a cool fall night in November. Stars shone over the river of marsh grass, their dim light filtered through the leaves of large live oaks that looked like they were about to topple over from the weight of the Spanish moss hanging from their limbs. A cool breeze blew off the water, rustling the palm fronds, and causing people to don their sweaters and jackets.

It was an informal party. People stood in small groups talking and drinking while children ran, chasing one another. The good ol' sound of Gregg Allman blared from the speakers. Picnic tables were covered with potluck macaroni salads, red velvet cakes, bowls of cocktail sauce and pots of chili and Brunswick stew. Kegs of beer and bottles of vodka, rum and whiskey sat on a makeshift bar made of an old tree stump. We had all the trimmings of a good party.

As Ian, Chris and Julie headed to the bar, I went in the opposite direction, to investigate the roasting of the oysters.

A red-hot fire burned. Half a dozen guests stood waiting to help. A weathered man dressed in a jean jacket and a John Deere green baseball cap set a large piece of steel on cinder blocks over the fire. Once hot, the oysters, still in their shells, were placed on the metal sheet, covered by wet burlap sacks. "This steams the oysters," the man said. "Then the shells will loosen."

True to his word, fifteen minutes later the shells opened like the mouth of an alligator. He picked up the steel plate and dumped the oysters on to a picnic table covered in newspaper. The crowd swarmed before he replaced the plate on the fire for round two. With oyster knives and gloves in hand, people began shucking. The feasting began.

These people knew exactly what to do. Instead of sitting down to a meal, they stood by the piles of oysters; grabbing one at a time, shucking it, spooning cocktail sauce, and slurping it out of the shell. They tossed the discarded oyster shells into a plastic garbage bin, and grabbed another oyster, repeating the procedure.

"Cool weather produces the plumpest oysters." The grill master laid a third round of oysters on the plate. "There ain't nothing better than standing around a fire on a crisp autumn night drinking cold beer. Good friends; good food."

Like magic, the oysters appeared from the fire as the pile on the table diminished.

"These are my friends Jimmy and Cathy." Jacqueline approached the fire with a couple.

"Well, hello there." Jimmy had a more pronounced Southern drawl. He smiled and laughed both at the same time.

"Nice to meet you."

"They sell the shrimp that comes off the boats." Jacqueline grabbed an oyster and began shucking.

"I've never seen a shrimp boat. How do you catch them?" I turned to Jimmy.

"You never seen a shrimp boat?" he asked. His face lit with surprise. "Shoot girl, you got to come down and see for yourself."

"Come out Sunday. Paul, the captain, would just die to meet you." Cathy added. "I'll make supper for you'all when you return." She had the look of a hard-working woman. Her green plaid jacket, jeans and boots all screamed of a life working on a shrimp boat, as did her rough and tough hands.

* * * *

The boat, *Bo-Nita*, had been out in Warsaw Sound for the past three days. Cathy arranged for Jacqueline's father, Bob, and I to take a tiller-driven flats boat called a Carolina Skiff out to meet her.

We met at Jimmy and Cathy's Sunday morning at eight. They couldn't join us, as they were busy getting their refrigerated shed ready for the haul *Bo-Nita* would bring in that night. Their house doubled as *Bo-Nita's* shrimp storage. Here the shrimp were weighed and heads removed before they were bagged and sold to local customers.

Cathy welcomed me in like a friend she'd known forever. "Now, you make sure them boys behave themselves. And Bob, you get her back here by dark. We're goin' have her first crab boil tonight."

"Jeez, Cathy. Don't you give me no grief." Bob and Cathy bantered with the familiarity of old friends. He had the same hardworking look, with a face carved by the sun, and long hair hidden beneath his trucker hat. An old pair of aviator glasses hid his eyes, but I knew from his tone of voice they held a mischievous sparkle. He, too, had owned shrimp boats in the past and had spent all his life on the water around Savannah.

With coffees in hand, we climbed into the skiff. We carried provisions and a newspaper to the crew. I waved over my shoulder as we set out for the day.

Georgia's coast is covered in meandering coastal creeks, inlets, coves, and peninsulas. After only a few minutes, it started to feel like we were in a labyrinth, turning corners left and right, willy-nilly, hoping to end up where we wanted to go. The marshland is home to thousands of birds, including a great blue heron that soared over the calm water ahead, seeming to lead us out. Iridescent blue dragonflies flitted around our heads as we wound our way through the marsh grass islands to the open water. A pelican flew low over the water, looking for fish. He swooped low like an airplane buzzing the ground. Bob expertly navigated the "roadway" and brought us out to open water.

Bo-Nita was a fifty-two-foot trawler, built, owned, and captained by Paul Gregory. Like most shrimp boats, she was rugged and well worked in appearance, her wooden hull battered from hauling equipment. She cruised the calm waters of the bay waiting for us to approach. A dozen seabirds, looking for discarded catch, followed *Bo-Nita*.

Once we tied up to *Bo-Nita's* stern, Bob toured me around the boat before I met the captain. The main cabin was forward, holding the wheelhouse, galley, bunks for crew, the head, and the all-precious TV. Three men fishing at sea for days on end still had to keep up with the score of the football game. Aft was the main deck used for dumping the nets and sorting the catch. Below was the ice storage and engines. The boat outriggers, used for nets and stabilization, were out to both port and starboard. Although, technically I lived on a boat too, this was a completely different world.

"This here is Paul," Bob said.

"Welcome aboard, miss." Paul tipped his ball cap. He was a broad, red-haired man with the physique of a linebacker. His huge shoulders showed how physical shrimping must be. I could actually see the sun burnt lines etched on the side of his face where his eyes creased in smile.

"So you're interested in shrimpin'?"

"I like to know where my food comes from."

"Well, this ain't no grocery store shrimp you're seeing here today." He launched into a complete description of his day's work. He was a jolly man, full of interesting stories and tales of life as a shrimper.

"Where do you go on that big boat of yours?" he asked, unable to comprehend life beyond the Georgian waters. He was as interested in my life aboard a yacht as I was of his.

When he sat behind the big wooden wheel, you could tell how comfortable Paul felt on the water. He was a true southern shrimper, having done this since high school. He leaned back in his chair, kept one eye on the game, one eye on the water, and his mind on the job.

Paul and his crew were there to catch wild shrimp. I tried not to get in the way. The nets were in the water long before Bob and I arrived. We were waiting for the boat to drag the nets up and down the area before bringing in their catch.

Paul was in control of where and when they would move. He stayed in constant contact with the forty other boats on the water that day, sharing information and discussing where the shrimp were. Every thirty minutes a smaller net was brought up and emptied to check what they were catching. "We estimate that for every shrimp in the small net, there will be one pound in the large net," He told me.

After estimating the catch so far, Paul picked up the radio to talk with other captains. "Falcons are down by twelve. They can't keep it together today. Looks like you owe me a round of beers," he said into the mike.

"Jacksonville's the team to put your money on today," the radio squawked back. Fishing wasn't the only important information shared by captains.

Bonita's catch were the Atlantic white shrimp, firm, sweet tasting, beige-tinted shrimp that are best in the fall when they are the largest. North Americans eat more shrimp than any other seafood, and white shrimp are considered a premium. There are several species of wild shrimp found in coastal waters. Northern shrimp off the coast of Maine, and pink shrimp in the Pacific waters close to Oregon. Brown and white shrimp come from the Carolinas down the east coast to the Gulf of Mexico. Pink shrimp are found off the south west coast of Florida and spot prawns in British Columbia.

Each of these varieties has a unique flavor because of their diet and the waters they inhabit. They all have a fresh aroma like an ocean breeze. Paul's catch, Atlantic white shrimp, go straight from sea to market—never frozen or injected with preservatives.

Many of the shrimp sold in grocery stores are farmed shrimp imported from such diverse places as India, Bangladesh and Central and South America after being hatched and raised in holding ponds. Environmental concerns with farmed shrimp center on the control of water quality. The water the shrimp are held in is usually poured off, often poisoning the local water supply, leaving water undrinkable, and affecting the natural waters and its environment. The other concern for me as a chef is that the shrimp are generic tasting and bland, due in part to a diet of meal instead of natural foods. They're also pumped with preservatives to last longer and stay firm.

Bo-Nita's outriggers held the trawls, large bag-like nets that are dragged through the water. They scoop up the shrimp as the boat moves along. After three hours of trawling the large nets were reeled in and dumped onto the boat's aft deck. The catch flopped wildly on the deck as the crew sprang to work. One man sorted the shrimp into baskets, while another rinsed the basket and a third transported them to the hold where ice was added to keep the shrimp fresh. The by-catch; jellyfish, sand dollars and starfish-were all quickly thrown back into the water.

A few blue crabs were in the mix that day. They were stored in a separate red bucket—a gift for dinner at Jimmy and Cathy's house.

The shrimp were transported back to shore each night on the same Carolina skiff that Bob and I arrived on. They'd spend the night on ice in Jimmy and Cathy's refrigerated shed. The next morning they were sorted, cleaned and ready for regular customers or the market.

"What about dolphins and turtles?" I asked. I didn't want to insult Paul, but I was concerned what such big nets were doing to the rest of the life in the ocean.

"I'll be honest. For years, we took up everything in these nets. Now, they have fancy gadgets to let the big stuff go free." Because of trawling regulations, Paul's nets were all equipped with extruder gear and guards to reduce the number of non-shrimp that were caught. There had been worldwide concerns that trawling nets kill 'by-catch,' other species of sea life that are not intended targets. But in recent years, the nets had been altered to reduce the catch of these unwanted species. Dolphins, turtles and sharks are now able to swim free of the nets with only a five to ten percent loss of shrimp.

Small independent shrimp boats like Paul's don't have anywhere near the impact on the ocean as commercial fishermen or longliners who can obliterate whole schools of breeding and migrating fish. Another reason to search out small local suppliers.

Half way through the day, I was treated to the best surprise of all. Paul pulled up a basket of shrimp from the cold water not ten minutes before and began cooking lunch for us. He set a large pot of water on the stove to boil with Old Bay Seasoning. The smells of peppercorns, allspice, and bay leaves seeped through the air. As the water came to a boil, Paul layered the ingredients in the pot, letting each addition cook for just the right amount of time before adding the next. First the onions and potatoes, than the keilbasa sausage for flavor. He returned the lid to the pot and asked, "Do you like a little heat?"

"Of course," I replied.

Turning back to the pot, Paul added the corn, still on the cob and broken in half. At the last minute the shrimp were added, so as not to overcook them—a real low-country boil.

We all lined up for the meal. Paul piled our plates high with corn, sausage, and potatoes. I took my cue from the others and poured a generous amount of cocktail sauce on the side of my plate for dipping.

We sat on the back deck among the nets and equipment. Just as the gamberi rosso from Vito in Italy had changed my mind about the taste of shrimp, these reinforced how good shrimp could taste. These Atlantic white shrimp were full of flavor that burst in my mouth when I bit into one. No one spoke as everyone was busy peeling, dipping and chewing.

These men had all grown up on this fare, but for me this was a first. Paul has a heavy hand with the Old Bay and had added a generous amount of pepper to the pot. Everything had a kick to it. Corn kernels burst with flavor. The moist kielbasa sausage drizzled down my chin, and the shrimp was plump and sweet, just as Paul had predicted.

After our second trawl of the day and six hundred pounds of shrimp later, Bob and I said our goodbyes and headed back through the creek maze as a tangerine sun set over the water. In our possession were shrimp for *Blue Moon*, fresh as you can get them, with no hormones, no antibiotics, no chemicals, and fifty blue crabs for dinner that night.

We returned to Jimmy and Cathy's to meet Jacqueline and the rest of the crew for a crab boil—another party. Cathy had more oysters, chicken and dumplings, and a delicious, moist carrot cake. We drank cold beers while the blue crabs went into the pot to boil. I helped Cathy lay newspaper over the table. Within minutes we began to feast again. I could get used to this Southern hospitality.

Paul's Low-Country Boil

This is the easiest recipe for a crowd. Everything is boiled in one pot and ready to eat. There are many brands of spice mix to use: Old Savannah Crab and Shrimp Boil is the brand of choice in the south but there is also McCormicks, Old Bay, and Zatarain's Crab and Shrimp Boil. Don't be afraid to leave the shells on the shrimp. Peeling them is half the fun. Make sure to put dishes out to collect the shells or place extra newspaper on the table to wrap it up in afterwards. The condiment to serve is cocktail sauce for dipping.

2 lemons
3 liters water
1/2 cup spice mix (see above)
2 tablespoons sea salt
2 white onions, chopped in 1-inch dice
2 pounds baby potatoes
4 cobs of corn, cut in 3
2 pounds kielbasa sausage, cut in 2-inch lengths
3 pounds medium-sized shrimp, head off, shell on

Cocktail Sauce:
1/4 cup horseradish
3/4 cup ketchup
2 tablespoons mayonnaise
1 tablespoon Dijon mustard
2 tablespoons Worcestershire sauce

In a large pot bring water, lemons, onions, potatoes, sea salt, and spice mix to a boil. Simmer for 10 minutes. Add sausage and corn and simmer another 7 minutes. Add shrimp. Bring back to a boil and strain. Mix ingredients for cocktail sauce and serve on the side for dipping. Serve with lots of bread and cold beer.

Serves 6

Island Cowboy

I've always had a romatic image of a cowboy. He should be rugged and strong, rough and tough, yet tender and courteous. He lives on a ranch surrounded by sprawling hills and valleys and spends his days outside riding the land. At night he sleeps near a campfire. I come from cowboy country after all.

After I began traveling, I met different versions of cowboys. And while some are the spitting image of Robert Redford, most are regular men who live life their own way. Some drive motorcycles down deserted highways, some ride waves on surfboards, and others set sail for far away islands.

But the quintessential cowboy lives on an island off the coast of Georgia. Twenty miles south of Savannah, inaccessible by car, Ossabaw is the second largest barrier island off the Georgia coast. It has eleven thousand acres of highland forests and fourteen thousand acres of marshland. Ossabaw is home to tall, sturdy pine trees, fragrant azaleas, tropical palms, bright blooming southern magnolias, and live oaks dripping with Spanish moss. Salt-water creeks and tidal rivers scribble the land. Thirteen-foot alligators inhabit the land, frequently sunning themselves on the banks and in the marsh grasses. Immense, shifting white sand dunes dominate the eastern side of the island, leading to vast stretches of deserted beach scattered with driftwood. These dunes are also the nesting ground for loggerhead turtles. The island is full of wild turkey, hogs, and deer. Endangered bald eagles fly overhead. The waters host oyster beds, shrimp, and fiddler crabs.

Amid this natural beauty lives an eccentric, beautiful woman named Mrs. West and her island cowboy, Roger Parker.

Mrs. Eleanor Torrey-West is the steward of Ossabaw Island. Her family bought the island and constructed their Spanish Revival style home there in 1924, when Mrs. West was just a girl. The large two-story, Bermuda pink stucco house with 40-foot ceilings and large picture windows overlooking the Atlantic was built as the family's summer home. The house sits at the end of an avenue of live oaks, so tall and full they create a tunnel leading to the entrance of the house.

Now in her ninety-third year, Mrs. West has lived on the island and taken care of it most of her life. She loves her island and doesn't believe in turning it into just another residential development, although she has been offered a pretty penny for it.

"Aristotle Onassis called one day and offered me millions," she said. "I never called him back."

With the charisma of a visionary, she has preserved her island in a unique way. In the sixties, Mrs. West and her husband, Clifford, created the Ossabaw Foundation. Four programs were established to bring together scientists, writers, and artists on the island for research retreats. Mrs. West's vision for Ossabaw has always been to share her island with like-minded people, enriching lives without destroying the island's nature.

Instead of bowing to development, she recently turned the island over to the Georgia Department of Natural Resources, with the understanding the land is to be used for educational, cultural, and scientific programs based in environmentally sound practices. The beaches are open to the public during the day, but there will never be any expansion or infrastructure on the island. Ossabaw will never be an overdeveloped condo-ridden resort destination.

Ossabaw Island has hosted such visitors as President Carter, Jack Leigh, Margaret Atwood, and Sandra Bullock. Henry Ford was the first person to sign the guest book. I, too, had the privilege to be a guest on this oasis. Jimmy and Cathy introduced me to shrimpin' and also to Ossabaw, where I found two remarkable people: Mrs. West and the honest-to-god cowboy who helps her.

"Watch out for Roger," Cathy warned. "He'll have you two-steppin' and shootin' whiskey before the weekend is through."

The tough-as-nails caretaker of Ossabaw Island has been working for Mrs. West and her family for the last fifty-nine years. He clears the trees that fall during hurricane season, rounds up the wild donkeys for penning, fishes the rivers, maintains the roads, and fixes things in the house. He is her link to the mainland by boat.

His ubiquitous black cowboy hat sits on top of his grey hair, pulled down low to hide his blue eyes, and shield the smile that plays on his lips when he speaks. Roger loves to tell a good story and charms everyone around him. His lively face alights with animation when he begins a tale.

"Last winter we had my birthday party here on the island. Now I ain't telling you how many candles was on the cake but I will tell you that Greg Allman was here and sang me Happy Birthday." His laugh was gruff. "Can you imagine that? The Allman Brothers singin' to me."

I loved hearing him speak. Not enough people just sit and listen. And sure enough, the next time I visited the island there was Greg Allman sitting and talking with Mrs. West. She had no idea who he was but everyone in Savannah knows Mrs. West.

During one of my visits to the island, Roger introduced me to Southern BBQ—Ossabaw style. Although Mrs. West is a vegetarian and wouldn't think of eating one of the thousand feral pigs that inhabit the island, Roger, is master of the flame and loves to throw a cookout. On the day of the BBQ, I began to understand that this was no ordinary afternoon meal. This was an all day event.

Early in the morning, Roger, his friend Richard, Jimmy and I went hunting for a hog. We piled into Roger's pickup truck and drove the dirt roads that crossed the island. Roger had built more than one hundred miles of road years before and knows every inch of the island. He knew exactly where to look for the wild pigs and had no trouble sighting one. Off the side of the road, digging under a bush, were three small hogs. Black rough hair covered their bodies. Small, beady eyes stared at us as we approached. They didn't run. They just watched.

We pulled over to the side of the road. Why, I'm not sure. It was unlikely there would be any traffic since there was only the four of us, Mrs. West and Cathy on the island that weekend. Roger reached into the bed of the truck and produced his rifle, not once taking his eye off the prize. He had his sights on one of the hogs; it was small but the smaller the better for eating. Roger shushed us while removing the straw from his mouth he'd been chewing. He brought the gun to the shoulder of his checkered shirt and fired. One shot was all it took, quick and precise to the head. One hog fell as the other two bolted for the forest behind them.

"I'll be damned if it ain't the best shot I ever seen," Jimmy drawled. "Roger, you is the man!"

A slight turn of the mouth was all the pride Roger showed. But it was easy to see: he liked being the man. "Load 'em up." His voce was like gravel as he replaced the rifle. Richard and Jimmy each took two of the pig's feet and swung him into the bed of the truck. Off we went, bouncing our way back to the abattoir on other side of the island.

Roger and Richard went to work bleeding, gutting, and skinning the hog. With the skill of a man who had done this numerous times before, Roger strung the pig up by its hind legs, then picked up his hunting knife and tested its sharpness against his thumb. Richard steadied the pig from swinging. Roger slit the pig's throat from ear to ear. Blood poured out of the cut and onto the floor. Directly under the pig was a drain that now swirled bright red. Jimmy picked up a hose coiled in the corner and began washing down the blood.

Roger made another long slash up the pig's belly, then reached in and pulled out its entrails. Like discarding lint from his sweater, he flicked them into a bucket by his feet. With fingers thick from years of manual work, Roger separated the skin from the flesh. Using a combination of knife cuts and a pulling motion the pig was skinned. Richard gathered the bucket of skin and guts to be thrown in the ocean for the fish as Jimmy continued to rinse the floor. Roger removed the pig from the hook and began butchering. It was all over in a few minutes.

I had never seen an animal slaughtered before. I had butchered many pieces of meat in my kitchen, but had never been involved in the whole process.

Although I am not squeamish, I did take a moment to contemplate vegetarianism. But not for long. There was dinner to make.

Southern BBQ is done traditionally in a pit, but Roger's ingenuity and a friend's construction skills combined to create a custom barbecue smoker. Roger loaded island-cut hard wood into the steel belly of the barbecue for a local authentic taste. Once burning, the wood would produce a low-temperature fire that sat just off to the side of where the meat would be grilled. The heat and smoke were designed to fill the grill area, indirectly passing tendrils of smoky flavor through the meat, saturating the meat, and rising out of the chimney on the far side of the barbecue.

BBQ is a way of life in the South, defined by the flavor of each region. North Carolina has a thin, vinegary sauce. South Carolina applies a mustard-style sauce to its meat. Memphis uses a dry rub of herbs and spices. Kentucky has a tomato-based black molasses-like sauce, and Texas likes thick and spicy tomato sauces. In Georgia you'll find both tomato and vinegar-based BBQ sauces. They're usually spicy and always mouth-watering. But wherever you are, the trick seems to be the long, slow cooking to produce tender, fall-off-the-bone meat. In the last phase of cooking, the preferred barbecue sauce is added to the meat so it won't burn, but the meat will pick up its taste and stay moist.

This is the South, where BBQ is as sacred as NASCAR, and recipes are as guarded as Fort Knox. Roger would only smile when I asked what was in the sauce he was using on the meat.

"It'll take a few more bottles of vodka to get the recipe outta me." He refused to reveal his secret, but he did let me observe the ritual. When Roger's barbecue grill reached three hundred and fifty degrees and the smoke was just right, he liberally coated the pork with salt and pepper and placed the pieces in the smoker. The gentle heat of the smoking wood worked its wonders on the meat for the next six hours.

During this time there was much talk of where the fish were biting, what was happening with the new motor for the pickup, and what the boy who helped on the island last year was doing for work. Drinks were poured, and all the while Roger held court while tending the barbecue. He frequently turned the pork, stoked the fire, and basted the meat with a mixture of pineapple juice, salt, vinegar, and water. It all seemed like second nature to this man. We spent the day sitting around the BBQ, eagerly awaiting his next story.

"Darlin', this here is going to be the best damn BBQ you ever had. I guarantee it beats them fancy restaurants you go to."

By smelling the air I knew he would be right. Roger always had a flirting smile on his face when speaking with me. I could never tell if it was his innate charm or the fact that I was enthralled by his cowboy manner, but even with him in his seventies, I couldn't help but blush as he spoke. I loved it when he called me darlin'.

As the day went on, Cathy and I started pulling together salads for dinner. Cathy made the batter for corn fritters and put together a crust for the red spot bass she'd caught earlier. Great fishing spots are just another of Ossabaw's amenities.

Just before sunset, Mrs. West wandered over from the main house. "Roger, what have you done now? You know I love those pigs, they're my guests here on this island and not for your smoker." The twinkle in her eye gave her away; she'd had this playful fight with Roger many times before. "These pigs were of pirate descent." Mrs. West turned to me me. "Three hundred years ago they were aboard a Spanish galleon that sunk just out there." She waved to the Atlantic in front of us. "Chased by none other than Blackbeard himself. These pigs swam all the way here." She turned back to Roger. "And now Roger salutes their heroics by cooking them." She swatted at him like he was a bird she was shooing away. "They're my gift from the King of Spain."

"Yes, ma'am but this one here just jumped into the back of my truck while I was runnin' this pretty lady around the island. He wanted to come to dinner." Roger winked at me. "Didn't he, darlin'"

"Oh, you. You know I never believe a word you say." She laughed. "Did you at least make me some fish?"

"That we did ma'am. Cathy's frying it up in the kitchen."

"Well, what are you folks waiting for then?" Mrs. West asked. "Dig in, don't let my little friend go to waste." And with that, the feasting began. Roger painted a last coat of his secret sauce on the pork and let it finish on the grill while he set himself up with a fresh drink. He then picked the choicest cut of meat for me.

"There you are darlin'. You tell me if that ain't the best BBQ you ever had." It was warm, juicy, melt-in-your-mouth pork. Roger's vinegar-based sauce was piquant and lighter than the ketchup-based sauce that I make. It didn't overpower the soft texture of the pork, and I was able to taste the smokiness of the meat instead of just the sweetness of the sauce. BBQ had never tasted so good.

"Roger, this is delicious!" I said, licking my fingers. "I'm going to start cooking all my pork this way."

Mrs. West cut in. "Honey, it just won't be the same." She shook her head. "That's the magic of Ossabaw you taste. Just look at where you are." She dramatically waved her arm to showcase the setting before us.

And she was right. We sat in the front yard, overlooking the Atlantic Ocean. Behind us the sun was setting through a veil of palm trees. The large, bright yellow ball that had filled the sky moments ago was now sinking at an alarming rate. The few clouds in the sky turned cobalt blue while the sky itself began its turn from baby blue to pastel pink.

———— VICTORIA ALLMAN ————

Rays of sunlight illuminated the clouds from below, creating a rim of light. Before I knew it the sun had completely disappeared behind the trees. The light held the shades of pastel while the ocean in front of us turned a darker hue of midnight blue. The pastels in the sky gave way to deeper mauves and dusty roses. The palms lost their green tones and became black. The whole sky started to change color again, becoming richer and more radiant as the night descended. A whippoorwill called in the distance. The cold night air grazed my cheek.

"You are right, Mrs. West. This place is magical," I said.

Roger still hasn't revealed his secret sauce to me, even after many straight vodkas and the promise of a two-step, but I can tell you it is delicious on Royal Ossabaw Island-raised hogs—especially sitting outside under one of the island's live oaks, listening to the rustle of wind through its leaves.

That night, I learned there are different types of cowboys. Some ride horses, some ride waves, and others, like Roger, preside over island paradises and tend to the barbecue. Jimmy says life is about making memories. This is one of my better ones.

Roger's BBQ Sauce

No idea.
I tried for this recipe but Roger would not reveal his secret. All the smiling and two-stepping I did that weekend, and many after have not softened his guard at all. I don't mind having to go back and try again.

Victoria's BBQ Sauce

1/4 cup vegetable oil
1/2 cup onions
4 cloves garlic
2 tablespoons chili powder
2 bay leaves
1 tablespoon dry mustard
1 tablespoon sea salt
1 teaspoon ground ginger
1 tablespoon curry powder
1 teaspoon ground pepper
2 cups ketchup
1/4 cup lemon juice
1/4 cup molasses
2 tablespoons Worcestershire
2 tablespoons soy sauce
1/2 cup sugar
1/2 cup apple cider vinegar
1/2 cup apple juice

Sauté onions and garlic in the vegetable oil in a heavy bottomed saucepot for 5 minutes over medium high heat. Add spices and stir. Add remaining ingredients and reduce on medium low for 30 minutes, stirring occasionally. Cool and slather over barbecued chicken, pork or steaks.

Makes 3 cups

Living in the Clouds

I first noticed Patrick's smile as he was walking down the dock. He beamed like a lighthouse. When his smile grew larger, his forget-me-not blue eyes danced like a moving ocean and his sun-tanned skin crinkled into laugh lines like the ridges of an accordion.

His uniform of khaki shorts and a white polo with *Lady Linda* stitched above his left breast blended him into the crowd. I wore similar garb, as did thousands of other crew wandering the docks at the show. But it was his brilliant smile that made him stand out.

That was the Lauderdale Boat Show, four years ago when I first started yachting. We had been dating on and off ever since. Like driftwood, he floated in and out of my life with the waves. It was the cliché relationship of seeing each other whenever our two boats were in the same port. We started with half a dozen dates in Lauderdale the first year I joined *Pari,* and then a moonlit night in Italy later that summer. The following year we stole away to Key Largo for a weekend of kayaking through the mangroves in April. But I didn't see him again until December in Palm Beach, for only a few hours.

To friends who asked, I described our relationship as intense, but sporadic. We would get together for a night or two but then inevitably one of us would sail away, and it would be another six months before we would see each other again.

It was either the healthiest relationship I had ever been in, or the strangest.

In April, spring fever hit the crew. We'd been in the shipyard in Savannah for six months. Mase and Ian both started dating girls on shore. Marisa left the boat to have a baby. Emile, as a doting new husband and father, bought a house. He redecorated and moved his new expanding family in. Chris and Julie announced they were moving to Colorado and get married. Everyone was in love.

"You know what this means?" Julie asked.

"Yeah, you're all leaving me," I wailed.

"No, it means there's a position open for Patrick." Leave it to Julie to think of my love life before I did. I enjoyed working on *Blue Moon* so much I hadn't considered leaving to work with Patrick. Here was an opportunity for him to come and work with me.

I don't know why it took so long for us to think of getting a job together. With Julie's prodding, I called Patrick. He called Emile. He was hired. Simple as that.

But before we entered into such an intense situation of living and working together we wanted to travel to see if we gelled for more than a night or two.

The fiftieth anniversary of the first Everest summit was in May. We both loved mountains and wanted to take part in the celebration. We planned to hike and camp our way to Everest base-camp through the Khumbu valley.

This was it; the first time I was sharing a travel experience with someone else. Until now, Patrick and I hadn't spent more than two consecutive nights together, and here we were about to spend three weeks crammed into a tent. I anticipated a very short-lived relationship. To call me nervous would be an understatement. Downright scared would be more like it. It had been a long time since I spent that much time with a man, and he was going to see me stinky and grubby from the trail.

* * * *

The Himilayas were exactly what I expected. They towered. They shot into the sky. They presided over us like monarchs. We hiked, supported by a Sherpa guide, Dinde, and Mars our porter, named for the Mars Bar hat he wore throughout the whole trip.

Dinde, a copper colored man with almond eyes and dark hair, pointed to the mountains as they came into view. "That is Ama Dablam. I guide it next season. Maybe make top." Sun worn, wrinkled, and weathered he had been helping trekkers hike through these mountains his whole life, but had yet to summit one of the legendary peaks.

"You do this every season?" I asked.

"For last thirty years," he answered. The mountain air must be a natural elixir, as he didn't look a day over thirty-five to me.

Grueling five to seven hour hikes up and down the dusty trail were our daily routine. Mars passed me on the trail as I struggled with my lone backpack. His head bowed with the weight of ninety pounds of equipment loaded in baskets and braced on his back by a strap across his forehead. He hiked quickly up and down the trails, calves bulging like those of a weightlifter. With boundless energy—not to mention strength and speed—he raced past me each day, his back bent over from the weight, an enthusiastic smile on his face.

The Himalayas are the youngest and highest mountains in the world. Dramatic, rugged peaks graced our backyard. Hundreds of miles of pure snow-covered mountains extended far past what I could see. We were trekking up the western valley of the Khumbu, across a glacier to Everest base-camp and down the other side of the valley. It was a trekking route that hosts hundreds of travelers who explore the region by foot each year. But for Patrick and I, who had been living at sea and spending more time below sea level than above it, it was a strenuous undertaking.

We traversed over white-water rivers, up steep dirt paths, down rock-strewn trails, over high swaying bridges and through rhododendron forests. Each day brought steep ascents, sheer cliff drop-offs and dusty, slippery footholds. The aching legs from climbing and back pain from carrying our gear was a small price to pay for the spectacular view of never-ending white-capped mountains.

Hiking in such terrain of challenging hills and sharp descents took time. We moved slowly, which gave me time to enjoy the scenery. I spent hours looking up at the snow covered-peaks while getting to know Patrick. Sometimes we hiked in silence; yet other times there wasn't enough time to tell all the stories we wanted to share.

"When I was in Hawaii, we used to hike like this into the bamboo forests. The sound was deafening when the wind blew." Patrick's life sounded romantic to me. When faced with the choice of universities, he picked Hawaii, believing if you had to go to school, there better be a wave near by.

My cheeks burned beet red when he spontaneously belted out his rendition of *Beast of Burden* as a group of Nepelese men passed us driving a herd of yaks, weighed down with a heavy load. Patrick's loud American voice echoed through the valley causing two of the men to just stare. *I'll never be your beast of burden*. Yet the next afternoon I swooned like a schoolgirl with a crush on a movie star when he spoke of his travels through Mexico. This was our time to really get to know one another, and it would be a long three weeks if we didn't like what we found.

Villages lined the trails, providing support for the trekkers, a chance to rest, and a glimpse into the Sherpa culture. Smiling children with grubby hands called out to us as we passed. *"Namaste!"* Good day. Many would follow for a time, eager for a treat of candy.

Teahouses built into the hills offered warm meals, drinks and snacks, or a bed to sleep in. Outhouse-style bathrooms were rarely more than a shed covering a hole in the floor over a pile of straw. If we were lucky, we got a bucket of somewhat warm water for showering.

This was as close to Western civilization as we'd find in these remote villages. Patrick spent the weeks on the trail growing a bushy blond beard and becoming a mountain man. He steadfastly refused to use the few and far between showers until we returned to our hotel room in Katmandu.

"I want to become one with nature," he said on more than one occasion, and by the smell of him, he succeeded. We decided to spend one night at a teahouse instead of camping in an effort to arrange a shower for me.

We arrived in Thore just after lunch, and Dinde introduced us to the woman who owned the teahouse. Tashi was dressed in a customary long woolen dress with her head wrapped in a colorful scarf, gold hoop earrings, and a North Face Fleece jacket for warmth. She spoke no English, but continuously smiled at us and laughed, making us feel welcomed and right at home.

"Namaste," I ventured.

"Namaste," she replied with a giggle. That was all we could communicate through words.

We arrived in early afternoon, thoroughly exhausted after the long traverse of the day. Clouds and cold weather rapidly closed in, filling the valley. Fog crept further up the canyon, blanketing the teahouse like a cozy quilt, lending an eerie feeling of isolation. As the sole guests at the teahouse that day, we felt like the only people on the earth. The afternoon invited us to curl up in the common room on a bench with a book and a cup of tea, soaking up the heat from the pot-bellied wood stove. Billows of smoke rose from the glowing flames, dissipating near the roof, lulling me into a trance.

——— VICTORIA ALLMAN ———

I was not long into my book when Tashi appeared from the kitchen with a Nepalese favorite of milk tea; tea brewed with buffalo milk, sugar, and sweet spices. "*Dhanyabad*," I butchered as thanks while she continued to smile and giggle. She also had two heaping plates of boiled potatoes, coarse salt and a green chili sauce, one for us and one for Dinde and Mars. Nothing fancy, no intricate garnish, no bone china dishes, no vintage wines; just boiled potatoes and a smile.

Patrick and I eagerly peeled them with our hands, liberally sprinkling the salt and dipping them into the subtle, homemade sauce. The small yellow-fleshed potatoes were waxy and sweet. The depth of flavor lingered in my mouth, but not the piquant heat I have grown to expect with hot sauces. It was soft and mild like the Sherpa people themselves. Roasted green chilies had been crushed in a stone bowl, along with a few herbs and spices. Simple.

Tashi, Dinde, and Mars sat at the other bench excitedly talking and exchanging news. With no newspapers, telephones or transportation available, Tashi received news from the outside world from the trekkers and guides coming through the teahouse. We sat and listened to the Sherpas bubbling about people they knew and what was happening on the mountain. Periodically, Dinde would translate for us, passing on the news of another successful summit of Everest by Apa Sherpa, the man with the record for the most ascents, or of how many summit teams had stayed in the teahouse. The excitement was infectious and even though most of the time we had no idea what they were saying, we soon found ourselves laughing along and smiling with them.

"Wouldn't this be perfect?" Patrick looked out the window.

"What, to live in the clouds?"

"Yeah, in the clouds, in the mountains, so far away from everything."

"It sure is peaceful here," I agreed.

"This is what I would like one day. A mountain retreat," he said.

Where had this man been all my life?

The next morning we awoke unfathomably early to hike to Tengboche. We trekked in the dark with the cold night air biting at us. The bright light of morning broke over the mountaintops, burning away the previous day's cloud and filtering down to warm our backs.

Before long, we were in range of Tengbouche, a Buddhist monastery strategically situated in the center of the Dudh Kosi valley. Sitting in a clearing on the side of a mountain under the shadow of Everest, Tengbouche's warm yellow walls and slanted red roof stood out against the green pastures of the hillside. Built of stone and carved with ancient Nepalese markings, the large three-story building stands as a symbol of peace and tranquility amidst the rugged jagged peaks of the Himalayas. It is the largest, most sacred, and active monastery in the Khumbu. This unique location has attracted many Nepalese and Tibetan monks who practice Buddhism, spending their lives in quiet meditation seeking their own truth.

We approached the monastery by a sharp curving trail, through blooming rhododendrons. Colorful prayer flags mounted on bamboo poles and piles of prayer stones lined the trail. The mantra OM MANI PADME HUM, "Hail the jewel in the lotus," was etched deep in the stones. Loosely translated it is a prayer that brings joy and peace through the easing of bad karma.

We arrived at Tengbouche on May 29th, exactly fifty years after Sir Edmund Hillary and Tenzing Norgay stood on top of Everest. Events were planned all over the world to celebrate this achievement but none so special as at Tengboche. The Sherpas gathered to pay respect to the mountain and to Sir Edmund for all he had done for the region. The guttural sound of the blowing sacred horns called all to assemble.

Surrounding the courtyard was an outer wall equipped with prayer wheels. As we entered the courtyard, Patrick ran his hand along the wall setting them spinning like a child's toy. We gathered on the large flat stones of the entrance to watch the rising sun. Prayer flags held aloft by a long pole in one corner fluttered in the breeze. We passed under statues of snow leopards mounted as protectors of the temple against evil forces. We entered the dark monastery lit by the glow of smoky, yak butter candles. Incense burned. Baskets overflowing with offerings of fruits for Buddha sat on the floor. Rich tapestries hung on the walls, and a large golden Buddha dominated the room.

A monk began the ritual with a morning prayer and an invitation to meditate. Several others sat chanting the same prayer OM MANI PADME HUM, like the hum of crickets on a quiet summer evening. We tried to settle our excitement and calmly meditate, but we couldn't help our restlessness. As the repetitive chant continued, we rose to explore the rest of the grounds.

Patrick, Dinde, and I found a place on the grounds in temporary stadium seats. Surrounded by green fields and the towering sentinel of Everest, we sat for the blessing by the *Rinpoche*, the Abbot of Tengboche.

"This blessing is to all who come to the celebration," Dinde translated. "He wish us a long and spiritual life. Next, a prayer to the Goddess of Everest and here, this place and all peoples in Nepal." Dinde shone with pride and spoke in a hushed, respectful voice. He kept us informed all afternoon as a rich pageant of celebration followed.

The Nepalese performed elaborate tales of the triumph of Buddhism over earlier religions, the teaching of Dharma, the call of religious duty and purification of evil spirits through mask dances. Women dressed in their very best and men in Tibetan caps and fur-lined coats from neighboring villages preformed traditional dances. Several monks and nuns, sat surrounding the *Rinpoche*. They blew into bugles, rang cymbals and beat drums.

The air was filled with emotion as a ceremonial white yak was offered as a symbolic sacrifice to the Goddess of Everest, Chomolungma. The animal had been smeared in butter and bathed in milk to cleanse him of his burdens. Adorned by a small silk scarf around its neck to symbolize that he was the chosen offering, he was set free of labor to roam the hills.

"No one can use this yak now," Dinde explained. "He is free man, just like we want to be."

In the closing ceremony the crowd surrounded the *Rinpoche* in a rush to be blessed by the High Priest. Dinde left us to place his *kata*, a white ceremonial scarf used as a goodwill offering, around the *Rinpoche's* neck. In exchange, he was blessed by holy water placed in his hand to drink, while the *Rinpoche* lay his hand on Dinde's bowed head.

The metallic gong of the monastery rang out, echoing through the hills, calling us to the traditional meal of *dal bhaat*. The monks had set up large tables with one pot of rice, one pot of lentil soup, and one pot of lightly curried potatoes and greens. Single grains of nutty rice were piled in bowls and topped with a mild yellow curry blend of potatoes and covered in a thick soup of brown lentils.

The *Rinpoche* blessed the food and everyone eagerly lined up, reminding me of a scene from a school cafeteria. That is until I looked around: the men serving lunch had clean-shaven heads and wore full robes of saffron and deep maroon down to their sandaled feet. Many guests were draped in *katas*. The strength of the sun reflected images through the hills; prayer flags fluttered in the breeze. Clearly I was a long way from any school cafeteria I'd ever been to.

Surrounding us, Nepalese and Westerners alike devoured the *dal bhaat* with their right hands as custom dictated. The curry wasn't strong in heat, but full of flavor. Nepalese food has been described as a milder version of Indian. The rice absorbed the soup and mixed with the potatoes, creating a soft, creamy texture. It all combined perfectly; just sticky enough to scoop up with your hand, but wet enough to still be considered moist while eating.

Patrick and I sat on the steps of the monastery, letting the sun warm our faces as we watched the spindrift blowing off Everest. We ate and listened to the rhythmic chanting and trumpets. I looked at Patrick. His blue eyes shone with complete delight. He looked like he belonged here and felt right at home.

"Do you realize that we've been together for almost three weeks, and we're still talking to each other?" I laughed.

"We might actually get through this," he responded. "Maybe even do it again."

I don't know what I'd been so worried about. We both had a similar way of traveling and an ease with each other I had yet to find with another person. If two people can live through long, exhausting days of climbing, dusty trails of mud, cold nights in a tent on a frozen ground, the smell of not showering, and the simplicity of life in Nepal, then maybe they could face everyday life together. Somewhere between the strenuous hikes, smelly clothes and bowls of *dal bhaat* I found someone to travel with for awhile.

"If you are this happy with a few boiled potatoes, rice and lentils, then I think I'll cancel our reservations at Charlie Trotter's when we get home."

"No way! I'm just as comfortable sipping champagne and slurping down oysters as I am sitting here in the mountains eating with my hands. Besides, after looking at you like this for three weeks, I want to see you clean shaven and bathed."

But, as long as the simple things in life taste good and made me happy, I was glad to be in my hiking boots instead of high heels, standing next to a man wearing the same Mountain Hardware t-shirt he had worn for the past five days. Boiled potatoes, lentils and rice—it's the simple things. And someone to share them with.

———— VICTORIA ALLMAN ————

The Lobster Commute

*I*t was a Tuesday night at five o'clock. As many people were leaving their mundane office jobs, loosening their ties, sighing heavily and slipping into their grey four-door Toyota Camry for the hour long commute home, I was in a twenty-three-foot center console boat with Patrick and his friends Jason and Wendy. We were making our own commute from work, out the intracoastal waterway in Ft. Lauderdale to the lobster honey hole.

The sun sat at a forty-five-degree angle, and we had at least two hours on the water, or under it, in this case, before it got dark.

Jason knew just where to go. He knew a secret spot and proudly led us there. Lobster season just opened but for weeks prior, Jason scouted the local waters, diving different locations, looking under each rock and into every crevice he came across for the telltale signs of lobsters.

Patrick knew Jason from Hawaii. They ran parasail boats together while Patrick was getting his Anthropology degree. When Patrick left to spend a season snowboarding in Tahoe, Jason and Wendy started yachting. It was these two who had been berthed next to *Pari* at the Lauderdale Boat Show. They had been there the day Patrick and I met.

****

"We're all going to the Dockwalk party," Jason had said to me. "Why don't you come along?"

"Yeah, Pat is coming with his crew," Wendy said.

It wasn't exactly a date but it was the first time Patrick and I had gone out. The four of us had been friends ever since.

* * * *

Somehow, Patrick and I made it through our three weeks together in Nepal in our seven- by eight-foot tent and still miraculously liked each other. When we returned to *Blue Moon*, he became first mate, my roommate, and my boyfriend. I was sad to see Chris and Julie go but excited to see where this would lead. No denying it now. We took the huge step from not spending any time together at all to spending every single day and night together. We were now officially a couple.

Mind you, we were not in your typical relationship. We weren't the ones stuck in traffic, rushing home to put dinner on the table before collapsing in front of the television to watch reruns of *Friends*. We weren't struggling to spend our two-week vacation on a beach somewhere drinking pink blender drinks with umbrellas in them. Instead, our life consisted of just your average Tuesday night, in full Scuba gear, lobster noose and underwater light in hand, going to corral dinner.

Although I cannot reveal the location of Jason's honey hole, I can tell you that our commute was short. Ocean breeze blew through my hair, sea salt spray misted my body. The declining sun warmed my skin. Not a bad commute, all things considered.

"This is the spot for bugs," Jason, a tall thirty-year-old sport fish captain, told us with authority. It was his brand new boat we commuted in.

I sat on the side of the boat and checked all my gear as Patrick turned my tank to flow. He checked that my BCD was tight and secure. He made sure my octopus, the back-up breathing device was easy to reach if I needed it and my weight belt was secure. His hand lingered on my hips as he adjusted the strap.

Even in the warmth of the sun my skin goose pimpled. My heart beat faster. I smiled at Patrick, glad we were together.

Patrick clipped my dive computer into place in front of my chest so I could easily see how much air I had left. I slid my feet into my fins and lowered my mask on my face. Patrick reached over, placed one hand on the back of my head, the other removed the red hair that had gotten caught in my mask. He looked into my eyes and smiled. "I'll meet you in the water."

I nodded and took a deep breath. I placed one hand on my weight belt and the other over my mask and regulator so they wouldn't fall out when I hit the water. I looked at Patrick.

"Clear. He signaled that it was safe for me to enter the water. I leaned back and lifted my legs as the weight of the tank pulled me over the side of the boat. I back-rolled into the water like a turtle stuck on his back. Underwater, I twisted awkwardly to right myself. Bubbles streamed from my regulator, clouding my view. I kicked with my fins and broke the surface headfirst. I fanned my arms to tread water.

"You okay?" Patrick asked from the deck of the boat.

I raised a hand to the top of my head, signaling to Patrick that all was okay. He signaled back. He pulled his mask down over his eyes and back-rolled gracefully into the water. Slowly, like an underwater gymnastic routine, he too surfaced. He grabbed me around the waist with one arm and filled my BCD with the other. He made a thumbs-down signal and we began our descent.

Patrick was a dive master and had completed more than three hundred dives. He also had his captain's license. He'd been working on boats for the past fifteen years, so this was all second nature to him. He and Jason got up early to surf and ran straight from work to the ocean to get wet again. Common for them, but for me this was a unique event. I may live on the ocean, but I'm not in it as much as I'd like. Long hours and mealtimes coincide with sunlight hours. But not today. Today I stole away early to hunt for dinner.

Florida spiny lobsters are found up the coast and in the tropical waters throughout the Caribbean. They are clawless but have sharp spines covering their bodies for protection. Reefs and wrecks are usually teeming with them and can easily be spotted on a dive if you know where to look.

Lobsters are night creatures. During the day they are usually hiding in pockets of coral, under ledges, and in caves. The telltale signs of their presence are their two long front antennae that poke out as sensors and their glowing red eyes when a flashlight is shone on them. Night dives can be particularly fun; when caught in a beam of light, they scurry across the ocean floor.

I pinched my nose and blew to clear my ears, then stretched my neck from side to side to adjust to the pressure of being underwater. All I saw was blue. Rays of sunlight slanted down from above as we disappeared into the depths.

When we hit the bottom, Patrick checked with me one last time to see if I was okay. He motioned to the left, grabbed my hand, and began swimming into the abyss. Fine particles of sand floated in the water, but I couldn't see a coral reef or any fish. We kicked some more. Suddenly, an object came into view. It was a custom-built structure of large star-shaped jacks that stretched along the sandy bottom like a snake. The concrete jacks were piled on top of each other intermingling to the left and right of where we were. I stopped kicking and looked around. I knew Lauderdale was famous for the artificial reefs that had been sunk to create homes for tropical fish and coral. This must be one of those, I thought. It was strange not being able to talk and ask Patrick.

Multi-colored tiny fish with violet fronts and golden rears flitted about, looking like two different fish stuck together. A three-foot silver barracuda watched us with steely grey eyes. I shuddered at the sight of his pointed teeth and under-slung jaw. It drifted above us menacingly. Wendy swam into view clutching a mesh bag for the lobsters.

Jason and Patrick were already inspecting the structure. They had their heads down. Jason spotted two antennae stuck out of a dark hole. He swam up to the opening and shone his light into the hole. He motioned me over. I could see three lobsters cowering in the far corner. A large coral-red lobster faced the entrance. I nodded as Jason dropped the light to the sandy bottom and reached for his looper, a three-foot stick with a wire loop at one end and a handle to tighten the noose at the other. A lobster cowboy's lasso. Jason gently placed the closed loop end of his stick behind the first lobster. Slowly he opened the loop and scooted it under and around the tail of the lobster. He jerked the handle and pulled the stick towards him. With lightning speed the loop closed around its body. The lobster bucked like a bull and tried to get away. It was too late. He was dinner.

Jason placed a gloved hand over the tail to steady the crustacean. He pulled out his measuring tool. It's illegal to keep lobsters that are too small or females bearing eggs. Careful not to injure it in case he had to put him back, Jason placed one end of the ruler between the lobster's horns on the top of his head and angled the tool directly down its back to the top of his tail. If the body was larger than the tool, then we could bag the lobster but if not, he was returned to his hole. The smile I saw behind Jason's mask and regulator told me this one was large enough. Jason had captured the first lobster of the day. He placed it in Wendy's bag and mimicked a smoking gun with his forefinger and thumb: a direct challenge to Patrick. Jason turned back to the other two lobsters that lay waiting for him as Patrick furiously began his own search under the jacks.

I swam a little way down the structure, making sure to stay in sight of the group. Black and grey angelfish with their bright lemon yellow stripes, as well as a few baby blue parrotfish meandered past. The forked tail of another fish I couldn't identify flashed by. I was enjoying being in the water and just lazily swimming along when I caught sight of a squirrelfish swimming into the reef. Just as he entered a hole he turned and darted away. Something in the hole had spooked him.

Swimming closer to get a better look, I saw a large coral red lobster sitting under the jack. He was backed into his cozy home, facing the entrance. It was propped up on his thin long legs like a spider. Maybe that is why they are commonly referred to as bugs. It was larger than Jason's first lobster. It sat by itself, looking out at the passing water, alert to danger.

I looked back to signal to Patrick, but all I could see of either him or Jason were two sets of legs and flippers sticking out of the reef while they battled each other to get at the lobsters. Patrick's looper was shuddering like it was having an epileptic fit; he was too occupied to come and see my lobster. I gave a little wave to the lobster and swam off again.

With all of the excitement, it wasn't long before Jason and Patrick's heavy breathing sucked their tanks dry of air, and we were forced to ascend. We all surfaced near he rear of the boat.

I removed my mask and regulator. "That was great!"

"And we have dinner too!" Wendy held up the bag. "Are you up for a lobster dinner?"

"I think we can manage that."

Patrick climbed the swim ladder and took off his gear. He reached down to help me with my equipment. "You still have air?"

"Yep," I said proudly. It was the first time I hadn't called the dive short because of breathing difficulties.

On the way home Jason and Patrick reviewed their dive. They tallied up their count and made plans to return the next day. "I need a bigger light," Patrick said. "And more weights to stay down."

"You could catch more if you had your own bag as well." Jason teased and taunted his victory. Jason eased the boat up to the dock. The guys rinsed and chamoised the boat, and organized all of our equipment.

Six large lobsters awaited me in the boat's hold, and within fifteen minutes I'd prepared them for cooking. The sun had long ago sunk and the heat of the day evaporated. We loaded our dinner and gear into the back of the truck, our excitement for the day coming to an end.

Back at their house, Wendy and I split the dinner preparations that night. I chopped fresh tomatoes, onions and chilies for a salsa while she picked up a pair of kitchen shears to split the tails. She pulled the jelly-soft meat from the shell, sliced it, and placed it back in the shell. I spooned a mixture of lime and cilantro over the top and popped them into the oven to roast. Wendy tossed a salad, and I picked up two dark avocadoes with textured skin to make fresh guacamole. I chopped emerald green cilantro for a lime yogurt sauce while tortilla shells warmed. To accompany our Lobster Tacos, we stirred up a pitcher of lime daiquiris.

Sitting down for dinner I raised my glass for a toast, "To the two best lobster cowboys I know."

"That was nothing. Tomorrow we'll take two tanks each and we can really clean up," Patrick planned. I could see the wheels turning and knew this would not be the last night we all dined on lobster.

I raised my wine glass in my own silent toast. If this is what my life would be like with Patrick, I was happy.

Lime Caesar Salad

1 head romaine lettuce
1/4 cup fresh grated Parmesan
1/3 cup Lime Caesar Salad Dressing

Wash and rip the romaine to bite-sized pieces. Gently toss the romaine with the Parmesan and dressing to evenly coat the leaves.

Lime Caesar Dressing:
1 clove garlic
4 anchovies
2 tablespoons Dijon mustard
1 egg yolk
1/3 cup lime juice
1 tablespoon Worcestershire sauce
1/4 cup fresh grated Parmesan
1 teaspoon sea salt
1/2 teaspoon black pepper
1-1/4 cups canola oil

In a cuisinart mix all ingredients except the canola oil. Process for 30 seconds. With Cuisinart running slowly stream canola oil into mixture—the line of oil entering the mixer should be no more than the size of a piece of string. The slower the better to thicken the dressing.

Makes 2 cups

Lobster Tacos

6 lobster tails
6 liters water
2 tablespoons sea salt

Herb Mix:
1 bunch cilantro
2 green onions
3 limes, zested
2 drops hot sauce
1/2 teaspoon sea salt
2 cloves garlic
3 tablespoons water
2 tablespoons olive oil
1 teaspoon Dijon mustard
1 head of romaine, sliced thin
12 corn tortillas

Cilantro Lime Yogurt Sauce:
1 cup plain yogurt
2 limes juiced
1/2 bunch chopped cilantro
2 cloves garlic
1/2 teaspoon sea salt
1 drop of hot sauce

Bring the water and sea salt to a boil in a large pot. Add lobster tails and boil for 1 minute. Drain and cool. Preheat oven to 350.

While cooling, mix the herb mixture together in a cuisinart until it is chopped into a paste. With cooking shears, gently cut down both sides of the lobster "bellies" removing the soft cartilage. Gently pull the tail away from the shell in one piece. Reserve the "top" of the shell, place shell on a baking tray forming a boat to cook lobster in. Place the tails right side up on a cutting board and cut a parallel slot down the center of the tail one quarter of the way through. Open the top of the tail up like a book. Spoon the herb mix into the tails evenly making sure you fill the newly made slot. Place tail back in its shell and roast in oven for 15 minutes. Remove from oven and slice. Return to shell for presentation.

Place the corn tortillas in the warm oven for 3 minutes.

Serve everything in family style bowls for people to build their own tacos of lobster, lettuce and sauce wrapped in the warm tortillas.

Serve with Lime Caesar Salad, Margaritas and Chips and Salsa.

Fins

"Victoria, you should come up here and see this." Emile called down from the bridge. I could hear the engines change speed and felt the boat slow.

We were traveling up the east coast, through the St. Lawrence River and across the Great Lakes to Chicago for the summer. It was day four of our two-week voyage. We were off the coast of Nova Scotia. Emile stood, scanning with his binoculars the water out the starboard windows.

"What's up?" I asked. It was just after seven. I assumed I was being called up to view the sunset, a favorite pastime of mine while underway. The setting sun was changing the ocean from its sapphire blue of only moments before to a cobalt grey color. But the view was from the port windows, not starboard. I was confused.

"Come look at this," he said, handing me the binoculars.

I couldn't believe my eyes.

"What is that?" On the surface of the water fifty fins stuck out, all within two hundred feet of the boat.

"Basking sharks," he said. "They skim the surface eating plankton. I've seen them in South Africa but never so many."

I handed Emile back the binoculars and opened the door to the outside deck to get a better view. The rest of the crew was gathered there watching the same scene. Spread out over the space of a football field, were grey dorsal fins followed by their tail fins. In some cases, you could even see their snout protruding from the depths below.

I stood mesmerized. The sharks cruised slowly right up to the boat. Their large mouths hung open like fishing nets trolling beneath them. Their gills looked like human ribcages inside the large round jaws. One by one each of the bulky shapes investigated *Blue Moon's* hull. They were as curious about us as we were about them.

"They can grow to be thirty-three feet long," Emile told us. "They're the second largest shark next to whale sharks." Emile had a photographic memory and could recite facts verbatim. "They swim in schools of up to one hundred."

I looked back at all the fins in the water. Amazingly, we were only seeing a small school.

The sun sank lower behind us, constantly changing the scene. The basking sharks circled. At last, they began to dive to greater depths than we could see. Emile brought *Blue Moon* up to speed again. It was time for us to continue our journey. I returned to the galley to finish cleaning up.

Such an encounter reminded me why I loved the water so much. Rare and un-expected things happened all the time.

Market Daze

I rolled out of bed at six in the morning. The alarm blared in my ear, my feet still ached from the night before. Patrick snored in the bunk beside me. The boat was quiet, the rest of the crew were still asleep, using every last minute they could before our eight o'clock start time. But not me.

It was market day in Chicago. The Green City Market was an organic haven for foodies; a source for the area's most outstanding meat, cheeses, flowers and produce. Chefs and home cooks alike flocked to the center of Lincoln Park to purchase directly from the farmers. Like a ritual, every Wednesday and Saturday I got up early to beat the crowds and the heat. I ventured out into morning traffic, still half asleep and blurry-eyed. My first stop was always a small independent coffee shop that brewed cups full of foam and robust richness.

"Latte?" The woman behind the counter remembered my order from earlier.

"Thank you." I smiled with gratitude.

Slowly my eyes began to open with the invigorating smell permeating the car. I whizzed down Lake Shore Drive and drove through the streets thinking about my menu for the day and how many people I needed to feed.

When I pulled into the park where the market was located and grabbed my sweater, I was nearly coherent. By the time I approached the first vendor, I was in a full food mindset.

Nick, a young agriculture student—a throwback to the sixties generation—greeted me like an old friend. He quickly steered me to what was perfectly ripe.

"These zucchinis were just picked yesterday." He caressed them lovingly. "These are the first of the summer tomatoes."

He helped me choose a variety of heirloom tomatoes ranging in color from stoplight green to Tour de France yellow. He talked me into cranberry beans for my salad, and I picked out the tiniest banana potatoes, no bigger than a child's finger. As I paid, Nick slipped a long seedless cumber into my bag. He assured me I would fall in love with its flavor, which I did.

Within minutes, I was on my way to my next friend who supplied me with local organic yogurts and goat cheeses, all hand crafted in a European style. Again I moved on, this time to the shyest man I'd ever met, who didn't even need to speak to convince me to try the honey from wild flowers just west of the city. Next I visited the woman who grew all her own herbs. I couldn't seem to escape the distinctive citric smell of lemon balm, the herbaceous smell of rosemary, and the lingering scent of fresh dill. This was the way to begin a day.

Brightly colored vegetables greeted me at every turn. Carrots, the color of Tigger, lay with their long feathery tops still attached beside piles of shiny purple eggplant. Sweet smelling fuzzy peaches sat next to a pyramid of blood red cherries on the fruit stand.

Halfway through, I stopped at a tent for a fresh baked croissant and more early morning greetings. Wiping the crumbs off my shirt, I was off to see the five-year-old girl with big bouncy ringlet curls who helped her mom with flower sales.

"I picked the sunflowers yesterday." Her innocent eyes turned me into a puddle, and I bought more than I could ever possibly use on the boat.

I quickly unloaded the bags at the car and headed back for one final sweep of the market. Mounds of sweet smelling basil filled the air. I couldn't resist buying several bunches for fresh pesto. I grabbed two pints of pencil thin green beans to toss with it and enough zucchini blossoms to stuff with a cheese mousse for an appetizer that night. I was off again.

As I motored along Lake Shore Drive, my mind raced, thinking about how best to use the great things I'd just procured. With ingredients that fresh and perfect, I'd keep the dishes simple to showcase the flavors.

After washing the lettuces, I'd roast the peppers and butcher the free-range chickens before starting on berries for the fruit salad. If I poached the peaches in champagne, I could preserve their sweetness without overpowering them. Half of the purple cauliflower should be used as a centerpiece but the rest I wanted to puree with the potatoes into a colorful soup for lunch. And the baby spinach would be perfect sautéed lightly to accompany a delicate white flaky fish.

As I wheeled into the marina parking lot, I called the boat. If they wanted to eat, they'd have to help bring the groceries inside. One of the new crew answered the phone. "Can you send the boys to help?" I asked.

The crew I'd worked with for years had slowly been changing. Emile left once we made it to Chicago. He moved to Holland with Marisa and his newborn son, Jacques. He was the build captain for the owners new bigger Feadship. Jacqueline had met a first mate on another boat and left to work with him. Mase was in Australia working on his house. Ian had given his notice and was leaving within the month.

I liked the new crew. I became great friends with our new chief stewardess Cynthia. The bosun Gareth and I spent our mornings running together and afternoons swimming laps. But, it no longer felt like my *Blue Moon*. Patrick had only been there a little while, but it felt like it was time for us to move on.

Patrick walked down the dock with a cart as I unloaded my cloth bags full of produce. "I missed you this morning." He laid a hand on the small of my back, not wanting to show affection in front of the new crew. After six months of living and working together we were conscious to remain professional during working hours.

"You're stuck with me twenty-four hours a day now. I'm sure you survived two hours alone."

"Hey, we're a team now. No more alone." I smiled, no longer nervous and jittery to be around him.

I sorted through the vegetables, placing them into the walk-in or on the counter as needed for the preparations ahead. I poured myself one more cup of coffee, nowhere near as tasty as the coffee shops and scribbled a quick menu before picking up my knife. It was just eight o'clock, and I was ready for another day. It was days like this I would miss about *Blue Moon*.

* * * *

"Hey, I came to see if there was a left over omelet in here?" Patrick smiled, the lines on his face creased deeper. His blue eyes shone.

"Left over omelet?" I asked.

"Yeah, you know. One that just happened to be lying around that you didn't want to throw out. Maybe one with some mushrooms and a little cheese."

I grabbed a Teflon pan from the cupboard behind me. "Does this mysterious omelet have toast with it?"

"I thought I saw some of last night's rice on a plate somewhere."

I cracked two of the brown eggs I'd bought at market. I could think of nothing I wanted to do more than cook breakfast for Patrick. I'd been happy on *Blue Moon* as a single woman, able to come and go as I pleased. But in Patrick I'd found someone who shared my same interests, and who I wanted to spend my life with.

He built me a Santa Cruz mountain bike for my birthday that year. Each Saturday we headed to the woods to ride. I packed picnics, and we sat grilling and talking. I had over thirty years of stories to tell, he nearly forty.

Fridays, we headed to the local bookstore and spent the evening reading and planning where we wanted to go. "Hey, there's a back trail up to Machu Picchu that's less touristy." He flipped through a copy of National Geographic Adventure. "We could climb it next year."

"What about Borneo? I would love to see the orangutans," I said.

"Or Tanzania to summit Kilimanjaro." The excitement built in his voice. "You were in South Africa, but I've never been."

It was a big world out there, and we were just getting started.

This is Vietnam

*T*he first thing I saw when leaving the Hanoi airport was a Vietnamese woman wearing a long flowing traditional dress and conical hat to shade the hot sun. She rode an old-fashioned rickety bicycle through a lush-green rice paddy. I stepped out of that same hot sun and onto an even hotter commuter bus. It stopped to allow a man leading a water buffalo and cart laden with harvested rice stalks to cross the road.

A few miles farther and we honked at a man on a Honda motorcycle, Vietnam's favorite mode of transportation, to let him know we intended to pass. With no regard for lanes, right of way or oncoming traffic, our driver proceeded. We passed without incident. There seemed to be no road rules in Vietnam. Kids played openly in the streets. Horns honked incessantly. People drove fast. There were few traffic lights. This was Vietnam.

A child brought me there. My lifestyle on yachts didn't afford me the time for my own children. Nor did my wanderlust allow for it. Over the years, I sought out other people's children to love. I spoiled my nieces, Mara and Ella. I baby-sat Race and Natasha for my friends Trish and Noah. I lived with Marisa for a few weeks, playing each day with Jacques. But most satisfying had been my connection with Foster Parents Plan. Years ago when I still lived at home, I started writing to and supporting foster children in Honduras, Haiti, and

Vietnam. For a small amount of money each month, I formed connections to children that sustained my maternal instincts.

For years I wrote letters and sent pictures to a little girl in Vietnam. With the organization, I helped support her family and further the community in the rural area of central Vietnam. They set up facilities to help educate the children, improve the community's drinking water, provide assistance with farming practices, and established a medical center. Programs helped to train people build better houses and install irrigation in the fields. My job was simple. I sent a check every month and, if I wanted, I could establish contact with one of the children through letters and a yearly gift.

I began writing to Cam when she was three. Her parents would write back with the help of a translator. Initially, the letters were about their home life on the small farm where they lived, the health of their two children, and how they were doing in school. Timidly, I wrote of my family, where I had traveled, and what Canada was like. It seemed so trivial to be talking of where I vacationed each year to people who had never been outside their community. It took little time and hardly any money by my standards.

As the years passed, I watched Cam grow up in her pictures. With the same help of a translator and the little English she learned in school, she began writing to me personally. She told me what she liked to do and asked about my life. She became a person instead of just a concept. The more letters I received, the more I felt I wanted to see exactly who she was, where she lived, and what her daily life was like. Was she happy? Did she play? Could she see a mountain from where she lived? Were there snakes in the fields?

Patrick and I left *Blue Moon*. He headed to Lauderdale to finish his captain's classes. He needed to accumulate more miles at sea before he could captain a yacht of larger size, but the classes were a start. He would be studying for six weeks straight. Time for me to travel.

I arrived at Cam's village at the time of the Mid-Autumn Festival, a Halloween-like event celebrating the end of the rice harvest and the importance of family. I traveled that day with a translator, set up by Foster Parents. We bumped along the dirt roads past dark green jungle filled with camouflage trees and stories from hundreds of years of war. We turned down a dry dusty path to a grey mortar-covered house. We were greeted in the yard by Cam's parents: Duong, a small thin man with yellowing teeth and scruffy haircut, and Trang, a young woman with long dark hair and latte-colored skin.

"Welcome to my home," Duong said proudly through the translator. Trang just giggled.

"It's a pleasure to finally meet you." I bowed. "You have such a beautiful county."

"You like it?" he asked. "So many come and see only war." He shook his head to clear the thought. "Come meet children."

A shy young Vietnamese girl, who I recognized instantly, entered the room. Cam had long dark shiny hair like her mother.

"Welcome to my country, Vietnam." She kept her almond eyes demurely downcast. "I am happy to see you, my family is pleased to host you." Her English was practiced and formal. She had obviously been rehearsing.

I wanted to say so much to this girl, but the formality of the occasion didn't allow me to just yet. I did, however, immediately begin to cry.

"I'm honored to be here. Thank you for your hospitality." This was translated for me; my Vietnamese was limited to *Cam on* (Thank you), and *Xin Chao* (hello). Cam seemed only brave enough to recite a script that she had learned. We stood awkwardly silent for a time. Slowly I gained composure and started in on my many questions.

"How are you?" I asked.

She was shy at first. Answering quietly, her eyes not even looking at me.

"Cam is thirteen." The translator mixed up my original question.

"Where is your school?"

Again, a pause as the translator thought of the proper words. "She walk half hour to school house in village."

"Do you like your teacher?"

Cam and the translator spoke back and forth without answering me. "Cam ask why you cry?"

I laughed and cried, both at the same time. I must have looked bizarre to this young girl.

With so much translating going on by the Foster Parents representative, it was a slow and drawn out conversation and lunch was starting to smell delicious.

Trang had prepared a traditional Vietnamese feast to commemorate my arrival. The family lived in a one-room, single-story cement house. Banana and mango trees grew out back. Rows of tomatoes and chilies were planted in a garden. Chickens wandered freely through the yard, and a thin black dog lazed in the midday heat under a low, flowering bush.

Like most Vietnamese houses, there was no kitchen to speak of, nor bedrooms or bathrooms. A cloth hanging from the ceiling separated the sleeping quarters for the family. Two wooden beds were all the furniture the bedrooms held. Each bed had one thin blanket covering them. One bed for the parents and one for the children. In the main room a rickety table surrounded by mismatched chairs sat beside two open windows along with a large door open to the backfield for air-conditioning. The only decorations were the pictures I sent from far-off lands and an altar set in the corner to worship Buddhist beliefs. Wealthy Vietnamese have sparse living space compared to Western houses, but this was meager living according to anyone's standards.

I watched as Trang cooked. She squatted on her haunches on the floor in the corner over a thick wooden cutting board. She chopped vegetables and mixed dipping sauces while a wood fire burned outside in a cement alcove. There was only one cupboard with few pantry articles inside and only three utensils for cooking. No refrigerator, no stove, no appliances. All food was fresh from the field and picked daily.

"It smells delicious." I attempted to ask about what she was making but she only giggled and looked away.

We gathered around the table to dishes teeming with catfish stewed in tomatoes and green onions, steamed rice, thin duck egg omelets cut in triangles, deep green water spinach, and crisp white bean sprouts stir-fried with fish sauce. Pork was baked with a dizzying array of fresh herbs: basil, cilantro, and mint. Crunchy bamboo sprouts were steamed with herbs and chilies. Everything was fresh and brimming with flavor, not hot but spiked with complex explosive flavors. A plate of fresh spring rolls sat ready to be dipped into hot salty nuoc cham sauce. Considering the size and limitations of the kitchen, I was amazed at the number and variety of dishes set on the table.

"Catfish from the pond." Duong indicated a dish in front of him. He pointed next to the pork dish. "This my pig."

The pork had been butchered from the family's pigs grazing in the backfields. They were self sufficient. The vegetables were grown in the gardens surrounding the house. The eggs came from the ducks on the pond, which was also home to the water spinach, a lily-like plant grown in fresh water with spinach-like leaves, harvested daily as a staple vegetable.

Eager to serve me, Trang piled food onto my plate. I smiled. She giggled again. Famished, I dug into each dish, savoring the explosion of new flavors.

—— VICTORIA ALLMAN ——

Trang refilled my plate with the flaky strong flavored catfish.

"This is unbelievable," I said. "I love this food." She blushed and hid when I complimented her bamboo shoots. They were crunchy and bursting with liquid. "You're a great cook."

I had encountered this shy giggling in women and children throughout Vietnam but had hoped to break that barrier with these people with whom I felt such a strong connection. I wanted to really speak with them, to be let into their world, to know what they were thinking. But, the constrictions of formal feasting and the struggles of language barriers prevented me from getting too close. However, once enough time passed, Trang quietly asked the translator about me.

"Why is she unmarried?" She hid behind her hand when she spoke.

"Why does she have no babies?" came before I had fully answered.

"Why is she traveling alone?" Like many others I had met in Vietnam she was amazed and confused by the strangeness of a thirty-one-year old woman, traveling without family. She had married young and bore two children right away. Here I was older than her, yet it was she who was looking out for me.

When I explained, she was just brave enough to say "Soon you become rotten fruit." Meaning … if not married with children soon, it would be too late.

My life is hard enough to explain in English let alone through an interpreter to someone from such a different culture. I thought about mentioning Patrick, how he had to study and could not come to Vietnam so I chose to come alone. I thought about explaining that although I had a boyfriend I lived with, we were not married and were in no rush to become married. I can't even imagine what my life would sound like to this woman.

Duong was a different story. Custom and etiquette led him to do most of the talking. "We build a new school house with Foster Parents last year," he said. He ran the family's farm and helped in the community. Although uneducated, he knew more about the land and the country than I'd been able to read in any book. "I lead men to put up walls. We take you to see after lunch." He nodded, eager to have my approval.

Duong's ancient father sat at the head of the table. The same thinness was apparent in his physique; the only difference in the two men was the whiteness of his hair, giving him an aura of wisdom. He was old enough to have lived through the Vietnam War (called the American War in Vietnam). I wanted to ask about his experience. I was interested in a Vietnamese's side of the story, but

I didn't. I couldn't find the courage to bring it up. I was too young to remember the war and being Canadian, I had no relatives who were involved. I didn't want to presume anything or make any faux pas by asking. Now, I wish I had.

Later, people from the community who worked for Foster Parents Plan surrounded us, each telling stories of the organization and the role they played. The men explained how life was improved by the organization's involvement. We spent most of the lunch sitting at the makeshift table on borrowed chairs, discussing what changes were being made to the local medical facility and how a recent purchase of an exotic strain of rice would help the local economy.

Cam politely sat with her hands folded in her lap, not really listening or moving but stealing glances at me. Trang flitted about the room, arranging plates, fussing over the food and giggling when she tripped over her son who followed her everywhere hiding behind her skirt.

Like most children her age, Cam sat obediently in her chair while we talked. Her younger brother hid behind her, occasionally sneaking peeks around the chair at the strange white woman who was dining with them. Neither said anything until asked directly and then it was obvious how shy they were by their whispered responses.

"What is your favorite game to play?" I asked.

"The family has the skipping rope you sent and a ball." It hadn't dawned on me the only toys they would have were those I had sent.

They called me Victory instead of Victoria, which was easier on their tongue. They stared at me when they thought I wasn't looking. They laughed at my use of chopsticks as I dropped rice into my lap—they'd probably been taught to use these fiddly sticks at two years old. I didn't care if they found my ineptitude laughable. It was a joy to see this family's delightful attitude.

My red hair often sticks out in a crowd, but these children had never seen anything but the dark Asian hair of their friends and family. My long red braid was bringing waves of laughter from Cam's brother, who was just brave enough to reach out and touch it before recoiling into a heap of giggles.

I produced gifts of schoolbooks and harmonicas that brought smiles to their faces. I tried to talk about their thoughts on the future. "I want to be a singer." Cam said. "He wants to be a fireman." I wondered if the little boy had ever seen a fire truck. Both loved school and playing with their friends. Apart from the shyness and formality, they were no different from talking to children in the west.

—— VICTORIA ALLMAN ——

As quickly as all the plates had appeared, they were whisked away. The table was cleared, and green tea was poured. The men settled in to discuss community news, and the children and I went out to the garden to play. Trang picked fresh mandarins and *rambutans,* a red porcupine looking, lychee-like fruit, but with less of a strong perfume taste for dessert. As this was a celebration, it was not long before the business news changed to talk of the night's festivities.

The Mid-Autumn Festival was a time for children. There would be music, a tug of war competition, a lantern making contest, and dragon dancing. It was a lunar celebration, when the moon was full and the harvest was complete. It was a time for children to have fun, the parents' way of making up for long hours in the fields away from them. The children performed traditional dances. They made facemasks and costumes and would compete for candy and monies handed out by elders. Parents told fairytales and folk stories and served mooncakes.

Cam was to sing that evening in front of the community. Her father was full of pride and had her practice one more time for us. She stood her eyes cast toward the floor. She took a deep breath and opened her mouth to sing. A soft sweet sound filled the room. Duong rapped his knuckles on the wooden table and drummed his fingers to keep time. It was a haunting song full of sadness. I needed no translation to bring a fresh round of tears to my eyes.

Her voice rose to a strength I didn't think possible for such a frail body. I could see why she wanted to be a singer. The whole room was captivated. Her voice faded to signal the end of the tale. The room erupted in applause.

"That was beautiful," I said. Without electricity this was the family's nightly entertainment.

Duong opened a bottle of rice wine and shots were poured for toasting. "Can Ly." He held his glass high.

Everyone chimed in "Can Ly." It was a Vietnamese saying for good health and success.

I shut my eyes and tilted my head back opening my throat. The sake-like drink burned. Fresh tears of a different kind rimmed my eyes. I sucked air in gasping for breath as my chest tightened. This was raw alcohol.

In too short a time, my afternoon visit was over and I had to head back to the city before it got dark. I said goodbye and a heartfelt thank you for such an enjoyable afternoon and the glimpse into their lives I had been longing for.

For the first time Cam approached me, unassisted. She hugged me and said, "I hope to see you again."

The translator told me that she promised to study hard so I would be proud of her, and she wished my family health and happiness. It was all too much for me. I left the house that afternoon fighting back tears. These people had opened their home to me, and we shared more than a meal. I felt a part of a Vietnamese family, if only for an afternoon.

During my journey back to the city, the smiles and giggles of reserved children dance in my mind. I thought of the hardworking, determined men who strived for a better future, and of the salty, sweet-sour fish sauce poured over stir-fried vegetables, sautéed with catfish and marinated with pork to be baked in clay pots. And the sweet sound of a young girl's voice singing a haunting melody in a foreign tongue. A family I had only known through pictures had come to life in front of my eyes.

This is *my* Vietnam.

Vietnamese Summer Rolls

2 pounds mahi-mahi, red snapper or tilapia (flaky white fish)
2 tablespoons olive oil
1 lime, juiced
3/4 teaspoon sea salt
1/4 teaspoon black pepper
1-250 gram package of rice vermicelli noodles
1 tablespoon sea salt
1 cup each mint, Thai or regular basil. and cilantro

16 Rice Paper Wrappers, have extra on-hand in case you rip some.

Combine fish, olive oil, lime juice, salt and pepper. Marinate 10 minutes. Pre-heat oven to 350. Heat a frying pan (or grill pan if you have one) over high heat and sear fish for 30 seconds on each side. Place in oven and bake for 10 minutes until cooked through. Cool and flake the fish.

In a soup pot, boil 1 liter of water with 1 tablespoon sea salt. Add rice noodles, stirring to separate. Cook for 3-5 minutes until soft. Drain. Rinse with cold water and drain again. Using scissors, cut into 5 inch lengths. Set aside.

Slice herbs into thin strips and mix together.

~Continued on next page

—— VICTORIA ALLMAN ——

Place 2 rice paper sheets in the soup pot and cover with 6 inches of lukewarm water to soften for 20 seconds. When soft and pliable remove one carefully and place on a piece of paper towel in front of you. Place 1 tablespoon of the herbs in the center of the circle 1/3 of the way from the bottom in a rectangular shape 6 inches long by 2 inches high. Place 2 tablespoons flaked fish on top and 2 tablespoons vermicelli noodles on top of that. Roll the bottom of the rice paper up and over the filling, tucking the ends in to close, like rolling a cigar. Fold both right and left flaps into the center creating blunt ends of a roll. Be careful not to roll too tightly or the rice paper will rip (which happens often until you get the hang of it). Roll the filling gently towards the top of the circle, taking care to tuck the filling in to make a snug package.

Repeat with next sheet of paper and add 2 more to the soup pot to soften.

Serve with a ramekin of Nuoc Cham for dipping.

Serves 16

Nuoc Cham

1/3 cup fresh lime juice
1/2 cup fish sauce
1/4 cup sugar
1 clove garlic minced
1 teaspoon sambal olek
1/2 cup water

Combine all together and stir. Taste and adjust flavors until they are balanced sweet, tart and salty.

Stinky Rotten Fish Sauce

"**Y**ou do not want to go there," Si said with authority—as if we had known each other longer than the twenty seconds it took me to ask about the Kim Hoa Fish Sauce Factory. "I take you to waterfall. In the jungle" He nodded eagerly. "Everyone love it there."

"No." I didn't want to see another waterfall, pagoda, or be any place where I might run into tourists. "I want to go see the fish sauce factory."

"It not pretty. No one goes there. It smells." Si leaned in to whisper, as if telling a family secret. The soft putter of his Honda Motorcycle on which he proposed to take me on an island tour of the pretty spots, purred while he tried to convince me. "The waterfall is pretty. Just one hour across island. I good driver. I show you. I guide."

"That's okay. I can just walk to the factory from here." I turned away, but not quickly enough. Si jumped in front of me like a rabbit

"Okay. Fish factory, but it not pretty."

Vietnam's largest island, Phu Quoc, was only thirty miles southwest of the mainland, but a world away in terms of the hustle and bustle of city life. Gone were the jam-packed streets of Ho Chi Minh City. Gone were the car horns. The rush of everyday life was replaced by dirt-strewn bumpy roads, jungle forests, and long stretches of undeveloped beach smattered with bungalows made of bamboo and palm. The azure ocean curled around the island, rhythmically tossing its waves against the shore. Palm trees along the shoreline stuck out at crazy angles.

My dislike of the touristy, and my love of the obscure found me seeking solitude on Phu Quoc island. After the crazy chaos of Hanoi and Ho Chi Mihn City (eighty-two million people can be overwhelming at times), I wanted to read books on the beach, collect my thoughts, and dine on fresh fish. The one activity I planned was to visit the island's fish sauce factory, where the world's greatest fish sauce is made. Time on Phu Quoc would give me a chance to discover the source of the ubiquitous flavor I tasted all over the country, in every dish, in all the foods.

Fish sauce is to Vietnamese food what soy is to Chinese—the seasoning and the universal flavor of the nation's cuisine. It replaces much of the body's needed salt after sweating all day in the humid tropical sun.

It lends a salty flavor to stir-fried vegetables. To pork that has been marinated in fish sauce and baked in clay pots, it produces a caramelized sweet flavor. Salad rolls are dipped in sauces made of fish sauce, lime juice, sugar, garlic, and chilies called *nuoc cham*. It is present in *pho*, a clear beef broth soup filled with rice noodles, green onions, basil, cilantro, mint, and bean sprouts spiked with ginger and garlic. Fish are stewed in a curry sauce of coconut, chilies, cilantro and lime leaves and finished with fish sauce.

Kim Hoa is the fish sauce produced on Phu Quoc Island. Every afternoon at three o'clock, the fishing boats leave the island for the Gulf of Thailand. A night's fishing brings in the small silver anchovies (ca com) that are used for this particular brand.

The next morning, fish brought in by the boats are rinsed and laid to dry in the sun. The anchovies are then layered in gigantic island hardwood vats, seasoned with salt from the surrounding sea, and left to ferment for a year before bottling. The liquid that oozes from the fish is filtered and aged in other wooden vats until the light brown liquid becomes fully flavored.

Like the best olive oils of the world, the first ferment and pressing is of the highest quality and used in the dipping sauces. But in order to increase profits, the fish are fermented and pressed a second time for a lesser grade fish sauce that is generally used in cooking.

Si brought me to the factory, but he wouldn't go through the gates. He was the only tour guide on the island, but his cargo shorts, flip-flops, and bare chest made me question his validity. Wouldn't a tour guide want to show me around? Instead, he stayed with the motorcycle, smoking cigarettes with a group of boys from the boats and making plans for the night. I explored on my own.

The place appeared normal enough. Like any fish factory, the warehouse sat next to the water with a rickety dock leading down to the fishing boats. Abandoned crates and piles of discarded nets were scattered in the yard. As I entered the factory, the smell hit me like a door being slammed in my face. It took my breath away. I now understood why Si didn't bring tourists here. This was no ordinary place. The appearance of the factory and the operation were all what one would expect, but the smell was another thing.

There is no nice way to put it. This was stinky rotting fish. Wooden vats, with spigots on the bottom to pour off the liquid, lined the warehouse walls. These weren't the small kegs often used in winemaking; these were much larger and shaped like round flowerpots. Each vat held twelve tons of anchovies. The cool, dark room also held a bottling conveyor belt for production, just like a winery. Stacked in the corner were cases of the finished product. This particular factory produced six million liters of fish sauce a year.

"You taste?" A factory worker held out a bottle for me to try. On an overturned vat sat a plate of salad rolls. She nodded and smiled, pouring a small amount of brown liquid into a bowl. I held it up to my nose to smell, then dipped my pinky into the dish and raised it to my lips.

Fermenting, rotten fish, squeezed to extract an aromatic liquid, doesn't sound appealing, but it tastes delicious. It is the essence of Vietnam. It adorns every table alongside plates of fresh herbs, lime or kumquat wedges, sliced red chilies, and a mixture of salt and pepper. People are expected to adjust each dish with these condiments, balancing flavors with a squeeze of citrus, a few more herbs, or a dash of fish sauce to suit the individual taste.

I devoured the roll in three bites. Perfectly balanced flavors of salty, sweet fish sauce hit my palate, filling my mouth with an explosion of taste. It punctuated my senses. This wasn't the overpowering concoction I bought in grocery stores in the west. The Thai fish sauce I bought at home tends to be very strong and pungent, but this amber liquid was smooth and intoxicating. The flavor was lighter and fresher than any other fish sauce I'd tasted, with the transparency of malt vinegar and the color of amber.

"Delicious." I said. "Can I buy a bottle?" I wanted to make a gift of this find to my friend David.

The woman laughed. "No can take on airplane." Flight regulations deemed this delicious elixir as toxic. Special flights and shipping procedures had to be followed to export the sauce. This particular food item would have to be a memory only.

It didn't hurt that the swordfish I ate that night was the same one I watched fishermen pull out of the Gulf of Thailand late that afternoon. I poured a generous amount of Kim Hoa fish sauce over my water spinach that had been sautéed in garlic. Stinky rotten fish never tasted so good.

Vietnamese Swordfish Curry

After a phenomenal meal on Phu Quoc Island, I went back to the kitchen and spoke with the woman cooking. Her son was getting married that weekend, and she wanted the green and pink Patagonia shirt I was wearing for the ceremony. I traded it for this recipe. I now use it for a quick and easy meal over steamed jasmine rice. I must admit to adding a greater amount of fish sauce over the top of the curry to remind myself of that night on the island.

2 stalks lemongrass
2 cans (400 ml) coconut milk
3 tablespoons vegetable oil
4 cloves garlic, minced
2 inches fresh ginger, grated
1 teaspoon sambal olek
1 teaspoon ground coriander
1/2 teaspoon white pepper
1 teaspoon cumin
1 teaspoon turmeric
1/2 teaspoon sea salt
1 white onion, sliced thin
2 tablespoons Vietnamese fish sauce
2 pounds swordfish, cut in large dice, the size of a silver dollar
1 firm green mango, sliced into matchsticks
1/2 cup cilantro, shredded
1/2 cup mint, shredded
1/2 cup basil, shredded

~Continued on next page

Place lemongrass and coconut milk in a large heavy-bottomed stockpot and simmer over medium-high heat until liquid has reduced by a third. Remove and reserve. Clean the pan and return to stove with vegetable oil. Heat vegetable oil, garlic, ginger, sambal olek, coriander, white pepper, cumin, turmeric , and sea salt for 2 minutes to toast until their smell fills the air. Stir constantly to avoid burning. Add onion and sauté a further 2 minutes until soft. Add fish sauce and coconut milk and bring to a boil. Remember the smell at this point will be strong but the finished product will be heavenly. Add swordfish and simmer for 5 minutes until cooked through. Remove lemongrass stalks. Stir in mango, and herbs and taste for seasoning. Adjust heat with more sambal olek or salt with more fish sauce. Serve over steamed jasmine rice.

Serves 4

Tribal Bartering

*P*apua New Guinea? It sounded vaguely familiar. But even with the amount of traveling I'd already done, I couldn't recall where Papua New Guinea was located or any concrete details. I did remember reading about jungles, tribal warriors, and cannibalism. Pictures flashed through my mind of lavishly painted faces, elaborate headdresses, and men with animal bones piercing their noses.

Papua New Guinea is the eastern half of the island of New Guinea, the second largest island in the world. Lying north of Australia, it is approximately one-ninth its size but closely related in flora and fauna. It is one of the least tourist-visited countries on earth as I found out by reading the *Lonely Planet*. But all my reading left me unprepared for what I was about to see.

* * * *

After four years on *Blue Moon* I was itching to break out of my comfort zone and travel to new places. *Blue Moon* had been a fabulous experience, one of my favorites, but it traveled the same route every year. I wanted to do more exploring. When my phone rang one day, Patrick and I were given that chance.

"How would you like to join an expedition boat headed to the South Pacific?" This was all the encouragement I needed. Both Patrick and I had known captain Michael for many years and jumped at the chance to join his new boat. We joined *Pangaea* in Australia.

Michael informed the crew that our first charter would be to the unique locale of Papua New Guinea, a place not many yachts traveled. We would start in Madang and voyage up the Sepik River to explore the inner regions of the country. It sounded simple enough, boats travel up rivers all the time, just not this river. The Sepik River, also called the Amazon of the Pacific, is one of the largest waterways in the world. Over six hundred and eighty miles long, it runs from the center of the country through some of the wildest and most remote terrain on earth. It twists through steamy mangrove jungles, untouched dense rainforests, and boggy swamps. Swift currents run the muddy brown water out to sea. It is home to large saltwater crocodiles and multitudes of fish that supply the local tribes living along its banks with food. Small dug-out canoes and tinned motorboats constantly travel the river bringing supplies and people through the maze of jungle. A houseboat tourist operation even runs for part of the river but nothing like the yacht we would be taking. We would be the first boat of our size to go this far into the jungles of Papua New Guinea.

This was literally a voyage into unchartered waters. We did not have any maps or charts on the section of river we would be traveling. None existed. The river constantly changes course as shifting sandbars and large batches of weeds drift downstream, take anchor, and create islands for the river to flow around. There was also the problem of varying depths. At some points there would be as little as six feet under our keel. Adding to the danger were logs that run in the strong current and would do much damage if we hit them. Not to mention the force of seven knots of current constantly flowing through the river.

This was not your typical charter excursion. Most white boats, as we begun calling the lavish yachts used for entertaining, visit the beautiful places on earth to swim, shop, or watch the sun set. That was what we were used to on *Blue Moon*. This was not one of those boats, or one of those charters. The information we were receiving about what the guests had in mind was the stuff right off the screen of an *Indiana Jones* movie. We would be going to areas where local children had rarely seen white people, where headhunting was rumored to be prevalent until recent years, and stories of cannibalism still rang in the hills. We would see tribal dances, visit spirit houses, and meet village chiefs. Not my typical workweek.

But *Pangaea* was not your typical yacht. Patrick and I joined this one-hundred-eighty-six-foot expedition-style yacht three months before and quickly had to adapt to a new side of yachting. This blue-hulled boat was so very different from *Blue Moon* or any other yacht I had been on. There was none of the refinement or obvious displays of wealth. This was a boat from which to explore and have fun. Instead of million dollar pieces of art, we had fishing boats and dive equipment. Instead of fine china and cut crystal, there were frozen drink machines for Jacuzzi parties. We had three tenders we transported on deck, all fitted to support a full schedule of water sports.

There was a thirty-six-foot sport fish boat for marlin and tuna deep-sea fishing, and a lazzerette full of dive equipment, four wave runners and three kayaks. Water-skis, wake-boards, surfboards, and kite-surfing equipment lined the walls along with rods, reels, lures, and gaffs. Our crew included a dive instructor and two dive masters, as well as a commercial fisherman and surfboard shaper. We would not be going to St. Barths to mingle with celebrities or display ourselves prominently on the pier at St. Tropez. We were going to the middle of nowhere.

Patrick and I fit in well. He was an anthropology major and had studied South Pacific cultures extensively. He was also an avid diver and surfer. The boat was perfect for him, and since I'm not really a cocktail party kind of girl, the adventurous style intrigued me. These people would understand my love of camping, kayaking and exploring. Finally, my wardrobe of Patagonia outdoor clothing would fit my surroundings.

The boat's schedule was to be in the South Pacific for the next two years traveling the distances between Australia and the Marquesas Islands. We were a charter boat based in Tahiti. There we would wait for people to rent the boat and decide where they wanted to go. We heard talk of Palau, Fiji, Bora Bora and Indonesia. The Pacific Ocean is huge and there are many places to see. *Pangaea's* ultimate goal was to see them all. This was the biggest reason Patrick and I were attracted to *Pangaea*, the chance to experience all these new places.

Patrick joined as first mate, second in charge after Michael. He spent his days driving the boat, plotting our course, running the deck crew and managing all the diving and fishing activities. As chef, I prepared meals for our twelve person crew and the twelve guests we accommodated.

Not having known even where Papua New Guinea was before this trip, I had no idea what to expect or what was available. I began researching a month earlier while in Australia. I phoned the few hotels and resorts in the tourist areas of Papua New Guinea and spoke to their chefs. I read everything I could get my hands on, but it wasn't much; this was a relatively little traveled area of the world. From what I could tell, there were markets in the larger towns and a few stores that resembled convenience shops more than grocery stores. The people chartering *Pangaea* were spending a lot of money to be on the boat, and I wanted to be prepared with the right supplies and doable recipes in my head.

We'd been working with a local guide company to coordinate all the activities for the guests, and they were to be my first point of reference. Customs and Quarantine would not allow me to bring in any citrus, pineapples or mangoes, but I was assured by the company that I could find them everywhere. That made sense on paper, as this was a tropical island after all.

"Don't worry," they said. "The local markets here are very abundant. You'll be surprised by what you can find." I'd heard that line before. I started having flashbacks to the "everything" I was told I could find in Mustique. My idea of abundant is often completely different from a local perspective, so their assurances did nothing to lessen my concern. After numerous disappointments in other areas where "everything" was available, I was unwilling to risk finding what I needed in the local markets. I arranged with a provision company in Australia to fly in all my lettuces, baby vegetables, and berries the day before the charter arrived. I purchased all the meat and fish in Australia and kept it in our freezers.

The *Lonely Planet* says that Madang is the prettiest town in the Pacific. Perhaps they should qualify what they mean by pretty. On the eastern shore of the island, Madang sat on a low flat peninsula surrounded by a natural deep-water harbor. A number of small lush islands and coves dotted the bay. The water was a sliding array of turquoise that lapped onto small beaches with palm trees leaning far out over the water. That may be a pretty picture, but Madang itself was anything but. This was a poor and rough town, with crime and corruption running rampant. Petty crime committed by *rascols* (bandits) occurred at an alarming rate, especially on Fridays when paychecks were issued. "Don't carry a purse," the guide told me. "And never walk alone. Always go with a group."

On our first day, Patrick and I walked into town. It consisted of two main streets that ran through a shantytown-style center. Crowds of people were everywhere, just standing around hanging out. No one seemed to be going anywhere or doing anything.

We were close to the equator. Sweat rolled down my body. Dust stuck to my damp skin. I lifted my pony-tail off the back of my neck with one hand and fanned my face with the other. It didn't help. It was stifling hot yet I wore long pants and sleeves to discourage malaria-carrying mosquitoes. Mosquitoes came out by the thousands in this town by the water. The heat blanketed me, weighing on my body like a wool sweater. The oppressive heat was making me wonder if it was worth the risk of malaria just to feel the air on my bare arms.

We walked to the middle of town where there was a daily market. It was a central gathering place. People milled about in the sultry heat. The muggy air left little energy for anything but staying in the shade of the marketplace. Women sat on blankets selling betel nut, and men stood around chewing, talking and spitting. Betel nut (*buai)* was the local favorite narcotic, an exotic stimulant. It was chewed, or more accurately sucked, between the cheek and the gum, like chewing tobacco. Men leave it there to soak for hours along with coral lime (ground from baked seashells) and mustard seed. It stimulated the nervous system and gave a euphoric feeling. It also stimulated the saliva glands.

Men leaned against the buildings, chewing the walnut-size nut, creating royal red juice. Petchew! They spit a long red velvet spew to the dirt below. The streets were covered with the brick red juice drying in the sun. Pretty? Hardly, but the barefoot men with their teeth stained red were not embarrassed by their appearance, their constant drooling and spitting, or the state of their town. They were quick to smile and laugh. Maybe that is the affect of the betel nut? The subtle and natural lifting of the spirits created good-humored people. This was a friendly town if not pretty.

Amy, our chief stew came with us to the market. I was looking for vegetables. She was along for the culture. Scotty, her Australian boyfriend stood guard. Patrick with his blond head of hair roamed behind. The four of us stood out like tomato sauce dripped on white shirts.

It was to this central marketplace the locals brought their produce to sell. I passed women and children of varying ages sitting lethargically on cement slabs, under the hot sun with their water spinach, coconuts and ginger scattered in front of them. Nothing was wrapped in plastic. There wasn't even a building to keep the dry dust of the streets away from the food. It was all laid out on a dirty worn wooden table or a tarp on the ground—the same ground on which the juice from the betel nut was drying. I thought back to North America and its sneeze guards, sterile grocery stores, and sanitation rules. I was definitely not in Kansas anymore.

I didn't see much money changing hands and the produce seemed to just sit on the tables or the ground waiting to be purchased. Still, the market was full. People were everywhere. This was the center of the community. As I passed by, women with mismatched t-shirts and skirts called out half-heartedly, "Five Kina," pointing to a pile of yams. Their teeth were in no better condition then the men's. Their breasts sagged. Their faces drooped with excess skin.

"Two Kina," another said gesturing to the chilies. I got the feeling the price was the only English they knew. There are over eight hundred official languages in Papua New Guinea. People learn the language of their tribe, the neighboring tribes they trade with, and perhaps Pidgin, the most commonly used language. English falls far down on the scale of importance.

Kina is the local currency. The coins used to be heavy and carved into disks out of rare pink shells. They were strung together on a cord and carried as a status symbol. Recently, because of Western influence, paper money has emerged. I was in the market with a pocket full of kina bills ready to spend more money than these villagers had ever seen, all to indulge in Papua New Guinea's "abundance."

The first stall had water spinach and about eight half green/half red tomatoes. The next had the same water spinach and six fat cucumbers. The next had water spinach, and four small measly green peppers. On and on the tables stretched, each loaded with water spinach and not much else. There was a stall in the corner with a few green mandarin oranges. I tried one. It was amazingly juicy and sweet but so full of seeds I could do little but suck the juice out. Next to the mandarins was more water spinach. Where were the pineapples? Where were the mangoes? What about the coffee I read about?

August, our guide with a flat wide face was with us. "June is not mango season and the coffee is in the highlands too far away for walking to market," he said. "It flies out to export, but not for us, we don't drink it."

"You buy your bananas and papaya here," he pointed out. There were cabbages and yams, the ubiquitous water spinach, but nothing else. Abundant was the word the guide had used. It was a good thing I had a plane loaded with organic vegetables from Australia coming that afternoon. The guests were paying a quarter of a million dollars to be on *Pangaea*. They wouldn't be thrilled to eat rice and water spinach for twelve meals straight.

Our trip up the Sepik River was as harrowing as we expected. This was one of the world's great rivers. It started high in the mountains and flowed through primitive villages. We spent four days passing riverbanks lined with clusters of wheat and wild sugarcane. Villages composed of small stilted one-room huts made of wood and thatch sat on shore. Most of the dwellings were raised platforms to avoid rising waters and were accessible by bamboo ladders leading up to the palm bark flooring. Their roof was made of palm fronds. The huts were surrounded by gardens full of vegetables, making each village self-sufficient.

Thick jungle forests stretched forever beyond the villages on either side of the river, dissolving into the thick cover of green. Small clearings were bordered by jungle on each side of the river. It was easy to see how tribes could be out of touch for years.

As recently as 1930, tribes living in the highlands were completely unaware of the outside world. Mick Leahy and Michael Dwyer, Australian explorers looking for gold, discovered more than a million people in areas previously thought of as uninhabited. This was the land time forgot.

Naked, dirty, smiling children with bloated bellies met us at every turn of the river. Screaming with excitement in an erratic but enthusiastic way, they laughed, called out, and chased us down the riverbanks. We were entertainment to them, a sight they had never seen and probably would not again for a long time to come. Many waved as we passed by, some just stared with expressionless eyes like the visions in Sally Struthers telethons. Others showed the innocent curiosity of children and were intently interested in everything we did. What did this twenty million dollar yacht look like to them? I imagined we were an unexpected sight. We attracted an equally strange entourage. Children of all ages and stages of dress were running to keep up with us. The stronger ones ran ahead, squealing and shouting news to warn the next village of our approach.

Villagers poured out of their huts, some taking to their dug out canoes to follow. Outboard motors propelled some of these canoes and men, women, and children paddled others. By the age of four, it appeared a boy could maneuver these crafts down the swift flowing river.

Each night we anchored, unable to navigate the waters in the dark. Canoes gathered around our aft deck. Whole villages came to see what strange goings on occurred on such a vessel.

Patrick befriended many of the young boys by giving them rides on our wave-runners. One by one he took each boy for a ride. Naked, they straddled the seat behind him. Smiling and waving they passed their village, showing off to those on shore waiting their turn. He taught them to drive our machines but they had trouble teaching thirty-nine-year old Patrick how to balance in their round-bottomed vessel.

"Stand in back. Just paddle," one boy instructed him. Patrick rose, balancing like he learned on his surfboard. The hollowed tree trunk swayed beneath him. He teetered right and corrected too quickly to the left. Splash!

He emerged from the muddy water with a wide grin on his face. Children and elders roared with laughter. To their immense pleasure, he ended up in the water many times, tipping out of the canoe before he mastered its balance. Not to be beaten by these children, he suffered many soggy falls while providing constant entertainment to those around him.

The canoes themselves were pieces of art. Carving is prevalent in the South Pacific and what the islands are renowned for. The canoes and paddles of Papua New Guinea were no exception. They were chiseled out of a single log. Each canoe had a puk puk, a crocodile carving on its bow. Paddles were also carved out of single pieces of wood for strength. We often sighted children paddling together, young ones seated in front, while a boy in the back stood to steer. Custom dictated that women paddle from the front or middle of the canoe, sitting down, while men stand and paddle from the back. This was a patriarchal society.

It was these dugout canoes that would approach our swim platform each afternoon; each boat carried many children, all eyes staring and speechless with bellies distended from a parasitic worm in their intestines. A man who knew enough rudimentary English to communicate with us would call for me. In the boats were bananas, papaya and more of the ubiquitous water spinach to trade. Money did these people little good in such a remote part of the country. What they needed were school supplies and batteries for their flashlights to navigate the river at night.

Every afternoon, I went down to where the mass of canoes sat waiting and would be approached by one or two of the boats in the crowd. The men had black skin, darker than any I had seen, with matching deep dark eyes and chiseled bone structure. The children tended to be naked but the men were of motley dress. T-shirts with American slogans, women in threadbare tops. One even had a pastel pink puffy winter jacket, circa 1970s, in the staggering heat. I wondered if the man who held out the papaya for me to see had even heard a Garth Brooks song? But, there he was wearing his concert t-shirt.

"How much for the papaya?" I asked a woman with no top on. She wore dozens of woven palm fronds around her neck. One breast was shriveled and dry from the sun. The other hung down past her belly button, long and flat like a tongue. She wore a skirt of dried palm. With more charade-like mimicking than speaking, I offered her a frying pan for the papayas. She smiled wide, cradling the cast-iron skillet to her bare breast like a child.

I bartered for fresh coconuts, papaya, and bananas—marketing at its best. Two AA batteries got me a hand of bananas. It seemed like a fair trade to me, but by the laughing smile on the men's faces I got the feeling they thought I was a sucker. Such a sought-after commodity for something that grew on trees everywhere. What a silly white girl. For me it was the other way around: two little batteries to help these people out. I was definitely getting the better end of the deal.

Pangaea T-shirts were given out and Cokes were handed to the children who erupted into fits of giggles.

Patrick and I had brought atlases with us. While I traded for food, he was busy showing the children where they were compared to where the boat came from. I hoped the books would make it around the village and into the rudimentary classrooms, but I held little faith the children understood what was being said. Nonetheless, the smile on their faces and the fits of giggles Patrick was producing was enough for me.

While I was busy trading smiles with the locals, our crew was having a different experience. Although we hired guides Chris and August to help us navigate the river, they had never been on this particular stretch before. They knew how to run a river, but were not familiar with the lower portion of the Sepik. Michael, Patrick, and the two men spent every hour of daylight trying to read the river and decide which way to go. The direct path was evident as the main river flowed in one direction. But the danger was the logs, the shifting currents, the floating islands of marsh grass, and the depth. Charts would have depths of the river marked on them so Michael and Patrick could navigate a path through the deepest waters, but we didn't have charts. Instead, one had to drive the boat while the other watched the depth sounder calling out numbers and hoping it would not be too late to change course if the numbers got too small. Getting into too shallow water would eventually get us stuck and would ruin the props and stabilizers on the bottom of the boat. It went unsaid that if we did get stuck there was little hope of help being able to reach us for some time. As it was, much of the sand and silt in the river was being sucked up into the engines, causing substantial damage. Scotty our engineer was kept busy with maintenance.

Each night we felt like we were in Conrad's *Heart of Darkness*. Michael worried about people coming aboard the boat and set a watch. One of the guys sat watching the aft deck all night long. It sounded like an easy job, just sitting down and reading a magazine for a few hours a night. But it really became a struggle for survival. Not from the headhunting cannibals we had imagined from our research, but from another, equally frightening predator. The mosquito. They sound harmless, and everyone has run into them all over the world. But these were different. These were mutant mosquitoes thriving in a lost world. I was sure they had taken on the cannibalistic characteristics of the region and were out for human flesh. They were big, numerous and vicious. Our poor crew each had two hours a night of sitting outside surrounded by these blood-thirsty sucking creatures.

Except for the mosquitoes, we hadn't encountered any cannibalism on this trip. All the guidebooks had dismissed this practice as something that had been abolished, but we were still curious. Chris and August laughed when we asked. Their coal-black faces and short frizzy curls of dark hair illuminated the whiteness of their teeth. These two men did not imbibe on betel nut. But when pressed, Chris told me he had an older uncle who still remembered eating flesh.

"It's a sweet meat," he told me. "Children are the juiciest and used to be farmed for eating. They taste a little like chicken." He howled with laughter. My culinary curiosity had finally reached its limit.

Cannibalism and headhunting stories still circulate in association with Papua New Guinea. These practices used to be performed as ceremonial rites. Skulls were collected as trophies in tribal wars, boiled clean, and hung for display on skull racks. The resulting soup was drunk to acquire the spiritual power of the enemy.

Patrick had bartered for a skull rack and purchased a stone used for headhunting. I hoped these were just part of his anthropology curiosity and not something he planned on using. During funerals, loved ones would eat the deceased brains as a way of retaining family history and stories. It was widely believed when Michael Rockefeller disappeared in 1964, on the western side of the island. He was, in fact, killed and eaten by headhunters.

Maybe it was a good thing we were seeing this country from the relative safety of a yacht.

The river, the canoes, the market, and the cannibalism all made this trip the most culturally exciting journey I had yet been on. *Pangaea's* three weeks in Papua New Guinea could easily be right out of the pages of *National Geographic* magazine. But I don't think their explorers ever traveled in such style, at least not onboard a twenty million dollar yacht.

Riding Out the Storm

*I*t was a day of tropical storms like none I'd ever seen. Rain fell hard from every direction. Large heavy drops bounced off a vengeful steel grey sea. Ominous purple-rimmed clouds blanketed low in the ever-darkening sky. The storm's noise vibrated through the hull of the boat, driving us all inside for cover. We pitched back and forth in the swell. Sleep was a challenge. The boat's continual motion, combined with the clanging of the anchor, kept all of us awake, praying for a break from the storm.

Pangaea left Papua New Guinea and was now traveling through the Solomon Islands to Tahiti on this 3,500-mile run from one end of the Pacific to the other, or so it felt. But the Pacific is the largest ocean in the world, covering sixty-four million square miles of blue and encompassing one third of the earth's surface. *Pangaea* was only covering a small part of it.

Still, it was a long and tedious voyage. As chef onboard I was responsible for putting out breakfast, lunch, and dinner for our crew. Since I usually do this as well as cook for the yacht's guests, the light duty left a lot of down time for me.

Pangaea had four levels of deck, six staterooms, a dining room, a gym, and two spacious living rooms; plenty of luxurious space for guests, but off-limits to crew. We could stay in our cabins, hang out in the crew mess to watch movies and eat our meals, or be on the decks, if weather allowed.

The first few days were spent pleasantly reading and catching up on sleep. Then the storm appeared. Confinement set in. The same twelve humans, in the same rooms, each hour of each day, every day for ten days. It felt like a prison sentence with no end in sight: just miles and miles of angry blue water and sky, wherever I looked.

The Pacific Ocean can be beautiful and calm like a glass mirror or rough and agitated like margaritas in a blender. We had seen it all on this trip. On some days I stared across the water, believing I could actually see the curve of the earth. The next day, I'd be stuck inside while the wind howled with such ferocity I feared being picked up like a newspaper and tossed into the water to drown.

Patrick was a surfer at heart and had the requisite 'the-world-is-my-playground' yachting attitude. Normally, one of the happiest men I had ever known, he was quick to produce a smile and had an optimistic outlook on life, but even he was showing signs of weariness after ten days of bad weather. As first officer onboard, part of his role entailed driving the boat. Twice a day he would go up to the bridge to stand watch for a four-hour shift. After relieving Michael, Patrick had to go over our location on the chart, adjust equipment, watch for other boats, and make any necessary course changes. I'm not sure if he had it easier or harder than me, but at least he saw the chart every day and plotted our course. He knew we were making headway and slicing through the endless blue waters with a generous amount of speed. But he was also forced to stare straight into that blue void for hours at a time, twice a day, before being relieved by another officer. Around and around their schedule went, like mice in a wheel: four on, eight off, four on, eight off. Even cheerful Patrick was feeling a little batty by day ten.

Throughout the night, the wind picked up to over forty knots and roared outside our porthole. Ten to fifteen feet waves crashed against the boat and sent us rocking. Those with a delicate constitution spent most of the night curled up beside the toilet, praying for it to be over. In such a state you can barely summon the energy to return to your bunk.

We'd just about had enough when Michael decided to seek cover and find an anchorage.

In the middle of this huge ocean, far from any major city or urban area, are the Solomon Islands, southeast of Papua New Guinea. The chain is composed of six main islands and hundreds of smaller islands and atolls—sunken volcanic islands with a fringing coral reef. Volcanic islands in varying degrees of activity are scattered throughout the region. In the center of the Solomon's is Marovo Lagoon. At eighty-seven miles long, it is considered the largest lagoon in the world. To *Pangaea* it was considered a heavenly hideout from the storm. I breathed a sigh of relief when Michael steered us inside and dropped anchor.

"Let's get out of here," Patrick said the next day, although the weather looked only marginally better outside. Clouds still threatened to explode on us, but there was at least a little light peeking through.

"Yes, please." I begged.

Amy and Scotty had taken Oceana, the fishing boat to explore one end of the lagoon. We decided to take the wave-runners and head the other way. We planned to have lunch at Uepi Lodge, seven miles and three islands away. I didn't care if we got rained on, I just wanted off that boat. I needed breathing room to clear my head. We put on sunscreen, more from habit than any chance the sun would break through the clouds, placed our money and a change of clothes in a dry-sac, and donned our life jackets.

The minute we left *Pangaea* we knew this was going to be tough going. The usual translucent blue waters turned ugly. Menacing gray waves grew larger and threatened to upend us, while whitecaps formed in the distance. I sat behind Patrick wrapping my arms around his waist and holding on for dear life. He'd thrown me once already, and I was trying to avoid a second swim. As the wave-runner rode up the crest of the wave and fell, crashing down into the water with alarming speed, it sent spray up and over the front of the ski. As quickly as we dropped, another wave appeared in front of us. I barely had time to wipe the saltwater from my glasses before we would drop again, sending another torrent of water up and over us.

After two hours of constant pounding, we arrived at Uepi Island. We had a map and a rough idea the lodge was located on the eastern side of the island, but little else to go on. We circled the area twice before we saw the sign, *Uepi Lodge* engraved on a piece of wood no larger than a paperback book. The lodge itself was obscured from view. Coconut palm trees concealed the building amidst the tropical rainforest. A single dock was all that signaled its existence.

Although we arrived unannounced and in an unconventional way, Jill and Grant, the lodge's owners, led us up a pebbled path, past green flowering bushes and bungalows to the main house. Lunch was being served in the open-air restaurant.

The timber veranda was shaded with a palm frond roof and overlooked the white sand bars and turquoise shallows of the lagoon. The ominous day disappeared. Half a dozen tables and chairs were set up, plus a hammock for reading. The relaxed atmosphere of the place screamed of total escapism from the outside world.

Jill was an Australian pixie of a woman. "I fell in love with Uepi Lodge twenty years ago, when we were here as guests. We bought the place and raised a family here," she said. While Patrick and Grant discussed fishing and diving possibilities in the area, Jill and I talked food.

"I grow everything we need here on the island." Her size was misleading. She was a strong woman full of fierce passion when she spoke of food and living on the island. After obtaining the lodge from the previous owners, she commandeered the kitchen and started creating the fabulous dishes and fastidious reputation that Uepi is known for. "Our guests are normally from Australia and are used to lots of fresh vegetables that aren't available in the Solomon Islands. I knew this wouldn't do, so I planted a garden. Today I grow my own herbs and lettuces for each meal."

Lunch arrived at the table as we spoke. A South Pacific yellowfin tuna pie, Jill's healthy version of an Australian meat pie, was placed before me. Enveloped in a flaky buttery crust were chunks of tender, sweet yellowfin tuna coated with coconut milk, ginger, lime, and cilantro. This was topped with fluffy mashed potatoes and baked until golden. I had never had anything like it. The coconut milk reminded me of Thai food but without the heat. I could distinctly pick out the taste of ginger and lime in the velvety smooth sauce. The yellowfin, a top quality tuna plentiful in South Pacific waters, was barely cooked so it was still moist and full of flavor. The pastry was crisp instead of soggy or overloaded with the sauce. I eagerly poured sweet chili sauce (an Asian staple used like ketchup) onto my plate to accompany the pie. It was delicious.

"There must be just a little of the sauce peeking out of the pie when you break the crust," Jill told me. "Too dry and it's gummy to eat and too much, it's a soggy mess. It must be just right."

I could barely concentrate on what Jill was saying as I took another bite. All I could think about was how I could re-create this dish on the boat for guests. It was that good. I had to replicate it. They say that imitation is the greatest form of flattery. I hoped Jill would be pleased I was planning on stealing her creation.

I forgot about our harrowing journey to get to Uepi and the endless hours I had spent on the boat as I sat on the porch surrounded by Jill and her guests.

I absorbed the quiet, laid-back atmosphere. There was no fuss or formality, just a feeling of comfort. This was Eden, our secret oasis, hidden not only from *Pangaea* but also from the world. No telephones rang, no television blared. The island had no movie theatre or Starbucks. Best of all, there was no crew around. Patrick and I were on solid ground that didn't sway and tilt beneath us. We had succeeded in escaping our floating prison.

Unfortunately, as the day progressed I was forced out of my euphoric state with a reminder of reality. No matter how good the tuna pie tasted, it could not stop time, and the daylight hours were dwindling fast. Patrick and I faced two more hours pounding through whitecaps on the wave-runner to return to the boat. Grant, who had been watching storms from this vantage point for twenty years, felt the weather was about to get worse; the next storm was approaching.

"You'd better get going mate, or you'll be here for the night." The idea of being stranded on the island appealed to me as I imagined devouring more of Jill's culinary creations. But Patrick was a little more responsible and insisted that we go now before it was too late.

With goodbyes from everyone and a rough idea of how Jill made such a fantastic lunch, we departed along the flower-laden path to the shallow warm water of the dock. I climbed onboard our wave-runner, and Patrick started the motor. We'd only gone fifty yards when I turned to wave goodbye. It was too late. Surrounded by the coconut palms, Uepi Lodge was lost from sight. Once again, hidden from the world.

We traveled a few miles further when I heard the rumbling of thunder, seconds later, a streak of lightning flashed across the sky. Huge black clouds were building on the horizon, dark and towering, like a Canadian mountain range. A sudden flash lit up the sky and a terrific boom rattled in my chest. Everything grew dark, and a strong wind began to blow.

"Hold on tight," Patrick instructed as he bent lower over the windscreen of the ski, trying to avoid the spray.

Raindrops the size of marbles fell with such force it felt like stones. With each direct hit I felt the sting and I winced. Plonk, plonk, plonk. Raindrops hurtled down around us. Within seconds, a heavy veil of water surrounded us like a waterfall. A cold, raw feeling sank deep into my bones and I curled up even tighter to Patrick, praying we'd soon be back to the boat.

The torrent of rain continued for the next twenty minutes of our journey. When we left, hours earlier, I had barely looked back, eager to escape the confines of the boat. When we finally arrived within sight of the yacht, it had transformed to a place of secure warmth. It now looked like the home I'd never been so happy to see. I felt like Dorothy waking up to see Aunt Em. Stepping onto the swim platform, I smiled at Patrick, glad to be securely back in my prison.

Uepi Fish Pie

1 pastry shell
2 cups mashed potato (left-overs are perfect for this)
2 tablespoons vegetable oil
3 cloves garlic
2 leeks, white part only sliced thin
1 tablespoon fresh ginger, grated
6 lime leaves, chopped fine (or zest and juice from 1 lime)
1 teaspoon sambal olek
1 cup chicken stock
1 400 ml can coconut milk
1 pound fresh tuna, diced into 1-inch cubes
1 teaspoon sea salt
1/3 cup fresh chopped cilantro

Pre-heat the oven to 350 degrees. Bake the pastry shell for 10 minutes until golden brown. In a large heavy-bottomed pot heat vegetable oil and sauté garlic for 5 minutes until golden. Add leeks and sauté an additional 5 minutes. Add ginger, lime leaves, sambal olek and chicken stock. Simmer 5 minutes. Add coconut milk and simmer 5 minutes more. Remove from heat and stir in tuna, salt and cilantro. Place all in pre-baked pastry shell and top with mashed potatoes. Bake at 350 degrees for 30 minutes until coconut milk bubbles under the potatoes.
Serve with Sweet Chili sauce and a big green salad.

Serves 8

Paradise

"*I*t certainly isn't paradise, is it?" Patrick's voice dripped with disenchantment. We'd been on the island paradise of Tahiti for a few weeks now.

Pape'ete, Tahiti's capital city, was crowded and dirty, the streets narrow and unappealing. The buildings lacked character and many were old and either falling down or boarded up. Ugly graffiti marred the scenery and garbage lined the streets. It was an industrial port, stuffed with commercial boats, cargo freighters, and copra ships (dried coconut meat used for making coconut oil). Stacks of containers, huge oil drums, and dilapidated sailboats completed the scene. I had to agree: it just wasn't what I pictured when I thought of Tahiti.

Tahiti is one of a group of islands called French Polynesia. They lie half way between Australia and California and cover the same area as Europe. Five different island groups and one hundred and eighteen islands in total are part of French Polynesia, but Tahiti is the largest and most populated. It's a volcanic island with mountain ranges of up to six thousand feet high.

These mountains tower over the island and are often covered by clouds that create heavy precipitation and keep the island fertile and green year round. Heavily scented tropical flowers of tiare, hibiscus, and the sharp spikes of helconia permeate the tropical air.

Banana trees with their large flat leaves create canopies overhead. Pineapple, papaya, breadfruit, mango, and passion fruit trees grow along the mountainsides. Seen from the water, the island has numerous sharp peaks, knife-edge ridges, and plateaus covered in green plants and white clouds. The rocky coastline, continually beaten with waves, is cut sharply, creating shallow bays for swimming. Aqua lagoons surrounded by coral reef are teeming with fish. Situated between the Equator and the Tropic of Capricorn, the island's tropical climate includes intense sunshine and cool trade winds. It really could be paradise.

Just the thought of Tahiti evokes images of vivid tropical flowers, exotic beach hideaways, and aquamarine waters for snorkeling. And it is all that. But the main city leaves more of an impression of hell than heaven.

As we navigated the tiny winding streets of Pape'ete to the waterfront, I had to step over drunks sleeping in the streets. We turned the corner, and I tripped on a man passed out in a flowerbed, his flip-flops sticking out in my path. It rained that afternoon, but instead of a cleansing rain, the water added to the dirty feeling. Rivers of water carried garbage and slime down the gutters and out into the harbor.

"The best thing in Pape'ete is the *roulottes*," Patrick spoke with the authority of someone who investigated all the avenues available in town.

As the sun set and the day's business came to an end, another side of this bustling town emerged. The wharf was the center for shipping during the day, but at night it turned into a lively street fair. *Roulottes* (caravans) are Tahiti's answer to fast food.

Trucks arrived every evening at six o'clock, curving along the waterfront, a cleaner area of town. They dropped the sides of their vans to reveal a kitchen inside. Each of these mobile diners set out four or five plastic tables and chairs for their customers. A wooden A-frame menu board was all that distinguished one from another. Each *roulotte* specialized in something different. One had a hibachi grill set up to barbeque *steak frites* and chicken; another had a powerful gas-fired wok to produce *chow meins* and stir-fried rice dishes. Next in line was one with griddles to form perfectly round *crêpes*, and yet another opened to a hot stone oven that baked thin-crust, made-to-order pizzas.

Because of limited space, most of the ingredients for the menu were stored in big white coolers stacked on the ground. These also doubled as a workspace for chopping vegetables or assembling plates. Dishes were produced at lightning speed so little prep room was required.

Patrick and I had our hearts set on *Poisson Cru,* Tahiti's national dish of raw tuna marinated in lime juice and coconut milk. It was a dish we saw on many menus everywhere in Tahiti, fresh fish being ever so available on the island.

As we read the menu and I struggled to summon my high school French to translate for Patrick, a Polynesian woman with a Frangipani flower tucked behind her ear approached us. *"Nous voudrions deux Poisson Cru, s'il vous plait, et deux thè glacè."* I butchered the words as well as the pronunciation. Tahiti was a long way from my classroom in rural Canada.

The woman smiled at my effort and responded in English. "Two salads and two ice teas, yes?"

"Oui." At least I could manage that much.

It would have been the perfect night to sit enjoying our meal while we watched the sun set over the Bay of the Moon and the distant island of Moorea, but too many cranes and cargo containers blocked our view. The food was heavenly, but this still wasn't paradise.

A band played loud Tahitian music on the nearby promenade. We absorbed the melodious sounds of ukuleles, rhythmic tribal drums, and guitars from the traditional Kaina band. Children dressed in the omnipresent tropical shirts and dresses ran, danced, and squealed in delight beside the stage. It was hard not to enjoy myself surrounded by their joyous dancing. Their smiles were infectious. Maybe Pape'ete wasn't so bad after all.

A screen in the center of the square displayed a video of Tahitian women dancing. Unlike America, where the video would have been censored for public display, here in Tahiti beautiful, bronze-skinned, bare-breasted Polynesian women with long, shiny black hair danced in bark skirts. Each woman wore a crown of tropical flowers. They shook and swung their hips in an amazing display of flexibility, agility, and seduction. A permanent smile played on each of their lips.

"How can they make their hips swing from side to side so quickly while their knees are fanning in and out at the same time?" Patrick asked.

On screen the beautiful topless women effortlessly swayed their hips while they kept their shoulders straight. With knees bent and heels together, they opened and closed their legs in a scissor-like motion in tempo with the drumbeat. Their hips rolled in slow, then quick, movements. The effect was intoxicatingly sensual. I found it hard to believe it was their knees that captivated Patrick.

Tahiti has a romantic and exotic allure, partly due to the tropical climate, cloud-draped volcanic mountains, and deep carved valleys surrounded by pastel ocean waves, but also in part for its laid-back sensuality. The legendary beauty of Tahitian women is known worldwide, having been immortalized in the pages of history by the fated voyage of the *Bounty*.

In 1789, the *Bounty* arrived in Tahiti in search of breadfruit to transport back to the Caribbean. The crew of sailors stayed in Tahiti for almost six months. They lived with Tahitian women, entranced by their free and easy sexual attitudes. When it was time to leave, the sailors fought with their captain to remain. Captain Bligh was tough and refused to stay or bring the women with them.

At sea, missing their Tahitian women, the men mutinied and set the captain adrift in a rowboat. They sailed back to Tahiti to pick up the women, then sailed for another South Pacific island to avoid repercussions from the law. This true story is better than the stuff of legends and has forever sealed the romantic vision of Tahiti and its women.

Patrick found it hard to take his eyes off the screen as our food arrived. Our own Tahitian beauty delivered our two plates and smiled as Patrick sat mesmerized by the screen. "Today we wear clothes while we dance. That was a long time ago." She nodded toward the video. Patrick looked crest-fallen. As a sailor he would have mutinied for any one of those women on the screen.

Poisson Cru is a dish of raw tuna, sliced thin and mixed with cucumbers, peppers, onions, carrots, and herbs. At the last minute, coconut milk is added to the mix to coat the tuna and protect the delicate flesh before the acidic lime juice, sea salt and pepper is added. The salad is mixed to order and served right away so as not to cook the fish with the lime.

The soft silky tuna melted in my mouth. I instantly forgot how much I disliked Pape'ete. This was worth coming to town for.

* * * *

The *roulottes* were a great way to try *Poisson Cru*, but it didn't compare to having it made fresh for us. Our second engineer, Schwack, had been a surfboard shaper in a previous life. When he shaped a board for local surfing legend Raimana years ago, the two became friends. Now Raimana and his wife, Yvonne, were our unofficial tour guides. They both had the dark golden skin and deep wide-set eyes of Polynesians. Just as Tahitian women were beautiful, the men were equally handsome. More than this, they were friendly and easy-going. Soon after arriving in Tahiti, we were invited to their house for dinner.

They greeted us with warm smiles and kisses on both cheek. "Babe, you've got to try Yvonne's tuna. It's insane," Raimana told me. "Just wait."

—— VICTORIA ALLMAN ——

Scotty, Patrick, and Schwack went to see Raimana's new stand-up surfboard, while Amy and I ventured into the kitchen to help Yvonne. A mass of dark curls and big curious brown eyes appeared from around a corner. Ragi-ei (pronounced Ren-yea) their five-year old daughter smiled brightly and greeted Amy and I with two kisses on the cheek. She soon climbed up on my knee, giggling at my poor attempt to ask her about school in French.

Raimana was a sponsored surfer with Quiksilver and had surfed the famous big wave of Teahupoo his whole life. His near disaster on the dangerous wave was the most photographed surfing picture of all time. It had even been displayed in Times Square. Patrick was excited to spend the evening hearing stories of Raimana surfing with Laird Hamilton and Kelly Slater.

But we were all impressed with Raimana's first statement: "I just got off the phone with Jack Johnson (multi-platinum singer and former pro-surfer). I'm going to have lunch him next week in Hawaii."

That was it. The conversation quickly turned to surfing and waves. Patrick was in his element where I, on the other hand, wanted a glimpse of Tahitian life. I had Ragi-ei show me around. Their modest house was simple and open. Coconut wood walls and a corrugated iron roof formed the structure. They lived on the water, of course, with a breath-taking view of the Pacific Ocean. I could hear the waves breaking from their backyard.

We set a table in the front room and a potluck dinner began to appear. A friend of Raimana's brought guava pie. I had brought a grilled vegetable rice salad, and Yvonne was providing the tuna from her family's fish shop. Raw tuna sashimi was piled high on top a subtle grated radish known as daikon. There was also Raimana's sashimi sauce to pour over the fish: a combination of raw ginger, garlic, oyster sauce, and soy. The French culture of Tahiti has a large Chinese influence from migrant workers who came years ago to work the agricultural fields.

Finally, the talk turned away from surfing. Raimana began describing the method of making traditional *Poisson Cru*. "After cutting the fresh tuna, you soak it in salt water. Then your sauce is not too thick, you know. You must wring the fresh grated coconut meat in a cloth to get the juice out. Then a little lime juice. I love this meal. It is insane, brother." There was something wonderful about this man; something kind, something engaging and genuine. He bubbled over with enthusiasm and love.

Raimana was like no surfer I had ever seen. My idea of blond, blue-eyed

California boys, who used surfer-speak long after it faded from being cool, was being replaced by this dark-skinned, thirty-year old Tahitian man with shining eyes and a wide, ever-present smile. He was short and stocky with curly dark hair. He was intelligent and witty, even in English, a third language for him. But at the core, he was a surfer, consumed with the sport that made him famous. So before the conversation changed from *Poisson Cru* back to surfing, Raimana leaned toward me and said, "Don't worry Babe, I come to *Pangaea* and show you."

Two weeks later, Raimana was aboard *Pangaea* to go surfing with the owners. Raimana set about making *Poisson Cru*. First, he cut the tuna into thin pieces, the size of a postage stamp, taking care to cut out the bright red bloodline.

"I be right back." He disappeared from the galley to get fresh seawater from the swim platform, straight out of the ocean. He strained the water and poured it over the tuna to soak. "This cleans the fish," he told me while the tuna soaked.

He sliced tomatoes, celery, cucumber, and white onion. He grated ginger and chopped garlic. Just before lunch was served, Raimana drained the tuna and gathered his vegetables. Earlier that day he'd been ashore and came back with a bottle of fresh, grated coconut milk from a friend. The bottle of thick sweet liquid was poured over the tuna and vegetables. He squeezed three limes and gently stirred the mixture. He tasted a little, added more salt, and tasted again.

"Babe, taste this. This is it." He was beaming.

It was delicious. The tuna was sweet and tender. Because it was raw, it melted in my mouth like that night at the *roulotte*. The coconut milk added just enough fat to coat the tuna without being heavy. The lime added enough acidity to sharpen the taste without overpowering the tuna. The vegetables were crunchy and added a great contrast to the silky smooth tuna. It was refreshing and light—the perfect combination of the best of Tahiti. The sea and the land combined in one dish. I reached for a second bowl and knew this would become an instant staple in my menu collection.

Granted, Pape'ete was not the prettiest spot on the island but when I now think of Tahiti, I think of its warm and generous people. I think about Raimana and Yvonne and how Ragi-ei's eyes sparkled when she smiled. When I think of Tahiti, I now think of paradise.

—— VICTORIA ALLMAN ——

Raimana's Poisson Cru

2 pounds fresh tuna loin
1 tomato
2 stalks celery
1/4 English cucumber, peeled
1/2 white onion
2 cloves garlic
1 inch piece of fresh ginger, grated
1-1/2 teaspoons sea salt
1/2 teaspoon black pepper
1-400 ml can coconut milk
3 limes, juiced

Slice tuna into thin squares, slightly larger than a quarter. Soak in water for 5 minutes and strain. Chop the tomato, cucumber and onion to bite size pieces, smaller than the tuna. Pour the coconut milk over the tuna and mix in vegetables, garlic, ginger, sea salt, and black pepper being careful not to mash the delicate fish. Gently fold lime juice in. Taste for salt and acidity and adjust if necessary. Serve immediately.

Serve as a salad or with cold rice as a hearty lunch.

Serves 4

Dolphin Carousel

At a snail's pace, Patrick and I descended into the Bombay blue water beneath us. My ears always hurt when I dove, so we were taking our time going down. Patrick was patient, staying parallel to me and looking in my eyes for signs of pain. We resembled two bobbing bowling pins. All of a sudden, Patrick's eyes grew wide. A boyish smile broke on his face, creating the deep crevice of laugh lines around his eyes.

He pointed behind me. I turned to see a lone bottlenose dolphin gliding around us like a carousel. I'd never seen a dolphin so close to divers.

In his mouth he held a leaf, fallen from a breadfruit tree on shore. He wiggled it back and forth a few times as if it were stuck before he bucked his head like a bull and tossed the leaf aside. His pectoral fin caught the leaf, and I swore I saw him smiling as he waved it back and forth at us.

For the finale of our underwater ballet, with the same air of a performance, the dolphin flipped the leaf from his pectoral fin through the water and caught it with his tail. He twisted his body to check and see he had the leaf before shooting away, into the depths of the Tahitian water.

One single photograph was all Patrick captured, a blurred close-up of my red hair and the corkscrew shape of a dolphin seconds before he departed from sight.

Varo Hunting

Varo is one of the world's deadliest creatures. They were the inspiration for the monster in the movie Aliens. Divers call them thumb splitters. They strike their prey with one lightning-quick blow. Knowing these scary creatures were what we were looking for made me question what I was doing, snorkeling in the turquoise shallows of Maupiti, in my bikini, searching for varo holes.

Varo is the Tahitian word for mantis shrimp, a centipede looking relative of a shrimp that seems more like a praying mantis. They carry deadly front appendages folded in front of its head. At the tip of both arms are razor sharp claws that extend out to slice and spear passing fish.

Nunu had been bringing me varo and mahi-mahi all season. Every time we entered the lagoon in Maupiti he would pull up alongside the back of *Pangaea* in his sleek yellow and white fishing boat with Tahitian designs stenciled on the side. He sold me mahi-mahi that he had speared right outside the pass only hours before. His boat was specially designed to drive from the bow with one hand while holding a spear with the other. He was a professional fisherman, adept at catching the flashing blue and green metallic fish as they raced the waves.

Nunu greeted me the same each time. "Iorana Victoria. Mahi now, varo soon." He'd drop two or three whole mahi on the deck before motoring off. He returned to his island house to retrieve his mask and hook to go hunting for varo. Within half an hour, while I was busy cleaning the mahi for dinner, Nunu returned again with varo swimming in a bucket, ready to delight our guests.

That evening before the fresh mahi dinner, all the guests gathered in the galley. Varo must be kept alive until they are cooked. As I explained what varo was and how Nunu caught them, I reached my tongs into the bucket of water and grabbed the varo around its body, away from the claws. I placed it on its back in a hot pan. The oil spat and hissed. The varo bucked and lashed out with its razor sharp claws. I held tight, slightly turning my head. I tried not to imagine it flying out of the pan towards me, ready to slice and dice my face. The pan sizzled while the heat burnt off the excess water on the varo's body. I held it in place for no more than twenty seconds before it ceased to fight and began cooking.

"Oh, I can't watch." One squeamish woman left the galley—more sweet succulent meat for the rest of us. The cooking was actually quite humane and quick, but not for the faint of heart.

After a minute in the frying pan, I added a dab of butter and chopped garlic to flavor the meat. Two minutes on each side was all the cooking they needed. I swirled the pan one last time with some chopped herbs and slid the varo onto a plate with the sauce.

Like a shrimp, varo are covered in a soft cartilage that must be removed to get to the white meat. Taking my sharpest paring knife and turning the varo on its back, I split the shell down the center, exposing the tender flesh inside. Just like breaking into a loaf of bread. Our guests each grabbed a cocktail fork to try a sample. The opaque flesh had the consistency of lobster, with a slightly less rich taste. It was delicate and full of flavor, so fresh and soft that it melted in my mouth. I was amazed at how much better it was than lobster or crab.

After numerous trips to Maupiti and presenting varo to guests this way, it wasn't long before I was asking Nunu to show me where they came from.

Maupiti, the smallest and most isolated of the Society Islands in French Polynesia, is a minuscule version of Bora Bora with its sharp ridgeline summit that dominates the middle of the tiny island. Tranquility and isolation dictate the feel of the island. The calm sapphire water of the lagoon and sleepy swaying palm trees of the surrounding motus, the smaller islands ringing the island, are what South Pacific dreams are made of.

But we had to fight for the peaceful feeling of paradise inside the lagoon.

VICTORIA ALLMAN

A storm had hit the area earlier that morning, creating rough waters to sail through.

The Maupiti pass is one of the tightest gaps we sailed all season. Most French Polynesian islands are ringed by submerged reefs, part of their volcanic evolution, having erupted from the ocean floor and cooled to create fertile mountain islands. Breaks in these reefs allow boats to enter and exit the lagoons. Many are wide enough to pass through without incident, but some, like Maupiti, are narrow and dangerous. The tides rush out daily, carrying extreme volumes of water through the small spaces and creating a monstrous standing wave with enough force to push even large boats like *Pangaea* up onto the reef. On top of that, a south swell from the storm ran against the outgoing tide, creating another challenge to get through.

Patrick and Michael surveyed the scene with binoculars, checking for wave breaks and currents before deciding to enter the lagoon. This was not a place to be shipwrecked and neither of them wanted to make the wrong call. But after careful consideration they decided it would be safe and exhilarating to enter.

"Come to starboard to line up the range," Patrick called to Michael while continuously reading the water for the slightest change that would send *Pangaea* off course. Churning white water lay out before us, paving the way through the pass.

"How far to the reef on starboard?" Michael asked without taking his eyes off the bow of the boat. He couldn't see everywhere and had no rearview mirrors. He relied solely on distances called to him by Patrick.

"You have a good line and should clear by fifteen feet."

We entered the pass at eight knots and quickly heeled to the right. I headed down to the galley to survey the scene. I had to make a grab for the bowl of noodles I was preparing as it began to slide off the counter. But just as quickly we righted and sharply turned to port. We made one final push through the choppy water. I went outside to the stern to look at the cut we had just passed through.

The waves were high, breaking with loud thunderous roars. Water rushed through the break with the speed of whitewater rapids.

But inside the lagoon we were sheltered—a hidden Eden. The day was bright and the crew relished the chance to enjoy the small piece of the paradise we offered guests. Within minutes, all our toys were in the water for the crew to have fun with. Patrick organized dives and surfing trips, Amy and our other stewardesses rode jet-skis. Schwack kayaked to explore the lagoon. Scotty went kite boarding on the far beach.

I prepared a barbecue on the sundeck that evening to watch the sunset and the emergence of the Southern Cross. These few days were our Polynesian holiday before we raced back to Tahiti to pick up our next set of guests.

When guests were onboard, I rarely had more time than to say a quick hello to Nunu and ask about his family, but now my days were filled with nothing but time. That day when Nunu came by with his fresh caught mahi for our evening barbecue, I invited myself along to look for the menacing creatures.

"Is it Varo season?" I asked.

He laughed. "Always Varo season, if you are a good fisherman."

So there I was, floating face down, four feet above the flat white sand desert lagoon. The sun burned strong above, creating clear water and a slight pink shade on the backs of my legs. Twenty feet away, Nunu walked through the shallows with a red plastic gas can tied to his waist to collect his varo. Armed only with a pair of goggles, a snorkel and a twelve-inch thin steel rod, he didn't seem like a man hunting the world's most formidable animal. Instead, he looked like a typical Tahitian with dark tribal tattoos of tikis, turtles and rays wrapping around his bicep and stretching down his muscular calves.

We had been out there for half an hour, scouring the ocean floor for the three-inch perfectly circular holes that are the burrows for varo. They are not abundant and typically are scattered far apart in the sand. So far, I'd only seen the occasional sea cucumber and a broken ragged hole of a wandering hermit crab. I was starting to get bored when I spotted my first hole—a clean, black hole with straight sides the size of a silver dollar descending into the sand, like a cookie cutter had punched out a part of the seabed. Instinctively, I backed up to avoid any "splitting" of my body parts and called for Nunu.

He waded over and smiled. "This is Varo's home." He pulled his stick out of the floating gas can. On the end of the rod were eight upward facing hooks looking like an upturned, naked miniature umbrella. Nunu threaded a piece of mahi through the hook, securing it with an elastic band and placed the tip inside the hole. The other end of the rod was tied to a string so he could stand back watching from above until the varo took the bait. He could then yank the rod up, grabbing the varo without unleashing the fury of its claws.

I was ready for the aggressive creature to come out swinging its sling blade arms and slashing at the mahi and Nunu. I was envisioning a scene right out of Aliens that would end in Nunu being filleted up his belly, spilling intestines into the sea. Thirty seconds passed, then one minute, then two. Finally, Nunu raised his head.

"Varo not home." He waded off through the chest high water in search of a new hole.

I let out the breath I hadn't realized I had been holding in anticipation of the ensuing massacre I would witness. Quite anticlimactic, I thought, as I swam off, checking behind me to make sure the illusive crustacean was not just waiting for Nunu to leave before coming out to shred my legs with its talons. The varo's action of unfurling it's barbed spears and striking prey is the fastest known animal movement. It strikes fifty times faster than a blink of an eye. The jackknife weapon imparts a blow with an impact only slightly less deadly than a .22 caliber bullet. I didn't want to meet one in the water.

For the next hour, Nunu waded and I snorkeled, keeping my eyes peeled for more varo holes. We found only one more and repeated the procedure of lowering the hook into the hole and waiting, me with nervous knots in my stomach. But it was not to be our victory over the murderous opponent. With a laugh Nunu declared, "No varo today. All sleeping," and began to pack his gear. We swam back to his skiff to return to *Pangaea*.

Not until the next day, alone, did Nunu had success. Eager to show me his catch, he winked as he pulled his boat alongside and threw three varo on our back deck. "Today, I am good fisherman."

The varo ranged from six to twelve inches long and two inches wide. They had the head of an insect with small legs and feelers alongside their elongated body. Their soft cartilage was translucent and revealed white flesh with black markings at each section, resembling the markings of a tiger. They hardly seemed all that menacing until Nunu showed me what else he had brought. From his backpack he produced a dried claw from a varo he caught six months before. It was only slightly smaller than my hand with one large eight-inch talon, sharp as a pinprick dominating three smaller curled hooks. If one didn't get you the others would. Nunu demonstrated the size of the varo by placing his hand all the way up his arm at his elbow. "Grandma varo!" He laughed.

All of the sudden I was glad that we didn't find any varo while I was in the water. Some things are better left to the professionals.

* * * *

The next day, *Pangaea's* crew was gathered around for the daily crew meeting, drinking coffee and slowly shedding off the veil of sleep. "I have some news from the owners." Michael said in an uncharacteristically somber tone. Michael's serious manner slapped us all awake.

"It seems that there's been a sizable offer made to buy *Pangaea*. The owners have decided to sell her." He took a breath. "The new owners have their own crew and will be taking over from us on the first of the month." Michael shut his leather binder and looked up with tears in his eyes. "It seems our job is finished here."

Suddenly, the rich and aromatic coffee had a decidedly bitter taste in my mouth. I put down the mug I'd drank from every morning for two years and studied the faces of my friends. Each of them was lost in private thoughts of what the future would hold. My gaze fell lastly on Patrick. He sat sullenly in the corner. His usual smiling face was scrunched up as though he had tasted something surprisingly sour. His emotions were obvious; he was thinking the same thing as everyone else. Our idyllic escape to paradise was over.

Within the month, we would all be heading home to various places, moving on to different adventures. A smile crept to the corner of my mouth. Only the slightest twitch of an upturn on the right side of my face betrayed what I was feeling.

I was going home.

Mahi-Mahi Corn Chowder

2 slices thick-cut bacon
4 cloves garlic, sliced thin
1 cup onion
2 stalks celery
1/2 red pepper
1 tablespoon fresh thyme, chopped
4 cups chicken stock
2 potatoes
1/2 serrano pepper
1 tablespoon sea salt
1 teaspoon black pepper
1 can (400 ml) coconut milk
4 ears of corn
2 pounds mahi-mahi
1/3 cup cilantro
1 lime juiced

Chop all vegetables no bigger than a kernel of corn. Slice bacon to similar size. Sauté bacon in a heavy bottomed soup pot, over medium-high heat, stirring often, for 5 minutes until crisp and golden. Add onion and garlic and sauté another 3 minutes until soft. Add celery, sauté 2 minutes. Add red pepper, sauté 2 minutes, stirring occasionally. Add thyme, chicken stock, potatoes, serrano pepper, salt and black pepper. Bring back to a boil and reduce the heat to medium. Simmer for 20 minutes. Add coconut milk and fresh corn from the cob. Simmer 5 more minutes. Slice mahi-mahi into 1-inch squares and add to the pot. Simmer 5 minutes until fish is cooked through. Add chopped cilantro and juice of a lime. Taste for seasoning and serve.

Serves 6

Returning Home

*E*xactly four months after Michael gave us the news that *Pangaea* was selling, my two worlds collided. I brought Patrick to Canada to see from where I came. We traveled through my childhood to Emerald Lake Lodge in the mountains of British Columbia. Jamie, a good friend from my days at *River Cafe* was marrying Justine the next day on the banks of the gem colored waters. I looked forward to introducing Patrick to him and his brother Dwayne. So much had changed since I left. When I was in Calgary, I hadn't had a serious relationship with anyone. Most of my time was spent with Dwayne, Jamie, and our friends. Eight years later, I finally had a relationship that worked. I felt like I was bringing a boy home to meet my older brothers for the first time.

* * * *

The first year I was at *River* I couldn't afford to go home for Christmas. I didn't have any family in Calgary. They were too far away to drive and flights were atrocious. I would be alone.

"Pack your bags. We're taking you to Saskatoon," Dwayne said.

"Nothing says Christmas like the Bryshun family table," Jamie added. "You don't mind hearing my dad's same jokes again do you?" A few months prior we spent Thanksgiving at Dwayne's house. I cooked for his mom, dad, sister, Jamie and Dwayne, their respective girlfriends and a few other friends. I was used to quiet holiday celebrations with just my sister and parents at a table. Holidays with the Bryshuns were loud and boisterous.

"Why can't you take a turkey to church?" Mr. Bryshun asked me, shouting to make sure the whole table heard.

Jamie rolled his eyes. "We hear this one every year."

"Why?" I asked.

"Because he uses such fowl language." Mr. Bryshun slugged me on the arm. "Eh? Eh?" He laughed, looking for his audience to do the same. I laughed too, grabbing my arm and rubbing at the same time. He thought of me as one of his football playing sons.

Mrs. Bryshun shook her head. She said to me. "He saves that joke for someone special each year." They made me feel like one of the family.

Dwayne was classic like the gin and tonics drunk by the stylish and slick Rat Pack characters in the original *Ocean's Eleven*. His zest for life was as piquant as the lime that garnished the glass. I loved being around him. He possessed charm and compassion. He made me feel like he would do anything for me. I felt the same about him.

People gravitated towards Dwayne. He glowed like a campfire, drawing people's attention to his internal flame. I was no exception. But I was captivated by something else. It was his genuine protectiveness of our friendship I cherished. Girlfriends came and went for him, I dated on and off, but at the end of the day it was always Dwayne who was there for me. When I was alone it was Dwayne that took me out. When I was down it was him who made me laugh.

Just before I left for Lauderdale, I'd been trying to catch the eye of a local bartender. Dwayne offered to come to the bar with me to keep me company. Exasperated, my exact words were, "The last thing I need is some good-looking Bryshun scaring the guy off." It would not have been the first time someone had mistaken our close friendship.

I sat alone at one end of the bar that night listening to the Celtic band playing, as I had many nights before. The waitress approached. "Um, Victoria, this guy in the corner wants to buy you a drink." She looked cautious and added, "I can get Andy to ask him to leave."

"Why?" I asked. I turned to wave thanks, but no further explanation was needed. In the corner sat a scruffy looking man with a camouflage trucker's ball cap hiding his mullet haircut. A package of cigarettes was rolled in the sleeve of his white t-shirt that had been smeared with grease across the front. It sported a crude saying across the breast. There was a scar on his left cheek that was only half covered by a band-aide. He was busy lecherously twirling the end of his black moustache into a swirl.

I turned back and faced the bar. "Why do I always get the weirdoes?" I asked the waitress, declining the drink. I focused on an intense conversation with the bartender, hoping the guy would realize I wasn't interested and just leave.

Within two minutes the waitress returned. "Victoria, the guy insists. I think he knows you." As I turned again the guy rose and started toward us. He walked with a pronounced limp, slightly staggering and speaking out of the side of his mouth like he had suffered a stroke.

"You said no good-looking Bryshun, right?" The man did make me laugh.

The morning I left Calgary for Lauderdale all those years ago, Dwayne and I reminisced about our fun together. I was petrified. He could see it in my eyes. Like a great bear protecting her cub, he swung an arm around my shoulder. With a voice like velvet he said, "Home will always be here."

It was those words I was counting on as I returned.

* * * *

"Wow, you are real!" It was the first thing Dwayne said to us as we walked through the doors of the hand-hewed timber lodge. Jamie and Justine were to be married out by the lake, but the reception would be here the next day. "Jamie and I bet that you were just a figment of Victoria's imagination." With a wink he gathered me in for one of his legendary bear hugs. His rich buttery voice rang with texture as he said into my ear, "Just so you know, I bet he was real."

"We never thought this day would come," Jamie shook Patrick's hand. "Welcome to the Bryshun family." Jamie had the same dark hair, piercing mahogany eyes, and big heart as Dwayne.

I was home.

The next morning we took a long hike through the Douglas fir trees surrounding the property. We hiked along twisting trails, gaining altitude and a better view of the lake below. It was October, so we hiked past the first tales of winter. Clumps of white lay in patches along the trail, and cold steam rose off the glacial run-off streams. I saw my breath rise in the cold air. "Long way from bikinis and rum drinks on a beach," I said to Patrick.

"Yeah, but wouldn't it be great to have a bit of both?" he asked. "I think we should look into a property here in the mountains to get away to. We could live on the yachts during the season and spend our vacations here. I could snowboard in the winter and go mountain biking in the summers. You could read, host dinner parties…" he trailed off. "We could build a home, just the two of us." They were the magic words, a combination of my two worlds. My love for traveling would be sated with yachting, but we would have my love of mountains as well, where we could relax and be ourselves.

That evening as the sun set over the ash-grey rugged rock ridges we all gathered to witness the exchange of vows. Mr. and Mrs. Bryshun held hands, still in love after forty-five years of marriage. Jamie held Justine's hand and looked deep into her eyes. I reached out and grabbed Patrick's hand. Up until this point in my life, friendship was the most important thing to me. Being surrounded by my friends again was like curling up with a fuzzy blanket and good book in front of a roaring fire. It just felt comfortable. Dwayne was right, home would always be here.

* * * *

It had been eight years since I packed my car and left Calgary, tears rolling down my cheeks while watching Dwayne wave in the rearview mirror. Armed with an insatiable appetite for life and the promise of adventure.

I began collecting experiences. I believe there is always something new to learn, in cooking as in life, and I continue to be a student of the world.

In the past eight years I've had remarkable adventures and met fascinating people, all of who enriched my life in one way or another. I have traveled to six different continents, crossed forty-five countries off my list of places to visit, and added about a hundred more. I have hit highs and lows. I wouldn't change any one of them. Patrick went from a part-time boyfriend to a full-time love. My cooking went from intricate and complicated to simple and clear. My love of food and travel increased exponentially with every experience.

It is the unpredictability of it all I love so much. Where will I be next week, next month, next year? What new places will I get to explore? What new food will I get to experience?

Food has the power to invoke vivid memories and transport me back to certain times and places. Every time I make Irma's Calalloo Soup, I smell the frangipani that bloomed all over the island of Mustique. When I make Jill's Yellow-fin Tuna Pie, I can feel the sting of saltwater spray burning my eyes. The taste of shimp always makes me think of Jimmy's laugh and Cathy's generosity. A bottle of Bandol brings back the feel of the warm Mediterranean air on my skin.

Entering yachting to travel has been the single best decision I ever made. End of story … or maybe it is just the beginning.

——— VICTORIA ALLMAN ———

River Café's Spring Asparagus and Brown Beech Mushroom Soup with Great Northern Beans

Spring comes late in Alberta, Canada and fresh local Asparagus from Elna and Doug of Edgar Farms heralds the new season. Brown Beech Mushrooms or Hon Shimji, are prized species of the oyster mushroom family. They are cultivated locally and add a rich, mildly sweet and nutty taste. This soup had become a seasonal favorite at River Café.

1 tablespoon vegetable oil
1 inch piece ginger root, minced
1 clove garlic
1 small shallot, minced
1 head fennel, minced
1/2 teaspoon whole black peppercorns
1 bay leaf
3-4 juniper berries
1/2 yellow onion, chopped
1/2 carrot, chopped
8 cups cold water
1 sprig fresh thyme, de-stemmed
1 teaspoon fresh lemon juice
1 teaspoon grainy mustard
2 cups Great Northern White Beans, cooked
1 Tablespoon vegetable oil
2 clusters or 2 cups brown beech mushrooms known al as Hon Shimji, chopped
1 tablespoon sea salt
24 spears fresh asparagus

In a medium to large saucepan, sauté the ginger, garlic, shallot, and fennel in the oil over medium heat for 10 minutes or until tender. Be careful not to let it brown. Place the peppercorns, bay leaf, juniper, onion, and carrot in a piece of cheese cloth and tie it up to make a sachet (spice bag). Add the water, thyme, lemon juice, mustard, cooked beans, and the sachet to the saucepan. Bring up to a low simmer.

In a hot frying pan, sauté the mushrooms quickly. Add them to the soup pot. Continue to simmer for 20 minutes. Remove the sachet and season generously with sea salt. In a pot of boiling salted water, blanch the asparagus and cut into 1-inch pieces. Just before serving the soup, add the asparagus and adjust the seasoning to taste.

Serves 8

About the Author

Victoria Allman has been following her stomach around the globe for twelve years as a yacht chef. In *Sea Fare: A Chef's Journey Across the Ocean* she writes about her floating culinary odyssey through Europe, the Caribbean, Nepal, Vietnam, Africa, and the South Pacific.

Victoria is a columnist for Dockwalk, an International magazine for crew members aboard yachts. Her column "Dishing It Up" is a humorous look at cooking for the rich and famous in an ever-moving galley.

A chapter from *Sea Fare* was reprinted in the anthology Female Nomad and Friends by Rita Golden Gelman.

She also regularly contributes tales of her tasty adventures to Marina Life Magazine and OceanLines.

In 2010, Victoria received a Royal Palm Literary Award from the Florida Writers Association. You can read more of her food-driven escapades through her web-site, www.victoriaallman.com

Victoria's second book, *SEAsoned: A Chef's Journey with Her Captain* was released January 2011, by NorLightsPress. Her jourey continues.

Acknowledgements

This book would not be a reality without the support of my family. Many thanks to Paul, and to my mother who didn't try to stop me when I went off to pursue a life on the sea.

Thanks to my father, who's become quite the yachtsman himself, and to my sister Nancy, who's living her own dream with her husband Jeff and my two nieces Mara and Ella. She is the best sister in the world, and the greatest friend I could ever wish for.

Thanks to my friends from home: Dwayne and Sarah, Jamie, Naomi and Simon, David Wyse, David Forestell and his wife Vivian, and Vic and Pete who encouraged me to run. I appreciate my new yachting friends Yaz, Ian, Julie and Chris, Emile, Marisa, Mase, Cynthia, Jacqueline, Gareth, Shannon, Belinda, Jason and Wendy, and Amy and Scotty, who experienced these adventures with me.

Thanks to land-based friends Karen, Trish and Noah, Maari, Jimmy, and Cathy who opened up their homes and lives to me.

My early cooking influences with Lawrence Bangay, Sal Howell, and Norman Van Aken contributed to this book.

Thanks to the yacht owners for enabling me to see the world, and to captains Mike, Emile, and Michael and the various crew with whom I've worked.

I received monumental help from Joyce Sweeney and her band of Thursday night writers. This manuscript went from a rough sea to smooth waters under their watchful eyes. Thanks to all involved with the Book Passage Travel Writers Conference. The excitement and inspiration from days spent with Larry Habegger, Don George, and Tony Cohan helped this book evolve from scribbled notes in a journal. Thanks to Elaine Petrocelli for organizing such a motivating event.

Thanks to my agent Sammie Justesen of Northern Lights Literary Agency, who believed in this project and put it out there. *Sea Fare* has been a labor of love and would not have seen the light of day without the enthusiasm and support of NorlightsPress. Dee, Sammie, and Nadene have worked tirelessly to see this project through to completion. I greatly appreciate all their efforts. Thank you!

Most of all, I thank Patrick for being my traveling partner. His unending enthusiasm and support keep me going. He's my biggest fan, not only through his stomach but also through his unwavering commitment and love. Patrick, I look forward to more exciting adventures with you.

Available from NorlightsPress and fine booksellers everywhere

Toll free: 888-558-4354   **Online:** www.norlightspress.com

Shipping Info: Add $2.95 for first item and $1.00 for each additional item

Name _____

Address _____

Daytime Phone _____

E-mail _____

No. Copies	Title	Price (each)	Total Cost
		Subtotal	
		Shipping	
		Total	

Payment by (circle one):

Check   Visa   Mastercard   Discover   Am Express

Card number_____3 digit code_____

Exp.date_____ Signature_____

Mailing Address:
2323 S.R. 252
Martinsville, IN 46151

Sign up to receive our catalogue at
www.norlightspress.com

8507729R00130

Printed in Great Britain
by Amazon.co.uk, Ltd.,
Marston Gate.